D1291607

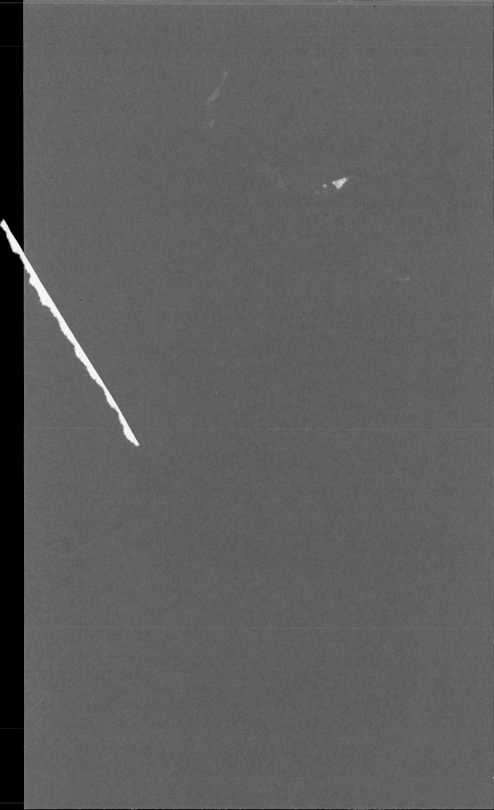

The Early History of Christianity

THE EARLY HISTORY
OF CHRISTIANITY

Covering the Period from 300 B. C.
to the Origin of the Papacy

BY *Alfred Honoré*

CHARLES GUIGNEBERT

PROFESSOR OF THE HISTORY OF CHRISTIANITY
UNIVERSITY OF PARIS

TWAYNE PUBLISHERS

NEW YORK 3

"I am not concerned about knowing whether what you have seen gives you pleasure; it is enough for me that it should be the truth. Science does not trouble about pleasing or displeasing: she is inhuman. It is not science, but poetry, that charms and comforts, and that is why poetry is more necessary than science."

Anatole France, *Honey-Bee.*

THE EARLY HISTORY OF CHRISTIANITY
consists of the first thirteen chapters of
CHRISTIANITY, PAST AND PRESENT
copyright, 1927 by THE MACMILLAN COMPANY

PREFACE

The main lines of thought followed in this book are the same as those of one of its predecessors, entitled "L'Evolution des Dogmes," [1] in which I endeavored to describe and account for the formation, successive modifications and final destruction of the articles of faith known as dogmas. Instead, however of considering the dogmatic assertions of religions in general *in abstracto,* the present volume seeks to understand and explain the life of one particular religion, studied as a concrete reality. It is above all with *facts,* their significance, consequences, and connections, that it deals. It is the main outlines of a history which it tries to delineate so as to prove, if possible, that not only in its dogmas, but also throughout the ramifications of its whole organism a religion undergoes the process of evolution.

From the social milieu in which it establishes itself it borrows the primary elements which form its substance and sustain it in organizing themselves. By undergoing more or less thorough transformations of its organs, it adapts itself to the demands of the diverse and successive spheres to which it is afterward transported. Like all living beings, it eliminates its worn-out and dead particles by degrees, and assimilates others derived from its surroundings which renew its flesh and blood until the day comes when, in the inevitable course of time, its powers of adaptation relax their activity and finally stop short. That means it has become unable to rid itself of the inert and noxious waste matters it is accumulating, unable also to nourish its life; death gradually takes possession of and congeals it, until at last the moment arrives when it is good for nothing but to

[1] Ch. Guignebert, *L'Evolution des Dogmes* (Paris, 1910).

engender, from its own decaying tissues, a new religious organism, destined to a similar fate.

No doubt it is a law of human mentality, by whose means religions are born, live and die, that though in certain respects the religious phenomenon may be different in itself, and perhaps, too, may raise itself from age to age toward an unconscious ideal of which some believe they have obtained a glimpse, yet it is really the same cycle that is being everlastingly developed and consummated, and then beginning once more.

The Christian religion will form the main object of our study here, and we shall endeavor first of all to account for its life during the earliest centuries of its existence. But, as in the little book I have mentioned, I shall by no means exclude comparisons between the facts of the history of Christianity and those of the history of other religions. A very powerful atavistic tendency, difficult to eradicate, exists in us; the Romano-Christian culture brought it into being. And it would have us believe that Christianity could never have been such a religion as the others; that its genesis and the course of its long career until the present day followed methods that were exceptional, and that it will never perish. Comparison alone can dispel this illusion, and replace it by a vision which, I do not deny, is disheartening, but is at least true to the historical reality. And is it not by venturing to look firmly in the face that which has been and that which is, rather than by endeavoring to conceal the real facts beneath the veil of his dreams and the adornments born of his desires, that man will rise to a clearer understanding of his destiny and his duty?

Is it necessary to add that the present essay does not presume to offer a complete picture of the history of Christianity, and that it only aims at presenting, in a form which all can understand, and in accordance with a scheme which he believes capable of demonstration, an ensemble of facts and considerations which will render the development of that history intelligible? It will happen more than once, especially in the earlier chapters, that I may make momentous statements without at the same time offering all their proofs. It will be understood that in a sketch of this kind a meticulous discussion of exegetics finds no place, and I trust that the reader who remembers that the critical study of the New Testament has been engaging my attention in the Sorbonne for the last twenty years, may have sufficient confidence in me to assume that I do not advance anything upon which I have not long and seriously reflected.[2]

[2] I have abandoned the idea of giving a bibliography, which would occupy unnecessary space, but I shall refer from time to time to works that are essential. Most of these are written in German, and the best summary on the history of Christianity that I know is that of G. Krüger, *Handbuch der Kirchengeschichte für Studierende* (Tübingen, 1909-1913), four volumes and index. The best account of the evolution of Christianity is to be found in the two works of Pfleiderer, *Die Entstehung des Christentums*, and *Die Entwickelung des Christentums*, (Munich, 1907), or in the large volume entitled *Geschichte der christlichen Religion*, published in Berlin and Leipzig in 1909, by Wellhausen, Julicher, Harnack, Bonwetsch, and others. As an excellent handbook with a very good bibliographical index I can recommend the book edited by Gerald Birney Smith, entitled *A Guide to the Study of the Christian Religion* (University of Chicago Press, 1917). This would be well read in connection with P. Wernle's *Einführung in das theologische Studium* (Tübingen, 1911), the title of which does not sufficiently indicate the variety of ideas or the wealth of information it contains.

CONTENTS

CHAPTER   PAGE

PREFACE vii

INTRODUCTION 1

I. The difficulty of defining "religion," and the need for insisting on an analysis of positive religions. —Wherein this task is already a complicated one.— How the religious and social strata correspond with each other in aggregates already developed.—The syncretistic nature of popular religion; its activity. —Examples from the history of Christianity.—*Endosmosis* between different religions established on the same social soil.—How a new religion may arise out of this condition.

II. Why the study of the history of Christianity is not more advanced. Reasons to be sought without and within.—Inadequacy of information; the problems badly formulated for so long a time.—The confusion caused by both adherents and opponents.— The present-day point of view.

III. How Christianity as a whole appears to the historian.

PART I

CHRISTIANITY IN CLASSICAL TIMES: THE CREED AND THE CHURCH

I. JESUS' INITIATIVE 21

I. The Jewish origin of Christianity.—Jesus the Nazarene; paucity of our information respecting him. —How and why his history soon gives place to legend. —Tradition and the sources of our Gospels.—How these Gospels were composed.—The gaps in the narrative filled in by faith.—How the problems of Jesus' rise presents itself.

II. The sphere from which Jesus issued.—The country of the Jews and its surroundings; the vast amount of religious material at the disposal of a fresh syncretism.—Jesus' training entirely Jewish.— The Palestinian world in the time of Herod the Great. —The priestly hierarchy and worship; the scribes and legalism; the people and the religion in force.—The

CONTENTS

expectation of the Messiah.—Characteristic features of Galilean Judaism.

III. The theory which accounts for Jesus' rise.—The Messianic hope.—Jesus in relation to the Baptist.—The themes on which he preached: the coming of the Kingdom and repentance.—Did he believe himself the Messiah?—The bearing of the Gospel designations Son of God, Son of David, Son of Man.—Various difficulties and probabilities.—Jesus a Jewish prophet.

II. JESUS' FAILURE   39

I. Jesus' failure inevitable.—His inability to present his mission in a way convincing to either people, scribes or priesthood.—The journey to Jerusalem and the death of Jesus.—Had the latter been foreseen by him?

II. The dispersion of the Apostles.—How their faith in Jesus' resurrection restored their courage.—The occurrences leading to this faith and its consequences with regard to the constitution of primitive Christology and the dawn of Christianity.

III. The disciples' faith reconstructed.—The idea of the speedy return of Jesus the Messiah.—Small likelihood of the success of the Apostolic doctrine.—Its survival assured by its transplantation to Greek soil.

III. THE WORK OF THE APOSTLES   51

I. The Apostles belong to Palestine; their point of view.—The Jews outside Palestine; the Diaspora.—How it is constituted.—The organization of its communities.—The propaganda of its synagogues.—How they arrive at an understanding with Hellenism.—The spirit of their proselytes; wherein it is favorable beforehand to Christian doctrine.

II. The syncretism of the Diaspora.—The Mandæism of Mesopotamia.—The Hypsistarians and the Sabians of Phrygia.—The Nazoreans of Perea, described by Epiphanus.—The influences favorable to Christianity wrought by these sects.

III. How the transit from the faith of the Apostles to the sphere of the Diaspora was accomplished; the story of the Acts.—Barnabas at Antioch.—The humbleness and apparently limited range of the work of the Palestinian Apostles.

IV. THE PAULINE MILIEU   63

I. Tarsus; its schools and their sphere of radiation.—The intellectual education of Paul.—How he becomes the Apostle of Jesus Christ.—His temperament.—How far it is original.—The elements of his doctrine: the importance of this point.

II. The redeeming Gods of the Hellenistic East.—In what respects they are alike and how they are confused.—The myth of their death and annual resurrection.—Its origin and first meaning.—Its application

CHAPTER   PAGE

to Mithra. Osiris, Tammuz, Adonis.—The drama of the life and death of the god.

III. The metaphysical interpretation of these stories of divinities: they typify the mystery of human destiny.—The necessity for man to associate himself with the destiny of the redeeming god to acquire eternal life; how this association operates.—The baptism of blood and the communion feast: the *taurobolium* and the banquet at the god's table.—The manducation of the god.—The resemblance between these rites and Christian baptism and the Eucharist. —The soteriology of the Mysteries and the Pauline soteriology.

IV. Was Paul acquainted with the Mysteries?—The religion of Tarsus: Baal-Tarz and Sandan.—Other Mysteries.—Hypotheses and probabilities.—The religious influences which Paul underwent at Tarsus.— Paul well prepared for his rôle of Apostle of Christianity to the Gentiles by his triple qualification as Greek, Jew and Roman.

V. PAUL'S TRAINING AS A CHRISTIAN 81

I. Paul had received a Christian training, though one that it is difficult to determine.—In what respect his injurious proceedings with regard to believers prepare the way for his conversion.—He has not been subjected to Apostolic influences, but to that of a Hellenistic community.

II. The faith of this community.—How it gathers force in Jerusalem and transforms the Apostolic faith. —The Church in Antioch; her importance and her spirit.—Her Christology: the conception of the *Lord Jesus*.—The part it plays in Paul's training.—His Hellenistic origin.—Worship and the Lord's presence in the Paulinian community.—The soteriology of the primitive Hellenist community and the Pauline soteriology.

III. How Paul's conversion was probably brought about.—How he regarded it himself.—What it must have been in reality.—How it led to his Apostolate and determined its direction.

VI. THE WORK OF THE APOSTLE PAUL 97

I. Paul's independence of the Palestinian Apostles. —His earlier position with regard to these.—How Barnabas directs his activity; his life as a missionary.

II. The teaching that this affords him.—The problem of the admission of the non-Jewish believers to the ranks of the Christians.—How its solution urges on Christian Messianism to become an Oriental religion.—Paul's Christology is an influence in the same direction.—How he conceives the person and the rôle of Christ.—The Savior and the Son of God; the work of redemption; in what respects this doctrine is a *gnosis*.

CHAPTER   PAGE

III. The influence of the Gentile converts' ritual
practices upon Pauline Baptism and Eucharist.—To
what extent Paul is the founder of Christianity.

VII. CHRISTIANITY AS AN AUTONOMOUS RELIGION   . . 108
I. Hellenistic influences unavoidable by the Christian faith.—The Johannine tide. The Judeo-Christian
resistance of Paulinism and Johannism. How they
are overcome by degrees.—The separation of the
Faith from the Law.—Separation of Church and
Synagogue.—The situation at the opening of the
fourth century.—The intellectual movement with
regard to religious matters from the first to the fourth
century.—The official Roman religion and religious
sentiment.—The urge of the East.—The individual-
istic syncretism of the third century.—Christianity
presents itself as an Oriental religion and addresses
itself to the individual.—It condemns syncretism, but
in appearance only; how far it is itself syncretistic.
—Its encounter with philosophy.
II. The Greco-Roman terrain.—The themes upon
which the school of metaphysicians ponders.
III. The influence of Hellenist culture urges the
faith in two different directions.—The transformation
of Christianity into a revealed and perfected philosophy.—The expansion of the *gnoses*.—The rôle of
heresy in the evolution of doctrine.—The influence of
pagan ritualism.
IV. How Christianity appears at the beginning of
the fourth century. It is an autonomous religion, very
hostile to Judaism.—The "rule of faith."—The Church
and the churches.—Christian exclusiveness.

VIII. THE FOUNDATION AND THE ORGANIZATION OF THE
CHURCH 125
I. Christ neither founded nor desired the Church.
—The Galilean Apostles do not seem to have thought
of her either.—The Gospel passages silent on this
point.—The myth of Peter's primacy.—Without desiring it the Apostles have prepared the Church.—The
body of the faithful and the Church of God.—Paul's
idea of it previous to any ecclesiastical organization.
—How the necessity of such an organization imposes
itself.—The idea of the Church at the beginning of the
second century.
II. The origin of the local churches. The models
followed in their organization.—Pagan associations
and synagogues. — Necessity creates functions.—
Rapidity of the movement.—Various influences favoring the institution of clergy and the advent of the
episcopate.
III. The monarchic episcopate. Its origin.—Causes
leading to the suppression of a plural episcopate. a
defense against heretics and a respect for Apostolic
tradition.—The bishop the president of the *presby-*

terion.—Ignatius' theory of episcopacy. — External causes which favor its general adoption.—The episcopal lists.

IV. The election of the bishop.—The conditions of his eligibility. His powers and their limits.—Clerical opposition.—The institution of the *ordo clericalis* and its degrees.—How the Christians distinguish the clergy from the laity.

V. The Catholic idea of the Church.—Its main components.—The rôle of the Apostolic Churches and the unique position of the Church of Rome.—The Church on the threshold of the third century.

IX. THE ESTABLISHMENT OF CHURCH DOCTRINE AND DISCIPLINE   144

I. Becoming a Christian in the beginning of the second century: baptism, its nature and its significance.—The three main types of the Christological speculative thought: *Paulinism, Johannism, Docetism.* —Their common tendency and how it developed among the generality of the faithful.—The demands of the faith in ethics and ritual.

II. The development of ritualism.—Complicates the entry into the Church.—The *catechumenate* and the *arcanum.*—The institution of the catechumenate.— The *competentes.*—The ritual complication of baptism.

III. The development of belief. Dominated both by the influence of the simple-minded and of the philosophers.—The illusion of fixity and the "rule of faith."—Its history.—How the problem of the Trinity is presented.—Its development in the second century. —The opposition to dogmatic evolution. — The Ebionites and the Alogi.

IV. The development of ecclesiastical life.—The life of the Christian tends to greater ritualism.—The origin of the Mass, and the significance which the Eucharist tends to assume.—Transubstantiation.

V. Penance.—Its character.—Its ritual regulation still very simple.—No other sacraments at the beginning of the third century.

X. THE CONFLICT WITH THE STATE AND WITH SOCIETY   162

I. How this conflict impedes Christianity.—The responsibility for it.—The Christians' rejection of the claims of the State.—Christianity opposed to social demands.—The current opinion concerning the Christians and its practical importance.

II. How the State regards Christianity in the third century: Christianity akin to anarchy.—Rulers who persecuted it; the reasons for the non-success of their persecutions.—How the change of front of the State and of society is prepared.—The compromise of Constantine, and the edict of Milan.—Its causes and the fundamental instability of its conditions.

III. The concessions made by the Church and their

CHAPTER   PAGE

limits.—Why Constantine's attitude had become
untenable.—The State Church at the end of the fourth
century.—The end of paganism.—How and why the
resistance of the aristocracy was overcome.—The
resistance of the intellectuals.—The resistance of the
country people; their apparent acceptance of Christianity.

XI.   THE SIGNIFICANCE OF THE TRIUMPH   177

I. The price of the victory of Christianity.—It is
the Church that triumphs.—The perfecting of clerical
organization.—The evolution of sacerdotalism and of
theology.—Doctrinal disputes and orthodoxy—Fundamental syncretism and the assumption of formality.
—The popular impulse.—The part played by monachism.—The first stages of Christian evolution; con-
trasts and coherences.

II. How the early Christian hope has been transformed; the effects of this change.—How the victory
accentuates these, though it is but in appearance only.
—The Church's responsibility; it becomes one aspect
of the Roman State, of which in the fifth century it is
the heir.—Material advantages and spiritual draw-
backs of this relationship.—How the idea, and the
fact, of the distinction between the "believers" and
the "perfect" is grounded in the Church, and its practical consequences.

III. The triumph considered from the point of view
of religious history.—The western world and primitive Christianity.—How the latter represents a syncretism resulting from the religious needs of the East.
—Rival cults: Mithra; Neoplatonism; Manicheism.

IV. The three religions and the fourth century.—
Resemblances between them; the practical inferiority
of Neoplatonism, and the superior position of Manicheism.—Why the Roman State proscribes it. and
why Christianity can cope with it.—The reason that it
triumphs over it.—The persistence of Neoplatonism
and Manicheism, even after the victory of Christianity; their influence in the future.

PART II
THE MIDDLE AGES
THEOLOGY AND THE PAPACY

CHAPTER   PAGE

XII. THE REMOTE MIDDLE AGES 201

I. The reasons why the *Western Church* hence-forth demands our attention.—The solidifying of the Eastern Church.—The separation of the two, and its consequences.

II. *St. Augustine,* as marking the end of classical times and the beginning of the Middle Ages.—The extent and profundity of his influence; his affirmation of the principle of the *authority* of the Church. —The necessity, for the unlearned, of such a principle, to them a guarantee of their faith.—The reality of movement and life in a setting regarded as fixed.

III. *What believers really are at the beginning of the fifth century.*—A fundamental paganism lies beneath the apparent Christianity; the entry of the barbarians into the faith, and the characteristics of their Christianity.—The Church's servitude, and its greatness, in the sixth and seventh centuries.—What the religion of the Middle Ages at their beginning really was.—The worship of saints and relics.—Various pagan survivals.—Dogma passes to a second plane.—How this religion comes to terms with the morals and the culture of the time.

IV. *The attempt to rise;* the monks and the rulers of the nations.—Charlemagne; Alfred the Great; the Othos.—The significance and the bearing of the *Carlovingian renascence.*—The exceptional and the anticipatory position of *Erigena Scotus.*—The difference between the religion of the learned and of the people; its disadvantage in the present, and its danger for the future.—The activity of the faith of the simple-minded in these days.

V. *The Carlovingian decadence and feudal disorder.*—Its effect upon religion, upon the Christian life, and upon the Church.—The life of the clergy.—The faith and the practice of the Christian laity.—The Church's reaction to feudal anarchy.—The monastic movement; the example of Cluny.—Its influence upon churchmanship and upon the establishment of papal power.

XIII. THE ORIGIN OF PAPACY 227

I. *The orthodox doctrine of the nature and origin of Papacy.*—The *historical* reality.—The preëminence of the bishop of Rome in the earlier centuries; its causes, nature, and limits.—Various examples: St. Cyprian and Stephen of Rome; the African bishops

CHAPTER   PAGE

and Zosimus; the affair of the Three Chapters.—The frequency of breaches with Rome.

II. *Patristic writings* a confirmation of facts; examples of this.—The independence of the ancient Councils with respect to Rome.—The scandals of Liberius and Honorius I.—The silence of St. Augustine, St. Vincent de Lérins, of the heresiologians, of Isodorus of Seville and of Dionysius the Areopagite with regard to the papal "primacy."—The hesitation of the bishop of Rome to lay claim to it.

III. *The causes which establish the Pope's primauté d'honneur and prepare the way for his primauté de jurisdiction.*—The government of the Church, in its evolution, apparently aiming at monarchy.—The concurrence of the Gospel passages, and the first appeal to them made by the Pope.

IV. *The historical bases for the success of the Pope;* their political character.—The Byzantine tutelage; the Lombard peril; the Frankish tutelage; the Roman anarchy; the German tutelage.—The theory of the Germanic Holy Roman Empire.—The advantages reaped by the Pope from all these.

V. *The establishing of pontifical doctrine.*—The juridical forgeries.—The forged decretals, and their importance.—How they continue to perfect themselves.—Gratianus, Martin of Troppau, etc.—The work juridical and not theological.

VI. *The political aspect of the doctrine.*—The temporal sovereignty of the Pope.—The monks' propaganda in his favor.—Similar action due to various external causes; the struggle of the priesthood with the Empire; the Crusades: their intellectual consequences.

THE EARLY HISTORY OF CHRISTIANITY

INTRODUCTION

It is a difficult undertaking to define "religion"—religion in itself, so as to cover that which exists beneath the different semblances of special religions, that which is common to them all and survives them all, and constitutes the indestructible foundation upon which each is established before it is arranged to suit the needs and the tastes of those who proclaim it. So difficult an undertaking is it that until now nobody has succeeded in accomplishing it in a way that satisfies everybody. It always seems as if the object overlaps its definition, at any rate on one side. So diverse, in fact, do the constituent elements of a religion, ever so slightly complex, reveal themselves when analyzed, and so widely varied the aspects in which they may be regarded, that one despairs of finding any formula elastic enough to contain or assume them all. On the other hand, when one has taken the trouble to study two or three religions closely, to take them to pieces, as it were, part by part, and to seek exact information about the methods and extent of their influence, one certainly discovers similar principles and agencies, common aspirations, the same ambition to rule the community and even to regulate the lives of individuals, as well as yet other resemblances. Nevertheless each, considered by itself, presents a special appearance of its own. It has its characteristic features, its way of life and method of action which often exclude those of others, its individual application to social or personal or family life, to action and thought; so that finally the differences which divide it from the

1

rest may appear more striking and really more essential than the resemblances between it and them. The cavern inhabited by the troglodyte, the hut of the savage, the tent of the nomad, the house, whether modest or sumptuous, of the settler, and the palace of his chiefs evidently all respond to the same essential need, that of providing a shelter from the tempestuous elements. They afford similar service to men whose needs vary greatly; and, as a matter of fact, they resemble each other sufficiently to be compared. Nevertheless, he who attempted to apply a common definition to them all would have to be satisfied with so restricted an indication that in it we could actually recognize nothing more than the most elementary form of human dwelling. So, too, it is impossible to characterize by the same terms the religion of an Australian aboriginal tribe and the Christian religion, for instance, except by disregarding all that the second contains more than the first. This is why I am inclined to believe that history has not much to hope for from these attempts at synthesis, however interesting they may appear at first sight, supported by noteworthy savants for the purpose of comprehending the Absolute Religion, and summing up its essence in a phrase. An exact analysis of each religion, and a comparison of it with the previous or contemporary beliefs and practices which may have affected it, form, in any case, the peculiar province of historical research.

In putting it to the test, we soon become convinced that it is a difficult task, not, to be sure, when one is dealing with a very simple form of religion, but when one is trying to account for the structure and existence of a religion that obtains in a sphere of advanced culture. The most superficial examination at once reveals that it is not *one;* that there is neither homogeneity in the diverse parts of its body, nor coherence in the varied manifestations of its activity, nor solidarity in the differing expressions of its ideas. We might say that it is composed of stratified layers, each of which corresponds with a social class, or if you prefer, with a

stage of social culture. However little we reflect upon
this, we soon cease to be astonished at it, for if it seems
natural that each community should create a religion
that suits it, it is no less true that in the same community each special social sphere, each "world," as we
say, should create for itself out of this religion the
variety which responds to its particular needs. It has
been rightly observed that in the last stages of the
Roman Republic the religion of the slaves was two or
three centuries behind that of their masters. This
remark may be more universally applied, and if history
shows us that religions, considered as a whole, are
developed and perfected along lines that are parallel
and contemporaneous with the progress of the culture,
one of the main aspects of which they are, it also enables
us to ascertain that the evolution of each of them, like
that of the community itself, is the result of a whole
series of movements, still parallel, but no longer contemporaneous, which are going on in the different social
strata.

Are these mere truisms? Undoubtedly, yet they are
truisms which must be repeated, because the best
informed of men often forget them, or at any rate, speak
of religions as if they had forgotten them.

Instinctively or, if you like it better thus, from a
mental incapacity to act otherwise, the populace that has
not learned, and does not know how, to reflect always
cleaves (even in communities which have a high standard
of refinement) to religious conceptions and practices
which do not correspond exactly either with the teachings of the recognized religion, nor with the mentality
of its learned ministrants, nor yet with the conception
of its dogmas and tenets which prevails among enlightened believers. This popular religion, when analyzed, is
revealed as a syncretism, a medley of beliefs and customs, differing in origin, age and meaning, and only
existing side by side because those who accept them
never compare them. We readily recognize, as soon
as we study the matter, that this syncretism is made up

of disconnected survivals, the débris of several religious organizations of past ages, upon which the present is established as well as it may be. The people, especially the rural populations, never make a clean sweep of their religious beliefs and rites; they spontaneously adapt them to the new religion imposed upon them, or else, should this religion refuse to entertain them, they drive them further back into the recesses of their consciousness and the depths of their inner being, where they remain as active superstitions. It will be understood that I am stating the case simply, and that the syncretism of which I am speaking has degrees, extending from the most ignorant boors to men who already possess a certain amount of culture, for superstition is by no means the exclusive privilege of the simple-minded. Our large towns have their magicians and their prophetesses, whose announcements are distributed in the highways or reach us by post, and their alluring promises are published by important newspapers. All this advertisement is not addressed to the people alone, but it is in the people, especially in the peasant class, that the religious memories of the past, transmitted from age to age, some of which go back to the most elementary conceptions of primitive religious belief, are to be found in the deeper layers, more or less openly combining with the tenets of the governing religion of the present.

These popular primitive heirlooms exist everywhere. They are objects of scorn and detestation for every religion which has not been directly derived from them, but they always react upon such a religion, and, to tell the truth, no religion can exist without coming to terms with them. Religion does not confess this; often, indeed, it does not suspect that this is the case; but it allows itself to be more or less profoundly affected by their influence; it assimilates part of their substance and thus contributes, in spite of itself, to insure their survival.

A religion, of whatever sort it may be, does not fall ready-made from heaven; it is born of some special

initiative or of some general need; then, as we have
already said, it organizes itself and nourishes itself
by what it imbibes from the various religious spheres in
which it is induced to live. It is not of this phenomenon
that I really desire to speak here, but rather of the more
or less active, and also more or less rapid, reaction of
the religious mentality of the ignorant, of these popular
primitive heirlooms to a religion which is completely
organized and, apparently, perfected. This is a constant
reaction, the effects of which, as is quite natural, make
themselves most felt at those periods in the life of religion when either by means of their numbers, by their zealous activities, or by the defection of the educated, simple,
ignorant folk exercise a predominating influence.

Is an example needed? Christianity, considered at a
given time, not only in the real effectiveness of its popular practice, but, if I may say so, in the entirety of its
religious and social life, submitted to a push from below
and yielded to the demands of the religious instincts
and of the superstitions which, in theory, it had tried
to overthrow, at three special moments in its history.
The first was in the fourth and fifth centuries, when
the entry of the urban commoners and the rural populations *en masse* into the Church was brought about, and
then that of the Germanic hordes. The second occurred
in the tenth and eleventh centuries, when the really
intellectual activity of the Western world, reduced to
the thought of a handful of monks, unresistingly left
a free field to popular religiosity and ignorant mysticism.
The third occasion, finally, is our own age in which all
active and fertile thought, because it necessarily adapts
itself to the demands of a science established outside the
faith, seems like a deadly danger to orthodoxy. An age
in which educated men one after another turn away from
the teachings and practices of the churches. Soon, no
doubt, the only "right-thinking" people will be the
believers who do not think at all, or think only in terms
of the past if the drift of a reasoned faith, the religious
expression of intellectual culture, tends to devotion, and

to forms of devotion in which the suggestions derived from popular primitive heirlooms alone seem to benefit. Moreover, the survey which will be developed in the various chapters of this book will produce for these preliminary considerations the *de facto* justification they need.

It may happen that many distinct religions exist side by side in the same community. At the outset they present one common feature, namely, that they are all based upon the popular primitive heirlooms of which we have spoken, except those which are limited to a small group of initiates who carry to an extreme the religious sentiment of their times. In the second place, though the points of contact between them differ, the results produced in all cases are clearly similar. By this I mean that, whether the attitude be one of hostility or sympathy, these contacts determine exchanges and syncretistic combinations of which those who effect them are, as a rule, unconscious. And they are, as it were, manifestations of an endosmosis which experience proves to be inevitable. They are produced, in the corresponding stages, between one religion and another. In other words, we find, for instance, a kind of sympathy and even solidarity established, which neither debates nor disputes can obscure, between the religions which are shared by "intellectuals." Within the differing schemes of dogma and liturgy, there are the same or nearly the same conceptions of religion developing, and the same mystic aspirations. We might even say that in these different religions, at this particular stage, the same level of religious sentiment is attained. For those who know how to look at it, the instinctive communion which tends to grow up between liberal Catholics and educated Protestants is an interesting spectacle. Most of them, in the one camp as in the other, show themselves very thoroughly surprised if this is mentioned: each side protests its independent standpoint and at once instances the disagreements. These undoubtedly exist; nevertheless the efforts of these men, still attached to different creeds betray such conformity that they lead alike, we might believe, to a religion under the control of science and reason, and to a pragmatism in both of the same nature and the same extent. The orthodox Catholics, held back by the fear of "modernism," are ready to believe this to be due to "Protestant infiltrations," whilst certain orthodox Protestants are troubled about "Catholic infiltrations"; the truth being that men of the same standards of culture on both sides are seeking the same balance between their science and their faith.

It is just the same with those in the lower standards of culture. There the phenomenon is no doubt less clearly visible, because there men's minds are less open, less supple; because they are not so given to reflection, and above all because religious questions, generally, are less discussed among them. It does occur, however. All else being equal, the sympathy which in these days we see establishing itself between the same social grades from one country to another, tending to an internationalism of the proletariat, the middle classes and the capitalists, at any rate as to their economic interests, may give us some idea of what is going on when the same general mentality, characteristic of the same intellectual or social class, is applied at the same time to several different religions in the same country. This also accounts for the unconsciously unifying sympathy which is created and developed between the corresponding strata of these parallel religions.

If this interchange is sufficiently active—and that depends upon the intensity of the religious life, which again is usually due to a variety of complex causes—it may determine the rise of a religious movement which may have for issue that coördination of borrowings from the past, and that re-formation of bygone elements, which is called a new religion, or at any rate, a renascence, a revival of the established religion. For that process to begin and to be pursued, there must first of all be a special exciting cause, and it must proceed either from the initiative of one man or the working of a group of persons; then one or two leading ideas must be emphasized to serve as rallying points in relation to which the others are established and organized. They need not necessarily be very original, these essential conceptions of the religion which is being born or reborn. On the contrary, they will have more likelihood of succeeding, of becoming more firmly implanted in men's consciousness if they are already somewhat familiar and express their aspirations and desires well, or rather, if they issue from them almost entirely. It has been maintained, and not without some reason apparently, that it is the milieu which creates the hero who is needed by it; it is also the milieu which engenders the prophet whom it must have; he it is who is the source of the pressure that causes the confession of faith which he feels to be more or less of a necessity to well forth. And every milieu to which it is transported tends to modify it, to fashion it in accordance with its own religious consciousness; and all carry it along in ceaseless transformation, through life and to death.

II

The critical study of the beginnings of Christianity and the evolution of the Church has now reached its proper place in the science of history. It is not, however, so advanced as the increasing number of books to its credit might make us believe, and many of its conclusions have not attained the degree of certainty to which other branches of erudition have already been raised. For this reason, among others, it still, in the minds of many learned men, and with the ordinary public who read and listen, has to submit to a great deal of mistrust and prejudice. Sometimes, indeed, still worse, it encounters complete indifference. Practically negligible, or nearly so, in the countries of Protestant formation and Germanic culture, these suspicions constitute, in countries which are of Catholic tradition and Latin mentality, a large and solid obstacle, very difficult to surmount, upon which much time and many efforts are spent in vain. The truth is, however, the science of past Christianity is not entirely responsible for its retardation, for it has made a great effort to make up for lost time, and thus far has attained results which are everywhere consider-able and, upon some essential points, decisive.

Until the earlier part of the nineteenth century, a veritable taboo forbade access to primitive Christianity for scholars who were disinterested and, quite uncon-cerned about the exploitation of truth in the interests of any particular religion, seek it for its own sake. Public opinion regarded the history of Christianity as the proper domain of clergy and theologians, and, since it was scarcely more than that it had some reason for consider-ing it as the complement, or rather, as one of the forms of apologetics, or a field of research reserved for pure erudition.[1] From the days of the Reformation long practice had accustomed it to seeing disputants, Papist or Huguenot, plunging both hands into the ancient text, as into a well-filled arsenal, where each might always find the arguments that suited him. In the course of the eighteenth century, the political enemies of the Catholic Church, and the ''philosophers'' who considered her dogmas obsolete, had followed the course and sometimes the method of Protestant polemics, but their criticism seemed no more disinterested than that of the ministers of the Reformed Church; it was only the spirit and the aim of it that were different. In short, at the beginning of the nineteenth century impartially minded men might justly imagine that the history of Christianity was studied only for the purpose of exalting or abasing the Catholic Church. This opinion led to consequences, differing according to previous individual prejudices, but all agreed that it established, with respect to such history, a mistrust difficult to overcome. Some, like the

[1] The works of the admirable savants of the sixteenth and seven-teenth centuries, such as Baronius, Thomassin, Tillemont, Mabillon, Ruinart, Richard Simon and others, prepared the way for a veracious history of the Church by propounding methods and principles and unraveling certain problems; but they did not knit it together.

simple-minded and ignorant, in thrall to the hereditary "hypnosis" of a Christian upbringing, which acquiesces in or merely suffers, but never criticizes or even reasons out, naïvely submitted to the domination of the taboo, and turned aside, as from a sacrilegious and damnable enterprise, from research that the Church's teaching rendered useless, as they believed, and which she condemned. Others, won over to scepticism by their natural disposition or through some superficial course of reasoning, laid down as unassailable the position, revived from Cicero, that religion is necessary for the common people, that it constitutes a guarantee of its morality and a restraint upon its baser appetites, and that to overthrow the established Church would be prejudicial to all classes of society. Lastly, others of sluggish mentality or rash in their judgments, inclined mistakenly to imagine every religion a vast medley of fraud and exploitation engineered by the priests, were persuaded that Christianity at best merited but a shrug of the shoulders and a jest.

Why not confess this to be so? In the Latin countries, what is called "le grand public" still stands up for the same old points of view in order to justify its attitude of indifference with regard to the history of Christian origins and of the Church, and its ignorance of the methods, the questions taken up, and the results attained. And up to now the attitude of public instruction also with regard to it has only too fully justified the prejudices of which it is the object. To speak only of France, three universities alone have been provided by the State with professors for the special purpose of studying Christian history, and although these attract many hearers, they still win but a small number of students. It cannot be otherwise as long as our young men come to the university without having had their attention drawn to such questions by their teachers in the secondary school (bound as these are by legal obligation to preserve a neutral attitude), questions which the scheme of studies evidently propounds, but which official duty and the quasi-general desire of the masters lead them to shuffle aside instead of treating.

In truth, the reality hidden beneath these things must in a measure also bear its degree of responsibility. By this I mean that such a study can become organized only at the expense of much painful effort, and by facing manifold difficulties, so hard as to discourage the student. Viewed from without and by the uninitiated, it possibly does not present a very attractive appearance. Its austere aspect, the hesitations and uncertainties involved, even its sober restraint, all concur in alienating the thoughtless, as well as those whom the positive conclusions of the exact sciences alone delight.

First of all, the sources of information at its disposal are, more than in other branches of history, mediocre, confused, and difficult of utilization. The oldest and on the whole the most interesting sources, since they relate to Jesus and the early days of the faith, collected in the New Testament have themselves exacted a preliminary critical inquiry, both long and meticulous, and not yet completed; far from it. For a long period it has been scarcely possible to seek for any elements or confirmations outside itself, so that the exegetical writers have found themselves obliged to interpret and commentate if they would understand. And if they sought to rise above textual details, they had to systematize and pile up hypotheses. It was a deplorable necessity, which only too often handicaps them still, unfortunately, and which too many of them light-heartedly accept! Now it sometimes happens that at the very moment when critical work seems to be on a fair way toward success, some decisive document is brought to light; a new hypothesis springs up, an original point of view gains acceptance, which entirely destroys the work done. In this way, in the last fifteen or twenty years, the synoptic problem embracing various problems concerning the first three Gospels has, so to speak, suffered an entire reverse; the Pauline problem has undergone renovation, and even that of the fourth Gospel, which might have been con-

sidered settled, has been propounded afresh in a different
form. These ficklenesses and doublings of criticism—
and examples would be easy to multiply—these perpetual
shifts in point of view and system have but one cause:
the documents by themselves furnish no connected and
coherent history of Christian origins; they make up only
fragmentary pictures of it, and the restoration of the
whole too often remains hypothetical.

Even outside the early days of the faith, the period
comprising the second, third and fourth centuries (in
which orthodox dogma was established, the clerical
hierarchy constituted, and the liturgy organized) is far
from being brought into strong relief in all its parts.
Our texts concerning it are rarely impartial and seldom
numerous enough to verify each other. The enemies of
the victorious Church of the fourth century, pagans and
various dissenters, had written a great deal against her,
or concerning her; this literature has almost entirely
disappeared and the little that remains is only enough
to show us how great would be the service it might
render. Because it has no alternative but to use (a)
polemical or exegetical writings mainly, badly emended
by accounts reputed to be historical, but written long
after the events and at a time when they were scarcely
understood, and (b) theological treatises, which reveal
more of the opinion of the learned than the living faith of
the simple layman, hardly helped at all by epigraphy
designedly fashioned to remain vague and imperfect, the
history of Christianity during the three centuries in
which the Church was constituted has been worse served
than any other branch of general history of the same
period. It is right and necessary that we should not
forget this fact. None of the difficulties which the history
of classic times encounters is spared a student of the
ancient Christian history, and it presents others which
are impediments peculiar to itself alone.

On the other hand, it must be admitted that the exegetists and the historians of primitive Christianity have
frequently lost a good deal of time through propounding

some of the problems badly. For example, to try to
extract from the collection of Christian documents alone
an exact idea of the early times of the Church was to
give way to a tantalizing delusion. Whether the fact was
realized or not, the undertaking was inspired by pre-
judgments of the faith. People could not make up their
minds to consider the Christian religion as *one* of the
religions of humanity; they endeavored to preserve its
old standing as an originality, and this desire was fed
from more than one root in the theological postulate of
revelation.

At the present time it is generally agreed that to drain
the Christian sources and give an exact account not only
of the state of the religious feeling, but of ethics and of
society in the Greco-Roman world in which the faith was
to make its way and find its sustenance, does not supply
material enough for us to understand its underlying
principle, or very essence, nor to grasp the reasons which
have given rise to it. It is thought that the secret of its
birth and early structure is to be found, for the most
part, in Syria, in Asia Minor, in Egypt, even in Mesopotamia, throughout the Eastern milieu in which it first
appeared or found its first vital elements. Meticulous
study given to the inscriptions, to the familiar documents
yielded by the papyri and ostraka,[2] begins to throw a
hitherto unsuspected light upon the New Testament
language and upon the mentality, customs, aspirations
and religious habits of the men by whom and for whom it
was written. The advance made in Eastern archeology,
properly so called, contributes to the same result.

Moreover, neither the Christian nor the anti-Christian

[2] This is the term used for the scraps of earthenware which, particularly in the Hellenistic world, have been used as writing material.
We find on them receipts, statements of account, extracts from classical
authors, various maxims and, among the Christians, verses of Scripture.
An exceedingly good dictionary, still uncompleted, places at the disposal of the erudite who apply themselves to the study of the New
Testament all the linguistic acquisitions which we owe to these various
documents, recently brought to bear upon the question. *Cf.* J. H. Moul-
ton and G. Milligan, *The Vocabulary of the Greek Testament Illustrated
from the Papyri and Other Non-Literary Sources* (London, New York,
Toronto, 1915).

writers have laid down their weapons. The Christians are not content with all their efforts to maintain in the minds of those who will listen to them—and they are many—the conviction that the liberal seekers after truth appear as enemies of the faith who are the more dangerous the more disinterested they seem. They put together, both in their schools and in their writings, a counter-history of Christianity. By this I mean that, while professing to adopt unreservedly the methods of scientific criticism, they apply these in their own way and in such a fashion that they always lead them— *mirabile dictu*—to conclusions that are in conformity with the assertions of tradition. And in the judgment of people who are not well informed, this history is as good as the other. On the other hand, the anti-clerical polemists turn the discoveries of the savants to account. It is impossible to prevent mischief of this kind, but the science of Christianity does not gain much standing from it, and even runs the risk of very annoying complications, as far as public opinion is concerned. The thoughtful man is not particularly astonished at this outcome, for he knows that it takes a long time to dispel appearances.

What I have just said applies particularly to the study of Christianity in classical times, but the history of the Church, in medieval, modern and present-day life, presents difficulties which, though slightly different, prove no less embarrassing. Documents are not wanting, and usually they seem fairly easy to interpret, but they are very scattered, and if they prove of sufficient interest to alter the opinion we are trying to form of the Church nowadays, passion and partisanship set to work upon them, and it often becomes very difficult to discern and determine their true meaning and import. To get a clear idea of what I mean, it is enough to think for a moment of the disputes concerning—taking things at haphazard—for instance monachism, the Inquisition, the causes of the Reformation, the personality of Luther, the spirit and the morals of the Papacy at diverse periods, casuistry, the Jesuits, the Syllabus of Pius IX, the doctrine of Infallibility, or the policy of Pius X. Little by little, time and scholarly patience perform their work, and the truth emerges from the strife and imposes itself upon the disputants.

Christian history, however, is far from having entered that happy sphere of entire scientific serenity in which the seeker, desirous only of finding out the facts, sees them as they are, and requires no other service from them than to add to his knowledge. Hereditary prejudices still taboo many great questions; diverse interests, religious, moral, or even political and social, lay a snare for scholarly curiosity; there is the legitimate dread of becoming unwillingly involved in polemics, which one may fear is not altogether honest and sincere. Other obstacles in its path are the gaps, doubts, and the disheartening ignorance, to which all true savants confess; rash presumptions, premature or shocking hypotheses, like those which would do away with the very existence of Christ; the clash of systems and the disputes of the erudite; and lastly, the necessity of the prolonged and painful effort necessary to follow up complicated research and tortuous arguments. All these are hindrances which serve to account, first, for the slowness with which the scientific history of Christianity is being built up; and, second, for the existence of a general feeling of indifference or distrust with regard to it, at least in the Latin countries, where the best educated almost all display ignorance of it, an ignorance both profound and deplorable.

Nevertheless, to anyone who deigns to look into the matter, it is clearly evident that the efforts of generations of scholars have not been useless. They have at least reached the point of propounding all questions at issue upon a basis of positive science. Even the number of those problems which they have solved is already large enough for their solutions to offer a solid foundation for some general conclusions. We do not know everything; on many questions we do not even know all the essentials; but we can at least determine the main lines of travel taken in the evolution of Christianity; we can distinguish its principal stages, analyze its essential factors, and also, in cases where positive evidence escapes us, we can advance with considerable assurance many important negations and definitely denounce the falsity of many traditions which have long led history astray. All this is indeed something of an achievement.

III

The genesis and progress of Christianity, viewed from without, setting aside not only every theological and metaphysical bias, but also any wish actually to comprehend them, appear to be a historical fact of a collective order, which may be broken up into parts somewhat as follows. In the reign of the emperor Tiberius, a certain Jesus of Nazareth arises in Galilee; he speaks and acts like a Jewish prophet, announcing the speedy advent of the Kingdom of God and exhorting men to become better, that they may secure for themselves a place in it; after he has gathered round him a few adherents his career is suddenly brought to a brutal end. But his work does not perish with him; it is carried on by his disciples. He is himself soon found to be the center of a really new religion, which spreads through the Greco-Roman world and, at the same time, severs itself from Judaism. By degrees this religion secures a better standing; it makes many converts, and finally proves disquieting to the Roman state, which persecutes it, but does not succeed in arresting its progress; it organizes and becomes a church which grows ever stronger; in Constantine's time it is tolerated by the emperor, then gains him to its side, and leads him to attack paganism. At the end of the fourth century it reigns, at least officially, throughout the Roman Empire. Since that time, the Christian faith has conquered Europe and spread throughout the world. And, at the first glance, these present themselves as such surprising results, compared with the modest proportions which Jesus seemed to have given to his work, that Christians feel that they can account for them only by representing them as the fulfilment of God's eternal plan for the salvation of men. Since Jesus, according to orthodox theology, is God, it must be believed that he willed this expansion, and that in spite of appearances, during his terrestrial existence, he organized implicitly a perfect religion, and that the entire Christian life is but the necessary development of the principles he laid down. In this way the establishing and evolution of Christianity throughout the ages are due entirely to his will, and, in the realm of things visible, setting aside the mystery of the Redemption, it was to found a creed of catholicity that he became incarnate, suffered, and died.

Do not let us dwell upon the reservations which a disinterested observer of the facts would not fail to formulate at once, namely, that the waverings, doublings, and changes more or less profound, the disputes, divisions and schisms which plentifully bestrew the history of the Christian Church, are scarcely reconcilable with the supposition of a distinctly defined plan, formed in the beginning by the Founder, and since followed out, point by point. But the sketch we have just given of the birth, growth and triumph of Christianity has taken account of the facts according to appearances only; it has not tried to penetrate their inmost recesses and actually explain them to us; it has only demonstrated their course and the connection between them, chronologically rather than logically. Apropos of these events, or among them, numerous questions of capital importance arise; these concern the foundation and the "essence" of Christianity, the meaning and the general disposition of the Christian evolution. It is questions of this nature which form the true material of the ancient history of the Church. Her medieval and her modern history, intimately bound up with general history, are much clearer to our vision than this time of her beginnings, in which so much uncertainty and doubt crowd to the surface.

PART I

CHRISTIANITY IN CLASSICAL TIMES: THE CREED AND THE CHURCH

CHAPTER I

CHRISTIANITY, therefore, was born of a Jewish movement. As it appears first of all, it was a development
solely of interest to the religious life of Israel, thoroughly
characteristic of the Palestinian milieu and rightly inconceivable outside the Jewish world. Although its growth
was destined in the course of time to be hastened on and
influenced by many different factors, its beginnings are
due to the initiative of a Galilean, Jesus the Nazarene—
that is, not the *man of Nazareth* apparently, but the *nazir*,
the *holy man of God*.[1]

To me it seems impossible to call his existence in question, as even in these days some endeavor to do.[2] But
directly we have affirmed it, we find ourselves involved,
to tell the truth, in doubt and uncertainty. To such an
extent is this so, that one of the main results of the
research to which in the last few years the primitive
documents have been subjected is that the impossibility
has been demonstrated of depicting the life of Jesus
with any real certainty. All the books which claim to
give us that history must be regarded as more or less
arbitrary and subjective. It is easy to give the reasons
for this conclusion. The men who had listened to the
words of the Christ and believed them after they had
given way to despair at his Passion and begun to proclaim his resurrection, did not feel any necessity for
setting down in writing their recollections and their
impressions. They took no thought for the instruction

[1] Upon this question of Nazareth, *see* Ch. Guignebert, *La vie cachée
de Jésus* (Paris, 1921), pp. 59 *et seq.*
[2] *Cf.* Ch. Guignebert, *Le problème de Jésus* (Paris, 1914); J. Case,
The Historicity of Jesus (Chicago, 1912); M. Goguel, *Jésus de Nazareth,
mythe ou histoire?* (Paris, 1925).

of posterity because they felt sure it would never come into being. At any moment the world of injustice and error, the world of the flesh, would come to an end; the human race would cease to exist, and the conquering Messiah would shine in glory in the clouds of heaven.

On the other hand, it was scarcely possible for their faith not to overmaster their recollections and distort them. They were sustained by the conviction that Jesus the Nazarene was indeed the Messiah promised to Israel *and* that he was enthroned on high on the right hand of God, awaiting the hour of his triumph. This conviction readily induced them to endow an apparently ordinary life, a very restricted success and a degrading death with profound meaning. It led them to seek instruction and portentous signs in its most minute incidents; to apply to their Master all the Scriptural passages thought to relate to the Blessed of Jahveh; and as a consequence to find in his life the fulfilment of all these prophecies. Thus their pious imagination mixed with the facts commentaries and additions imposed upon them, by this same conviction, as necessary and absolutely true, so to speak, since they were but fitting Jesus out with the nature and function of the Messiah. In the simplicity of their hearts, they very quickly became unable to distinguish these addenda from the data vouched for by their memories; at any rate, they are confounded in the teaching done by them, and their disciples were literally incapable of separating them again. Above all, the ecstasy of their faith left them powerless to suspend judgment in face of suggested special revelations and visions. That which any one of them learned by a direct communication from the Holy Ghost showed a power to impose itself upon him and the others with an imperative certitude which even the most direct of ''historical'' recollections did not surpass, even if they equaled it. What St. Paul, for instance, had learnt ''in the spirit'' from the Lord Jesus seemed to him more direct and much more certain than that which the Apostles Peter and James could tell him.

It was, therefore, from elements that were heterogeneous and very unequal in value that the tradition (*paradosis*) was fashioned which the believers in the first generation after Christ accepted as the authentic history of the Master. It was only after those belonging to the first generation were in their graves that this disappearance of the direct *witnesses* of Jesus, one after another, gave rise to doubts as to the imminence of the expected coming of the Lord. Then it was that the more prudent Christians deemed it expedient to commit to writing the recollections which oral tradition was reputed to have preserved.[3]

First to be formed, probably, were little books of memoranda in which each writer collected what he deemed specially interesting: connected sayings attributed to the Master; accounts of episodes in his life which were characteristic or edifying; descriptions of the "signs," that is, the miracles which he had performed to confound the incredulous. Nobody troubled about what we term historical exactitude, which presumes scruples unknown or indifferent to men of an ardent faith, who are therefore as devoid as possible of a critical spirit; on the other hand, each one aimed at establishing the soundness of the Christian hopes, at convincing the doubters and edifying the believers.

These little books constituted the ancient sources of our Gospels. The collection of the Logia or Sayings of the Lord Jesus, attributed to Matthew, and the narrative recital attributed to Mark which were, it appears, the chief of them, could at most only contain the scattered and already very mixed elements of a life of Jesus, such as it would be imagined to have been toward the close of the Apostolic generation. The successive writers of our Gospels, in the final third of the first century at

[3] Upon all that concerns synoptic tradition and the constitution of the Gospels, see the bibliography in G. B. Smith, *A Guide*, etc., p. 199 *et seq.;* and M. Goguel, *Introduction au Nouveau Testament*, Vol. I, *Les Evangiles synoptiques* (Paris, 1923), Vol. II, *Le Quatrième Evangile* (1924). An English translation of the New Testament specially to be recommended is that of J. Moffatt, *The New Testament* (New York, 1918).

earliest, evidently sought to make their story a coherent one. But, besides the fact that it would doubtless have been impossible to separate the real facts from the comments which modified them, to distinguish between what had happened and what faith imagined to have happened "that the Scriptures might be fulfilled," between that which they remembered and that which the Spirit had suggested to them, they had no desire to carry out such a sifting. Moreover, they found themselves dealing with material which it was very difficult to utilize. The collection of sayings preceding their own took no account of the circumstances in which the Lord had uttered them; the grouping in the various memoranda which is everywhere artificial, would probably be dissimilar. It was the same with accounts in them of events, properly so called, for these related episodes only and with considerable variance between one writer and another. They found it necessary to pick and choose, and then combine into a connected narrative fragments which were fairly incongruous.

We have only to peruse the three synoptic Gospels to be convinced that their authors have arrived at perceptibly different combinations of the same facts and of discourses which are identical or similar. We must conclude, therefore, that they have not been actuated by objective truth. They have not taken into account a chronological order of events sufficiently stable to impose itself upon them all, but on the contrary each one has followed a scheme of his own in the arrangement of his work. It is just as plain that not one of them had at his command a complete sequence of facts sufficiently condensed to permit him to give a satisfactory picture of the entire life of Christ. Not one of them has done anything but tie and fasten together, more or less skilfully, scraps of tradition which form an apparent ensemble but do not make a whole. In the development of the Gospel narrative immense gaps are either perceptible or to be divined, even in that of Mark, who is, however, prudent enough to say nothing about the birth or childhood of Jesus.

Now faith does not want to remain in ignorance, and it always learns what it needs to know; pious imagination is ever at its service. This is why the first, third and fourth Gospels give us accounts which are truly dissimilar, even contradictory, but all wonderful and very instructive respecting the period upon which the second is silent. Each fills up the gaps in its own way. The only thing is that these have not much in common, it is very evident, with history. It even appears probable that the recollections relating to the Passion had already been somewhat similarly impaired before the editing of our Gospels. Apparently they had been influenced by various legends known throughout the East and thus early had been interpreted in such a way as to give them a new complexion on many important points. And on the other hand, why not bring them into line with the initiative of the Master, add and incorporate in his traditional teaching all that the living faith of his disciples (obliged, so to speak, by his death and resurrection to see past, present and future only in the Messianic perspective) could fruitfully bring forth? Why not, for instance, attribute to the Master the order to baptize and the institution of the Eucharist, since baptism constitutes the seal of the faith even from Apostolic times, and the Eucharist the visible bond of brotherhood one with another, as well as that of Christ with them all, according to the interpretation of St. Paul?

Thus we can no longer see clearly the figure of the historical Jesus; no longer have we the means of depicting his life to ourselves correctly. Of the historical Jesus we may say that something may still be divined beneath diverse features of evangelical tradition, and of a correct biography we may hope to retain some episodes. Upon the one as on the other, and indeed upon all that relates to that which Jesus is reputed to have taught, it is expedient to affirm nothing save with the utmost caution.

Nevertheless, we know that upon a certain day this same Jesus left his family and began to traverse Galilee and to preach. Wherefore? Was it only because he felt the need of doing it in response to a vocation spontaneously created in him, though it is inexplicable to us, which urged him irresistibly onward? Undoubtedly, to some extent; but unless we accept the postulate of divine inspiration, which history cannot take into consideration because it is beyond verification and does away with all discussion, a vocation of such a nature cannot be understood save as the result of the influences of a milieu. The originality of an inspired person depends wholly upon the form he gives to the working over and assembling of the influences he has undergone which have unconsciously been performed in him. The problem of the rise of Jesus, therefore, leads us back historically to the intellectual milieu whence he sprang.

II

This milieu is not yet thoroughly familiar to us, but we are beginning to know it. We note that it presents itself under two aspects, or rather, that it is twofold. Christ was born a Jew; he grew up in Jewish circles from which, as far as we can judge, he derived the elements of his intellectual and religious training exclusively. Israel, it must be remembered, had not been able to isolate itself completely from the Syro-Chaldean peoples among whom it lived, or not enough so to succeed in escaping the stamp of their influence entirely. It had also retained some traces of its prolonged contact (a) with the conquering Greeks who had come from the kingdom of the Ptolemies and from the Seleucid kingdom of Syria, and (b) with its own sons who were established on Greek soil whom the great feasts brought each year, in varying numbers, to Jerusalem. In the two or three centuries, therefore, which precede the Christian era, it had domesticated more than one foreign idea and made it its own.

In the second place, be it noted that all around the Jewish world of Palestine was a pagan milieu. If it did not directly influence Jesus, it was to attract and influence his disciples almost immediately after his death. Bordering on Palestine to the north, west and southwest it was a Syrian and Phenician milieu which we divine more than clearly see, whence came mingled beliefs, forms of worship, superstitions and the prejudices, or perhaps merely mementoes, of various religions past and present. To the east it was a Mesopotamian milieu, in which the religious influences of India and Persia mingled on Babylonian soil. This region was the parent of many ancient myths current throughout the Semitic world, and also of forms of speculative thought in which metaphysics and astrology combined to offer an explanation of the universe and of human destiny. To the south it was an Egyptian milieu, where ancient national cults were revamped, expanded and, as it were, universalized under the fertilizing influence of Greek thought. Finally, to the north there was a Hellenistic milieu (in that section which we know as Asia Minor), a still more complicated one, but also more richly stored because it formed a kind of crossroad of religions. Besides the local cults, many of which were still active and powerful, the myths of the Olympian religion, and the theories and dogmas, more or less popularized, of the Greek philosophers, many other "contaminating influences" flowed in from all the milieus just mentioned, including even the Jewish.

Here was, so to speak, a vast and partly amorphous conglomerate of religious material which was not only already being organized into syncretistic combinations, more or less unusual, but lent itself indefinitely to all kinds of exploitation. For the future of Christianity, therefore, it constituted an almost inexhaustible reserve. But, I must repeat, Christ himself was, to all appearances, exclusively molded in the Jewish milieu,—for there is no vestige of proof for the theory sometimes advanced, of direct formative influence by Buddhism or Hellenism over him—and it was through the Jews, as intermedi-

aries, that the Christian religion first spread beyond
Palestine. Let us then cast a glance upon that Jewish
world before we try to take into account the religious
aspect of the other terrains to which we shall find the
Christian doctrine spreading.

The Jewish milieu in itself was an extremely complex
assemblage of influences at the time of Herod the Great
(who died four years before the birth of Christ).
Beneath an apparent uniformity of race, customs and
religion, the population of Judea in reality formed two
peoples of somewhat differing mentality and dissimilar
religious tendencies.[*]

The remote cause of this condition of things must be
sought very far back. When the king of Babylon had
deemed it wise to transport the Jews whom he had vanquished to the banks of the Euphrates, *super flumina
Babylonis,* he had taken account only of the families of
some importance. The country folk, the smaller fry, had
remained at home and continued no doubt to practice the
ancient religion of Israel in pious fashion, trustful of
Jahveh, but at any rate not so strict that they were unable
to compromise with the deities around them and their
adherents. Since the ancient Jahvehism was essentially
a man's religion, these worthy Jewish peasants did not
shun the making of mixed marriages, which mingled the
blood of foreign women with that of the elect people.
On the other hand, the exiles, or those at least whom
despair did not drive into the idolatry of their conquerors, rapidly developed. They found themselves
forced to reconsider the Covenant concluded between
Jahveh and his people in an endeavor to account for
their present misfortunes, to imagine a more consoling
future, and to use all the means at their command of
avoiding the repetition of such calamities. And they
convinced themselves that the ills under which Israel was

[*] The essential work here is Schürer's, *Geschichte des jüdischen
Volkes im Zeitalter Jesu Christi* (Leipzig, 1901-1909). Shailer Mathew's
A History of New Testament Times in Palestine (New York, London,
1902), may also be consulted with advantage. *Cf.* G. B. Smith's *A
Guide,* p. 179.

suffering arose out of its faithlessness to the Covenant.
There was only one way for them to appease an offended
God, and that was to put themselves under a regimen of
the utmost rigor in their devotional observances. This
meant in practice for them to set up and establish a very
strict ritual which should render idolatry an impossibility. The composition of this ritual, the establishment
of this strict legalism, strengthened by a new edition of
the Law in conformity to fresh needs, were the work of
prophets of the Exile, Ezekiel in particular. When
through the favor of Cyrus consent was given in 538
B.C. that these exiles might return to their country, they
did not all profit by the permission, but those who did
brought with them into Judea the new Law and the new
spirit and—an essential detail—they remained in close
relations with their brethren in Babylon, who helped
them, by their influence with the king of Persia, and
their money and moral support, to impose these imported
rules upon the resident population. The reorganizers of
the Temple and its worship and the implacable foes of
mixed marriages and concessions to foreigners were the
Jews Esdras and Nehemiah, envoys from Babylon. They
were already scribes, that is, men who had studied the
Law. They expounded the new edition and began to
institute, side by side with it, a complete jurisprudence
to settle those matters of conscience which could not fail
to multiply the moment that absolute legal exactitude of
compliance was set down, as the first requirement of
real piety.

The period which extends from the return from exile
to the birth of Jesus thus witnessed, in the first place,
the growth of a vast priesthood, a sacerdotal caste, which
hovered around the Temple without a rival and insured
the regularity of its service, but neither specially studied
nor taught the Law. From a natural propensity, it was
inclined to attach importance to rites and formulas only.
In the second place, the period was marked by the rise
of the scribes, or doctors of the Law, between whom
there was the keenest rivalry in ingenious probings into

all the recesses of the Sacred Writings. They comment, wrangle, and very often, despite their sincere and deep personal piety, end in stifling the free and spontaneous religion of the heart beneath the accumulation of their overscrupulous formalism. Certain among them, for instance, were concerned to know whether an egg laid upon the Sabbath could be considered clean, or if clean water, falling into an unclean vessel, was not thereby rendered unclean right from its very source.

Some of them, indeed, unconsciously influenced by Greek speculation concerning God, the world and man, enlarge and sublimate the ancient idea of Jahveh, and he becomes the God *per se,* not to be defined and not even to be named. Their tendency is to adopt a dualistic cosmology and anthropology, in which two contrary elements, matter and spirit, body and soul, are opposed. And in this way, quite counter to the influence of the finally exaggerated legalism, the nationalistic religion of Israel begins to be universalized and really to be humanized. This work is naturally carried further and accomplished more speedily in the Jewish colonies on pagan soil, where we shall find it later on, but from the beginning of the Christian era it had already been going on for some time in Palestine itself, and had there yielded appreciable results.

The people obey the priests because they are its national leaders: the High Priest alone is qualified to represent Israel to the Persian or Greek overlord. Judea thus becomes a theocratic state, and even during the Asmonean epoch,[5] although it believes itself independent, it remains theocratic, since the king is at the same time High Priest. On the other hand, this same people admires the learned scribes given to many scruples. In reality, however, neither the sceptical ritualism of the priests nor the haughty pedantry of the scribes touches the nation profoundly or satisfies its piety. Little by

[5] That is, in the time of the Maccabees, Judas, Jonathan, Simon; John Hyrcanus, Aristobulus and Alexander Jannaeus, between 165 and 70 B. C., for from the death of Jannaeus to the coming of Herod the Arab, in 40 B. C., there was a period of anarchy and decadence.

little it submits to the urge of rigorism. It debars strangers as far as it can and even is incensed at seeing its leaders at times becoming excessively "Grecianized." But it continues to love Jahveh with its whole heart, and in its days of tribulation to pray with a fervor inspired by the piety of former days and not imprisoned within the newer forms. In other words, its religion lives and develops. It takes up several ideas which are not properly Jewish but have come from the East—conceptions of the part played by angels and demons and the idea of a future life and of a last judgment. Then also, even the misfortunes of their times—for the Jews suffered much at the hands of the Egyptians, Syrians, Romans and from troubles of their own making during the four centuries which preceded the coming of Christ—served their religion. From them it reaps more complete domination for an ancient hope: it awaits, it calls at the top of its throat, for the Messiah, who is to restore to Israel more than its splendor of the time of David. These preoccupations of the popular faith are at last accepted by the scribes themselves; they expound, and to some extent, consecrate them. And the more that events seem to prove them in the wrong, the harder the yoke of the foreigner becomes, the more does this idea entrench itself within the minds of the plain people, the larger the place it occupies in their convictions.

We must not forget that at this time the Jews, as well as many others in the world, have not the least idea of what we call "natural laws," of the necessary and invariable connection between causes and effects. Convinced that with God all things are possible, they perceive no boundary line between fact and miracle. Indeed, they live altogether on the plane of the marvelous, for anything that is a "surprise" to them appears for that reason the direct act of God or of the Devil. This explains why they are easily persuaded that the amazing revolution which they hope for will be unfailingly accomplished as soon as Jahveh wills it, and that their restless anticipations await its announcement with ever increasing nervous tension. This Messianic hope, from which Israel expected signal amends for its misfortunes and oblivion for its humiliations, was on the contrary destined to lead it into most disastrous adventures, upon which it would plunge full tilt, because it was convinced that thus the Great Day would dawn and help from heaven arrive, if only they helped themselves. The fearful rebellions of the first and second centuries A. D. which decimated the Jews and consummated the ruin of their nation all proceeded from the persuasion that the time was fulfilled, and that the promise formerly proclaimed by the prophets was at length to be realized.

Now, in Galilee, in that northern part of Palestine where Jesus was born, the majority of the people were simple folk. The district had only been induced to participate in the new Jewish life in the time of the Maccabees; it had never viewed the sacerdotal hierarchy save from afar. If the scribes did not avoid it altogether, they did not swarm there as they did in Jerusalem or in Judea, properly so called, and they had not acquired the reputation and influence there which were the lot of the masters of the Judean schools. It was commonly said that the Galileans were unmanageable, doubtless because in the early times of the Roman domination some very resolute nationalistic gangs had taken refuge in their mountains. Fun was made, too, of them on account of their provincial accent. As a matter of fact, their piety retained, it seems, a spontaneity, ardor and profundity which testified to an intensely fervent religious life which was missing in the scrupulosity of Judean Pharisaism.

Jesus, therefore, was born and grew up in a district in which the majority of minds were preoccupied with religious interests. He sprang from a sphere in which the habit of life was one of simple hope and of anxious expectation of a certain miraculous event, procurable by the Jews, through their piety alone, which would render them masters of the world. But this people is governed by priests who do not share this hope and are mistrustful of the difficulties it may create for them with their foreign political masters. It is to some extent hemmed in by teachers of the stamp that can say that no ignorant person could be pious, and who feel scarcely any sympathy for a popular movement.

III

We have given, therefore, a profoundly pious man of the people whose mentality has not been withered in any way by the doctrine of the scribes, but from earliest childhood has been imbued with the prevailing ideas of his milieu, one who has acquired no intellectual or religious or moral life save through them. If he is also endowed with that singularly marvelous faculty of mustering within himself thoughts which are floating in the air he breathes and re-creating them, as it were, by his meditation upon them (and that must be the case with all who are inspired), it is easy to understand how he should come to translate his convictions into actions. An inspired Galilean of that epoch could not fail to announce in a more or less personal and original way the imminent realization of the hopes of the age. And such appears to have been, in fact, the origin of the "rise" of Jesus.[6]

Documents which would enable us to explore the material of details of his intellectual development and grasp the precise determining causes of the path taken by his initiative are lacking. It is not necessary, however, to assume that there was anything complicated about either. All our Gospels note an ill-defined but .real relation between the opening of his public life and the preaching of another inspired layman who proclaimed the necessity for repentance in view of the near approach of the promised era. It may be that Jesus had known John the

[6] Renan's *Vie de Jésus* is negligible from the scientific point of view. Loisy, *Jésus et la tradition évangélique* (Paris, 1910) and Bousset, *Kyrios Christos* (Göttingen, 1913), Chaps. i and ii may be read, as well as Barth, *Die Hauptprobleme des Lebens Jesu* (Gutersloh, 1911) and O. Schmiedel, *Die Hauptprobleme der Leben-Jesu-Forschung* (Tübingen, 1906). *Cf.* G. B. Smith's *A Guide*, pp. 268 *et seq.*, which gives a critical bibliography.

Baptist and had been to hear him, and that through his example the vocation slowly and mysteriously preparing in the depths of his consciousness was irresistibly imposed upon his will. It may be that at the news of the imprisonment of John by Herod Antipas Jesus began to preach, in order that the Kingdom should not lack a herald. After all, he only renewed the prophetic tradition of Israel which had been suspended since the return from exile, but which many *nebim* before him, the Baptist among them, had already sought to restore. His initiative, however original its form may appear at first sight, was not in itself exceptional or unexpected.

Whether he knew from the very beginning what he really wanted, or even what he represented, may be doubted. Proceeding on different lines from the Baptist, for he had entirely renounced the ascetic life and the menacing language of his predecessor, Jesus developed the same main themes: The Kingdom is at hand, that great transformation which shall rid the world of injustice and evil; repent, if you would have a place among the elect. Why did he say this? He said it because he was urged thereto by a secret force, because he felt the Lord within him, as had all the inspired Jewish prophets. And what did he mean by it? How did he picture the Kingdom and its coming, in his own mind? We do not know; for our texts date from a time when the delay in the coming of the Kingdom had already modified the portrait of it in the minds of Christians. He doubtless imagined it in conformity with what was said about it around himself as the advent of materialized joy for Israel and a dazzling manifestation of the benediction of Jahveh, the form of which popular imagination had never really determined exactly and which he himself, possibly, did not strictly define. There is nothing to assure us that in the beginning he did not make allusions to Messianic upheavals of the warfare which, according to majority opinion, the Messiah was to bring upon the world. Our Gospels carry some traces of this frame of mind, but it is natural that these features should have gradually disappeared and little be left of them in writings designed to prove that in him, so mild and peace-loving, would be found he "who should come."

Did he believe himself to be the Messiah? It has been doubted; it is still doubted, and with considerable show of reason: never did he openly apply the title "Messiah" (in Greek, *Christos*) to himself. Close study of the passages in our Gospels in which the word appears does not allow us to refer a single case to either of the two main earliest sources: the collected sayings or Logia of the Lord, and the first Gospel, called Mark's.[7] And those which are apparently most convincing are the very ones which stand up the poorest under criticism: the famous confession of Messiahship before Caiphas the High Priest (Mk. xiv. 61), for instance, of which no guarantee of its wording exists nor does it appear to correspond with any context in historical reality. But at the time when the Gospel texts which we have at our command received their final form, it was inevitable, since faith in the Messiahship of Jesus had become the very foundation of Christianity, it should be affirmed in them in a conspicuous manner and made to appear authenticated by the Master in person. At any rate, "the words of the Gospel" and "the words of Jesus" are still two distinct and separate authorities for exegetists, and they come to a very certain exegetical conclusion that Jesus did *not* proclaim his Messiahship.

He never called himself "Son of God," an expression, moreover, which the judgment of a Jew would declare shocking nonsense as well as actual blasphemy. Not a single Gospel passage permits us to attribute it to Jesus with any certainty. It belongs rather to the language of

---

[7] In Mk. ix. 41 we certainly read: "For whosoever shall give you a cup of water to drink because ye are Christ's" (ὅτι Χριστοῦ ἐστε), but the authenticity of the characteristic words is renounced even by conservative exegists like Father Lagrange or H. Monnier, because the use of *Christos* without the article pertains to the language of St. Paul and not to that of the Synoptics, and because Matt. x. 42, the parallel passage with this, reads: "Whosoever shall give to drink unto one of these little ones a cup of cold water only, in the name of a disciple. . ." (εἰς ὄνομα μαθῆτου) a rendering that is much more likely to be the older one.

Hellenized Christians, such as St. Paul and the author of the fourth Gospel, by whom it would be regarded as profound sense and abundantly intelligible.[8]

He did not assume the title, "Son of David," which was well understood throughout Israel as essentially Messianic; he did not even make use of the designation which our Gospels seem to regard as characteristic of his personality and his mission, that of "Son of Man," or at any rate he did not employ it in the Messianic sense. This meaning for it was unknown to the Jews, for no reference from the noteworthy passage in the Book of Daniel (vii. 13-14), "I saw in the night visions, and behold there came with the clouds of heaven one like unto a son of man. . ." had yet been drawn by the rabbis to the appearance of the Messiah. Not till long after this, was it so referred to in the synagogue, and then it was due to the influence of the similar use made of it by the Christians. After a time believers understood so imperfectly the Aramaic language as to imagine a "son of man" (*bar nascha*) which means simply "a man," as found in the Logia or Sayings of the Lord, contained some mysterious meaning. They linked it with the use made of it by Daniel, which they did not understand either, and in both passages declared it to be a specially Christian equivalent for "Messiah." That this is an error cannot be doubted after examination of the text; and, in nearly all the passages of our Synoptics in which the expression occurs, it has been inserted by a redactor. In five or six passages only [9] is there a likelihood of its resting upon an authentic saying of Jesus, incorrectly translated, and even there it must be understood as if it read "a man."

[8] A Jew might call himself the "Servant of Jahveh," but not his "Son," and I think it probable that Jesus did, in fact, consider and represent himself as the Servant of God, according to the Psalmist.

The Hebrew word *Ebed*, which means "servant," is often translated in the Greek by the word παῖς, which means both "a servant" and "a child." The verbal transition from παῖς, "child," to υἱός, "son," was accordingly very simple, but the idea of "Son of God" is derived from the Hellenistic world.

[9] Matt. viii. 20 (Luke ix. 50); Matt. xi. 19 (Luke vii. 34); Matt. xii. 32 (Luke xii. 10); Matt. ix. 6 (Mark ii, 10; Luke v. 24); Matt. xii. 8 (Mk. ii. 28; Luke vi. 3).

For instance: "The foxes have holes . . . man has not where to lay his head"; or again: "And whosoever shall speak a word against the man it shall be forgiven him, but whosoever shall speak against the Holy Spirit, it shall not be forgiven him, neither in this world nor in that which is to come."

It is therefore an assured fact that primitive tradition had never openly declared that Jesus had given out that he was the Messiah, and we gain an impression of the same kind from that which is called the "Messianic secret," that is, the urgent (almost, according to Mark, menacing) command said to have been given on more than one occasion by the Master to his disciples, enjoining them to reveal nought of what they may divine, or learn, or catch a glimpse of, respecting his real status. What interest, therefore, would he have in disguising his identity and preserving silence about his mission, at the very moment when sense and meaning could only be made out of the contents of his preaching by proclaiming these very things? On the other hand, it is a problem bristling with difficulties set the historian to show the necessity of admitting that a Galilean peasant had so transformed the ideal hero upon whom the hopes of his nation were fixed as to have changed into a humble and resigned martyr the victorious king who was to become the Messiah. Certain commentators have tried to offset these contradictory difficulties by various suggestions which aim at proving that, if Jesus did not openly avow himself the Messiah, he believed that he was; he allowed his disciples to believe it; he perished because he had allowed Pilate to believe it. Had it been otherwise, they say, the Apostles would never have been able to conceive that the Crucified should have risen from the dead. None of these reasons is really very convincing. We may continue to find it surprising that Jesus did not explain himself more clearly upon this essential point. We may interpret the half avowals and the insinuations which the passages imply as devices of redactors which authentic tradition had renounced. We may infer that the Roman procurator had no need of any Messianic avowal to get rid of a Jewish agitator who was preaching the near advent of the Kingdom, which meant the imminent end of the Roman domination as a matter of course. Or lastly, we may believe that the love of the Apostles for their Master and the confidence they had in him sufficed to induce visions which implanted in them the absolute certainty of his resurrection and that the conviction that he had been "made Christ" by the will of God, as St. Peter is reputed to have said (Acts, ii. 36) grew out of the need of accounting for the miracle of the resurrection.

In short, there are fairly solid reasons for concluding that Jesus simply regarded himself and behaved *as a prophet,* who felt himself urged by the Spirit of Jahveh to proclaim the speedy realization of the great hope of Israel and the necessity of preparing for it. However, even in this case we may ask ourselves if he was not persuaded that a choice place was reserved for him in the *future* Kingdom, a status, therefore, which could scarcely fail to get confounded with the post of the Messiah itself. Many well-known exegetists, such as Loisy,[10] answer this question in the affirmative. But, if it is difficult to combat their reasons with assurance, it is equally so, in my opinion, to endorse them unreservedly. On this point, as on so many others, certitude of the truth escapes us.

[10] A. Loisy, *Les Evangiles synoptiques,* Vol. I, pp. 203-253.

CHAPTER II

The Gospel passages which are available, therefore, leave us in a state of uncertainty as to what Jesus himself thought about the guiding principle of his mission, the nature of his own personality and the scope of his own part. On the other hand, they make it clear that he was unsuccessful and that his Palestinian compatriots did not believe him in regard to his mission nor did they conform to the moral appeals made by him. During the time—a very brief one moreover—that he spent among them,[1] they looked upon his comings and goings with curiosity or with indifference, but no attempt to follow him took place. At the most, perhaps, he won over a few hundreds of simple Galileans. Although the Gospels portray crowds fascinated by his discourses thronging around him, that does not cause us to forget what they tell us elsewhere, with much more truth, of the hard hearts of the Jews. Indeed, Jesus himself seems to have despaired of softening them. The reasons for his failure are self-evident.

To the populace he did not speak in the terms they had anticipated. He preached self-examination, love of one's neighbor, humbleness of heart and a son's faith in God to people who were expecting an appeal to arms and the announcement of the final struggle preceding an everlasting triumph. He did not say to them: "Arise! the Messiah of Jahveh is in your midst," but: "Prepare yourselves by repentance to make a good showing in the Judgment which is at hand." He did not ask them

---

[1] Jesus' public ministry must not be calculated according to the data of the fourth gospel, which would allow us to attribute to it a duration of about three years. It actually lasted but a few months, possibly a few weeks only; upon this point we cannot be certain.

to act, but merely to mark time in a specified moral and religious attitude, which changed expectation into constraint. Though a son of Israel, he probably displayed a comparatively mild exclusiveness only. The heartfelt piety and the confiding faith of the Roman centurion or the woman of Canaan seemed to him to be worth as much as pure Jewish descent. Or rather, a heathen who believed through his words was considered by him as far superior to a well-born Jew who was an unbeliever. He said a good deal about justice, peace, devotion to the Father, and also spoke of resignation and patience. But of rebellion and of the triumph of the chosen people over other nations he never said a word. And although all this constitutes for us his originality and his charm, it could in no way please the ardent Messianists of Palestine.

To the Scribes he appeared to be an ignorant pretender, who naïvely assumed that good sense could take the place of learning and the heart act as a substitute for the reason. He spoke "with authority" although he had not frequented the schools, because he felt within himself the inspiration of the Father. Their spirit was a trial to him; the spontaneity characteristic of his religion felt itself under constraint face to face with the formalism of theirs, and this antipathy could not fail to be mutual. Surely we ought not to forget that our Gospels reflect the ideas and prepossessions of a time when Jewish legalism was no longer considered binding by Christians. They even regarded it as their chief foe, and this would consequently incline them to attribute to the Master the same aversion which they themselves felt toward it. Nevertheless, from the numerous passages in which Christ takes the scribes to task, and, conversely, from those in which they seek to entrap him by insidious questions, it is scarcely possible not to obtain a distinct impression that a dormant conflict existed between them and him. According to all the evidence, he respected the Law and paid attention to its demands, but he did not pay them exclusive attention, and he showed himself disposed to give his own pious inspirations precedence over rabbinical injunctions.

And as for the priests of Jerusalem and the Sadducean aristocracy, to them he seemed to be the most dangerous and embarrassing of agitators. He was dangerous, because in the end he might incite the people to one of those violent and irrational revolts which the Roman authorities were always rigorously repressing. The commotions connected with it would also disturb the peace of the Temple hierarchy. He was embarrassing, because he went so far as inconsiderately to parade before the populace comparisons and expostulations which were definitely to the disadvantage of the priesthood.

Possibly the people were more inclined to hesitate than to pass adverse judgment upon the *nabi* (prophet). It was said that Jesus multiplied "signs," *i.e.*, miracles, like healing the sick and those possessed by devils; they may have already attributed to him—a thing common enough in that country in those days—the raising to life of a few dead persons. His enemies ascribed all these marvels to the influence of Beelzebub, *i.e.*, the devil. Plain folks did not blindly believe their words, but they remained irresolute and perplexed. At any rate, if Jesus did not excite their enthusiasm, he did nothing to alter their kindly feeling. On the other hand, both scribes and priests detested him directly they knew him, and he committed the imprudence of letting himself fall into their hands.

We do not clearly perceive what it was that decided him to go to Jerusalem. It is probable that it was something more than the desire to celebrate the Passover in the Holy City. The Evangelists wrote at a time in which all the "mystery" of the life of Jesus centered in a death accepted by him for the redemption and regeneration of humanity. They assume that their Lord for some time preceding had explained the necessity for his Passion. This is why they do not hesitate to declare that Jesus went up to Jerusalem to complete his divine work upon the cross of Calvary there. To the historian his state of mind and his actual intentions seem more obscure.

Had he a definite impression that he had failed? We are justified in thinking so, for the facts speak eloquently enough. Indeed, it is not easy to imagine that he could have succeeded in carrying out his desire. His moral injunctions had no meaning and could bear no fruit save through confirmation by signs heralding the great event he declared to be imminent; the fulfilment of his announcer..ents alone could justify him. Now the signs were not forthcoming and his announcements have not yet been fulfilled, so that his later followers have long been obliged to maintain that the early disciples did not understand him aright, and that he had not told them the things he seemed to say to them. Firmly persuaded as he was that what he stood for and predicted was the truth, he may have convinced himself that its truthfulness would be made manifest at Jerusalem, that there alone the Great Day would dawn. That is what we should be influenced to believe if we were to credit the account of his Messianic entry into the city amidst the acclamations of the populace, but for my part I do not think it veracious.

Whatever may have been the intentions or the expectations of Jesus, he made an ill-advised move when he betook himself to a spot which was not home to him, but one where his natural enemies were masters. Did he commit some rash act there, such as giving himself up to an open demonstration against the sellers of doves and the money-changers established on the Outer Court in front of the Temple? It may be so.[2] At any rate, the Roman procurator had learned to be suspicious of inspired Jews, and it was by no means difficult for the priests and scribes to persuade him that it was to his

[2] The account of the cleansing of the Temple (Mk. xi. 15-18) scarcely inspires confidence, and it may well be only an editorial illustration of the passage from Is. lvi. 7, which Jesus is reported to have recalled to mind.

interest, for the sake of order, to put an end to the excitation of tumults by an insignificant Galilean. Pilate, therefore, had Jesus arrested, judged and convicted him, and crucified him. The people offered no resistance. According to all appearances, the efforts of our Evangelists to absolve the Roman of guilt, and lay upon the Jews the entire responsibility for the crime, are not inspired by a desire to be true to the facts, but by a desire to humor the Roman authorities, for they were writing at a time when these authorities were the sole support of the Christians against the animosity displayed toward them by the synagogues.

Jesus had not foreseen what would happen. The terror and flight of his disciples are plain proof that he was taken by surprise. Pilate's decisive blow caught him still deeply dreaming and seemed to shatter his work to bits. It is probable that in his last days on earth anxiety about the future, the uncertainties of the existing situation and—who knows?—a doubt of himself may all have invaded his thinking and kept the thought of his approaching death which weighed heavily upon his spirit company. But nothing warrants us in believing that at that time he considered the sacrifice of himself was expedient for the achievement of his mission, while everything forces us to think that he said nothing of the kind. Indeed, since the miracle predicted did not take place, and Jahveh did not manifest himself, what else could he do save either to escape at once to Galilee or bow his head and submit to his fate? Perhaps he did, in fact, think of fleeing back to his own district; it has been supposed so, since, according to Matthew (xxviii. 10) he told his disciples to meet him in Galilee. In any case, he had no time to carry out his intention, if he formed it.

II

The "stumbling-block of the cross," as St. Paul was to call it,[3] ought, it would seem likely, to put an end to

[3] Gal. v. 11.

the undertaking of Jesus. He had stood forth to announce an event which had not occurred; he had perished; his disciples, filled with dread, were scattered. Ought not they themselves to be expected to abandon the hope he had aroused in their hearts, and to pity or curse his error and their own? Do not let us forget that *he had established nothing*. He did not come bearing a new religion, nor even a new rite, but only a conception personal rather than original of the piety embedded in the Jewish religion. Nor did he aim at changing either its creed or its Law or its worship.[*] The central point of his teaching was the Messianic idea, which was common property to nearly all his compatriots as much as to him, and only his conception of it was his own. Let it be noted, too, that it is impossible to affirm that his conception itself was actually peculiar to him. To attribute to him the desire to found a Church, his Church, to provide it with rites and sacraments, visible signs of his grace, and to prepare it for the conquest of the whole world—these are just anachronisms. I prefer to say they are distortions of his ideas which would have shocked him, had he known them. But, then, what could possibly remain of him except some moral maxims valuable, certainly, but less original than they are ordinarily said to be, and the touching recollection of his virtues and his personal charm? Logic answers: nothing. Nevertheless, the history of events seems to prove logic wrong.

The trusting faith of the Apostles triumphed over death itself. And here we come into contact with the most obscure of problems. They found themselves in Galilee once more, in the familiar haunts where they had lived with him; they believed they saw him again there and became persuaded that he was no longer dead. This is the fact, though its details are not known to us. As was inevitable, tradition has sought to throw further

[*] It seems probable that his religious spirit was that of those known as *anavim*, *i.e.*, *the* "Poor of Israel," pious persons, little esteemed by the scribes, who were attached to Jahveh more by their love and filial confidence than by exactitude of legalist observance.

light upon it, but by mingling with it marvelous and improbable episodes of verification impossible through textual contradictions, it has rendered it unintelligible. The Gospel accounts of the Resurrection at our command to-day seem to the critic like so many mixed collections of confused memories, of invented sharper details, of old "histories" that were fictions which had become commonplace and trite in the Oriental world. But what *is* there at their base, for there certainly is some residuum that is historically accurate? To all appearances, there is a vision of Peter, followed by collective visions, an example of mental contagion by no means unique in the history of religions.

Let it not be forgotten that even if the Apostles did return from Jerusalem in great fear and perplexity, discouraged for the time being not only because that which they had surely anticipated had not occurred, but because a heavy, unexpected blow had been struck at them, they might nevertheless not have been reduced to quite hopeless despair. They attached too great confidence to the promise made them by Jesus to abandon it. The first moment of anxiety passed and they, back again in the milieu in which that promise had lately impressed them so strongly, reacted to it powerfully again, especially Peter. Now, in their minds the promise of Jesus was bound up with Jesus in person, and to confess that this person had disappeared for ever would have been equivalent to acquiescence in the loss of all hope. Their faith fixed itself upon, and, one might say, was hypnotized by, this one idea: "it is simply impossible that he should have abandoned us, that he should be actually dead." The inevitable culmination of concentration upon the same constant or fixed idea in the brains of men both uncultured and mystical, which were keyed high by great expectations and keen longings, is a vision. That is why Peter *sees* Jesus, and the others afterward see him as Peter has seen him. Whether it was an open case of visual hallucinations or of visual appearances of any kind whatsoever interpreted as hallucinations, matters little; fishermen from the Sea of Galilee would be equally foiled by both these phenomena.

The visions convince the Apostles that Jesus is *alive*, that he is living at least as respects *his spirit*, which has been glorified by God. But in order to be alive, it must be that he is no longer dead, and, if he be no longer dead, to the Jews of that era no hesitation is possible over the conclusion that he has been resuscitated. I do not mean to say risen to life *in the body laid in the grave*, but risen with a body. Assuming that the Apostles thought at first the apparitions which they had seen were of his *spirit* only, they could not, we may be sure, retain this opinion long, since popular belief construed resurrection to mean complete resumption of the life on earth.[5] Also various passages of Scripture, in which they looked to find the resurrection of Jesus announced and the justification for it, forced the belief upon them that he had issued from the tomb at the end of three days, or the third day.[6] This conviction of the Apostles is the foundation of the story, and it was upon Greek soil that the larger part of it first saw the light.

For the time being I am not laying stress upon this enlarged construction just put upon the story by inference. Let it merely be noted that the only Apostolic affirmation of it: "We have beheld him; God has revived him from the dead," contains a conclusion: Why should God have withdrawn him from the place of the departed if it were not that he reserved for him a rôle of prime importance in a great work in the future? This work could be none other than the establishment of the Kingdom, which the Master had proclaimed, and his rôle, that of the Messiah. This time it is two verses from the Acts of the Apostles (ii. 32 and 36) which permit us to grasp the Apostolic argument in action, as it

---

[5] Thus during his lifetime certain people believed Jesus to be John the Baptist risen from the dead (*cf.* Mk. vi. 14).

[6] Hosea vi. 2: "After two days will he revive us: on the third day he will raise us up"; Jonah ii. 1: "And Jonah was in the belly of the fish three days and three nights" (*cf.* Matt. xii. 40). We think too of **Ps. xvi.** 10 (*cf.* Acts. ii. 27, 31).

were: "This Jesus hath God raised up, whereof we all are witnesses," reads the one, and the other concludes: "Let all the house of Israel therefore know assuredly, that God hath made him both Lord and Christ, this Jesus whom ye crucified." I do not guarantee, be it understood, that the expression put into St. Peter's mouth here is authentic, and I even believe the contrary, for the use of the word Lord (*Kyrios*) reveals apparently, a Hellenizing redactor—I mean that it pertains to the Christology of Hellenistic communities—but the occurrence side by side of the two affirmations certainly corresponds to a particular psychological background.

If this faith of the Apostles in their Master's restoration to life had not been published abroad, *there would have been no Christianity.* It is from this point of view that Wellhausen felt justified in saying that, *without his death,* Jesus would have had no place in history. Conversely, can we maintain that the essential doctrine of Christianity rests upon his resurrection? From the standpoint of dogma, it would be difficult to exaggerate its importance, and it would seem justifiable to use as an inscription beneath the title of every statement of the orthodox faith St. Paul's words in I Cor. (xv. 17): "If Christ hath not been raised, your faith is vain." [7]

Moreover, for those who seek to discover the factors that determined what Christianity became and its spread from the purely historical standpoint, this belief in the resurrection of Jesus seems scarcely less important, for it is through it that faith in the Lord Jesus became the foundation of a new religion which shortly after separated from Judaism and was offered to all men as the Divine Way of Salvation. Through it again, the influence of the old Oriental myth of the God dying and rising again to lead his followers to life immortal will penetrate the consciousness of Christian communities, at any rate the Hellenizing ones, and promptly take the Jewish Messiah, a national hero, unintelligible and a matter of indifference to the Greeks, and transform

[7] Or "futile," as in Moffatt's excellent translation.

48

him into Jesus Christ, the Lord and Savior, the Son of God and his ambassador in the world, upon whose name, as St. Paul says again, all believers call, and before whom the entire creation ought to bow the knee.[8]

III

To begin with, the moment that it accepted the resurrection, the faith of the disciples could not fail to struggle to its feet and start to reorganize itself.

I say, reorganize itself, for it is indeed evident that it could not longer live supported by the declarations of Jesus alone. His death altered the whole situation for it preëmpted from choice or necessity a place in the eschatological perspective.[9] It was first of all given out that the death was decreed to make the resurrection possible, proof supreme of the Messianic dignity of the Crucified, and this explanation passed during the interim while it was worked over into the great mystery, the necessary fulfilment, the aim and end of the whole work. So they said: "Jesus the Nazarene showed himself to be a man inspired of God, who went about multiplying signs and wonders and doing good; he perished at the hands of wicked men; but he was the destined Messiah; God proved this by raising him up on the third day, and he will shortly come again in his celestial glory to inaugurate the Kingdom he has promised." In the preaching of Christ the near advent of the Kingdom seems to be the essential point, but in the Apostolic preaching it is the Messianic dignity of Jesus and his speedy return. These are the two themes, according to the Acts of the Apostles which the Twelve will shortly return to Jerusalem to develop.[10]

[8] I Cor. i. 2; Phil. ii. 9 *et seq.*
[9] That is, the final stages, the Last Things, in the description of the end of the world (from the Greek ἔδχχτος, "last").
[10] I am not discussing here the question whether the choice of the Twelve Apostles was actually due to Jesus' initiative, or whether it is to be referred to the action of the first community of Christians, when they experienced a need for administrators. Critics are equally divided upon this point.

We are obliged to believe that they possessed powers of imagination above the ordinary, for, *a priori,* everything should have led them to suppose that they would meet with still less success than their Master, and that a like fate awaited them. If the Jews had not believed in Jesus during his lifetime, how could they be expected to adhere to him now that everything inclined them to believe that he had been mistaken, that he had not even been able to save himself in the hour of torture and that he had died a miserable death in the sight of the people? He was living again, they were told. But who were they who had seen him? His disciples. But *that* was very feeble evidence. And the facts are that Jerusalem gave the Twelve the kind of reception which any others than themselves would have foreseen: they gained a few scores of adherents, as the least important of sects might have done; as long as they did not preach openly and spread abroad their heresy, they retained the good will of the people through the strictness of their piety as Jews and their assiduity at the Temple services (which well proves how little idea their Master had had of severing himself from the religion of Israel). When better known, they aroused the contemptuous animosity of the priests and scribes and suffered much indignity at their hands. Their mean condition and their peaceable nature—possibly, also, the correctness of their Jewish practices—warded off death from them, however; though, for several of them, this proved but a respite. They may have gained some recruits in the small towns near Jerusalem, but, according to all the evidence, they soon reached the crest of their success among those of Jewish race. This success seemed so limited in the eyes of those least prejudiced that it appeared to them likely that the Christian heresy would not survive the generation which had witnessed its birth, and that soon the followers of Jesus the Nazarene would be lost in oblivion, like those of many another *nabi.*

This was not what happened, however, for a new element now intervened which entirely altered the complexion of things. Unable to take root in Jewish soil, the Apostolic seedling found itself transplanted to a Greek terrain; we shall see how. It flourished there; and we shall understand why. Right here, truthfully speaking, it is that search must be made for the first period in the evolution of Christianity. This will explain how it became oriented with its face turned away from Judaism, and toward a constitution for itself as a special religion.

CHAPTER III

The Apostles and the disciples, reassured by the firm faith of St. Peter, reassembled, as soon as their early fears had been dissipated, to try to reconstruct their shattered dream and to revive in their hearts the hopes that the Master had put there. They were, it must be remembered, Jews in mean circumstances and without culture. Their horizon could not be wider than that of Christ, and their ambition was confined to urging "the sheep of the house of Israel" into the way of salvation. Everything leads us to believe that, in the beginning at least, their Jewish exclusiveness was even disposed to show itself stricter in temper than that of Jesus. Nothing could have been further removed from their thoughts than the intention to carry the Good Tidings to the heathen; and, to tell the truth, it was impossible for them to conceive of the acceptance of the Gospel by Gentiles without their acceptance beforehand of the Jewish faith. But at that time a large number of Jews lived outside Palestine, and they were all counted in as members of the flock of Israel.[1]

[1] The important work is that of J. Juster, *Les Juifs dans l'Empire romain* (Paris, 1914); see also in the *Dictionnaire des Antiquités*, by Daremberg and Saglio, the article "Judaei," by Th. Reinach, and Schürer, *Geschichte des jüdischen Volkes*, Vol. III. Upon the early beginnings of Christianity, its transplantation in the Greco-Roman countries and its establishment as an original religion. Pfleiderer's *Die Entstehung des Christentums* may be read with profit, also Case, *The Evolution of Early Christianity* (Chicago, 1914), and K. Lake, *Landmarks in the History of Early Christianity* (New York, 1920). The following should be consulted: Bousset, *Kyrios Christos*, Chaps. iii and iv; J. Weiss, *Das Urchristentum* (Göttingen, 1914), Vol I; A. Loisy, *Les Actes des Apôtres* (Paris, 1920), and F. J. F. Jackson and K. Lake, *The Beginnings of Christianity*, Vol. I, Chap. i (New York, 1920).
Upon the discussion raised by the Acts see M. Goguel, *Introduction*, Vol. III, *Le livre des Actes* (1922), and Jackson and Lake, *op. cit.*, Vol. II (New York, 1922).

During the four centuries preceding the Christian era, many causes had led the ancestors of these emigrant Jews away from their homes. Necessity, first of all; their district, situated between the Ptolemaic kingdom of Egypt and the Seleucid kingdom of Syria, had frequently served as a battlefield for the Egyptians and Syrians. In the course of their raiding expeditions both sides had made many prisoners who had never returned again. Similar incidents had happened several times during the long struggle for independence waged by the Maccabees against the Syrian kings. These were repeated to their own advantage by the Romans when they made war upon Antiochus the Great, and later when they took part in the internecine strife of Judea. On the other hand, when they were well treated the Jews showed themselves industrious, loyal and zealous. For this reason the Ptolemies and the Seleucids sought to attract them to settle themselves in large groups, an endeavor in which they succeeded. Some colonies established themselves in the Nile delta and in Cyrene; others in Antioch, Lydia and Phrygia. Lastly, the resources of Palestine were not inexhaustible, and the Jews were a prolific race. Feeling themselves crowded on a soil which frequently offered little return for their labor, many Jews, since Palestine itself was under foreign rule, went to seek their livelihood in countries under the same domination, and some found wealth there. Even in the second century B.C. an Alexandrian Jew, addressing his nation, was at most guilty of poetical exaggeration when he wrote: "The whole earth is filled with thee, and the sea alike." [2] Strabo, the Greek geographer, a contemporary of Christ, was also under the impression that Jews were to be found everywhere. It was true that they had spread throughout the Mediterranean countries, but they did not form compact groups save in the large towns of the Grecian world, in Mesopotamia and in Rome where, under Augustus, about twelve thousands could be reckoned.

[2] Oracles Sibyllins iii. 271.

Wherever they were, as a rule they forgot neither their origin nor their religion. They stuck together; they sought to obtain from the authorities a legal right to control their own internal affairs, and to organize among themselves. They formed a *temporal* corporation, with its own selected leaders, its elected magistrates, its court of justice and its customs; and a *spiritual* corporation, a synagogue,[2] whither all came to hear the Law read, to pray and for common edification; and this too had a small governing body of its own. Larger Jewish communities, like that of Rome, would sometimes divide their members up into several synagogues. The Greek, Syrian and Egyptian rulers had let their Jewish subjects live according to their own customs and had even granted them various privileges. The Romans followed this example, and a veritable charter protected the sons of Israel throughout the Empire, a charter which not only sanctioned their religion and legalized their assemblies, but took their dislikes and prejudices into account, and and as far as possible treated their religious susceptibilities with respect.

This exceptional state of things their natural pride still further accentuated in these ways: in the contempt for the municipal forms of worship which it almost excused them for showing, and other defects or absurdities which they took no pains to conceal, especially the peculiarities connected with the services of the synagogue, which the common people regarded as the temple without any ritual dedicated to a god without an image or a name; the rite of circumcision; the food restrictions of the Mosaic Law. Piled upon top of these, several abominable but greedily accepted calumnies spread with regard to them—for instance, of practicing ritual murder and adoring an ass's head. These oddities and calumnies had given birth, among the people of the cities where Jews were to be found in numbers, to very hostile sentiments with regard to them. The Greco-Roman world experienced a

---

[2] This word, like "church," means both a place where people gather together and also the gathering that takes place in it.

veritable epidemic of anti-Semitism, which would have proceeded to the most violent measures if the Roman authorities had not restrained it, and which did occasionally outwit them. It is as well to note this in the very beginning, for very soon that hostility will be transferred from the Jew to the Christian.[*]

On the other hand, the Israelites, as a rule favorably regarded by the authorities on account of their submissiveness and their industrious and sober demeanor, also attracted the sympathetic notice of those to whom the mythological puerilities, the coarseness of the rites, the metaphysical inadequacies and the low state of morals in the current pagan religion were offensive. At a time when the emotional religions of the East began to be the vogue, Jahvehism seemed to those predestined by temperament to comprehend it as the simplest, the loftiest and purest of all. Besides, the Jews, though very exclusive, suspicious and unapproachable at home, had acquired better manners among the Gentiles. They did not rigidly close their synagogues to all non-Jews; they tolerated the "proselytes of the gate." Nor did they refuse to instruct those who wished to become acquainted with the Law, and moreover, since this had been translated into Greek, any educated man could study it by himself. In this way each synagogue acquired, little by little, a clientele of proselytes. Certain of them went so far as to become converts; they received the baptism of purification, accepted circumcision, sent their ritual offering to the Temple at Jerusalem, and thus became true sons of Israel. Others, not proceeding quite so far, used to frequent the outer court of the synagogue fairly regularly; they contributed some portion of their means to its up-keep and "lived the life of Jews" as far as their social status permitted. These were called the "God-fearers" and they were certainly very numerous in the large Jewries of the East and in Egypt; in Rome

[*] All the Greek and Roman testimony relating to the Jews has been collected, translated and annotated by Th. Reinach, *Fontes rerum judaicarum*, Vol I, *Textes d'auteurs grecs et romains* (Paris, 1895).

they were recruited even from the higher classes, especially among the women.

The Jews of the Dispersion had not preserved entire either the customs or the spirit of their Palestinian brethren. The homeland exclusiveness, hatred of what was Gentile and morbid fear of contact with the ritually impure had been forced to give way somewhat in a milieu in which they would have made life impossible. These Jews were daily associates of "sinners," and above all subjected as they were to its influence, they were also attracted by the Greek culture in which their surroundings were steeped. Setting aside religious convictions and the chief practices imposed by them, two or three generations after their emigration these Jews resembled the Greeks of the same social class in language, demeanor and in intellectual caliber. The most learned among them professed profound admiration for Hellenic literature and philosophy; they felt its influence to such an extent that they were no more capable of discounting them to the glory of the Law than of discounting the Law to their glory. For this reason, Philo, the type of these Hellenized Jews, busied himself demonstrating in all good faith, in Alexandria, that the revelations made to Moses and his Laws were in complete harmony with the speculative thought of Plato and Zeno. To him this admission was merely a question of understanding them aright.[5]

Ideas considered of supreme importance by the Palestinian Jews grew worn and faded among those who were Hellenized: their Messianism for instance, instead of decking itself out in the garments of a narrow and aggressive nationalism, tended to go on dress parade as the conquest of the world for the truth. On the other hand, fresh ideas, foreign to their race, made a home for themselves in their minds. For example, they became more and more imbued with the Greek conception of the dualism of human nature. They no longer attached

---

[5] E. Brehier, *Les idées philosophiques et religieuses de Philon d'Alexandrie* (Paris, 1907).

great importance to the future fate of the body, but concentrated all their solicitude on the destiny of the soul, a matter upon which the Palestinians had never professed any definite and clear doctrine.

There was a stronger reason still which kept the Jewish proselytes faithful to the culture and spirit of their milieu, for nothing would have induced them to be disdainful of that civilization which their education rated as the finest ever known and the most worthy of reasoning men. While adopting Judaism more or less entirely, they maintained that they were *adapting* it, and only banishing from their minds, as from their lives, that which seemed to be utterly incompatible with what they borrowed from it. This is why the Jews of the Dispersion and the "God-fearers" were found (especially the latter class) to be much more inclined than the Palestinians to discuss the statements of the Apostles and, eventually, to accept them. This, too, is why the very simple Apostolic doctrine, which experience showed to be very plastic, would be exposed to the risk of serious modification were it made known in the Hellenic synagogues.

II

This risk seemed all the greater, since, in some districts of the Diaspora, the Jews had not stopped short at adapting themselves to the social needs of their milieu and organizing their religious faith, or, at least, restating it in terms of their newer culture, whilst maintaining it in its integrity. Little by little they allowed some portion to become mingled with it of the ideas and beliefs of the surrounding paganism, whilst some of the pagans accepted in turn many important ideas from the Jewish faith and incorporated them with their own religion. We are ill informed respecting the syncretistic* com-

---

* This is the name given by common consent to all religious embodiments in which elements which have come from different religions are organized. The special work upon the synagogues of the Diaspora, considered from the point of view that is of interest to us at the moment, is that of M. Friedländer, *Synagoge und Kirche in ihren Anfängen* (Berlin, 1908). It must be read cautiously, for its statements sometimes go beyond the import of the text.

binations which were the result of such infiltrations, but what we can glean is quite sufficient to show us their importance.

The Jewish colony in Mesopotamia, for instance, was very favorably situated for undergoing, while believing itself to be combating them, infiltrations from Iran and from Babylon, those generators of amazing theories to explain the world and life in general, which are organized into more or less coherent systems, or *gnoses,* as they are to be called later in the Christian Church.[7] There is at least one of the combinations born in this strange milieu, into which Judaism enters as an element which we must name, that is, *mandaism,* a Judeo-Babylonian syncretism which seems to have served as the foundation of several subsequent composites which are of importance in the history of Christianity.

Another Jewish colony which interests us strongly from the same standpoint is the one settled in Phrygia. In this district which, throughout antiquity, was distinguished by the intensity of its religious life, the Jews at first form one or more isolated groups in the midst of pagan populations; but they finally surrender to the pressure of their surroundings and react upon these in their turn, so much so that we perceive pretty clearly that many of their religious conceptions, adopted by the pagans, are fused with their own indigenous beliefs. The really Phrygian cult is that of the Great Mother, Cybele, and of Attis, her lover. Attis now receives the title of Hypsistos, the Most-High, which is of Jewish origin and corresponds moreover with a Chaldean belief, according to which the abode of the gods is to be found *above* the seven planetary spheres and the starry heaven. On the other hand, a facile and tempting play upon words identifies Sabazios (Jupiter) or the Phrygian Dionysos, with Sabaoth; and we perceive, unfortunately only hazily, in the half-light thrown by the documents,

[7] The word *gnosis* means "knowledge," yet implies that this knowledge escapes ordinary men, and is only arrived at by revelation or initiation. *Cf.* Legge, *Forerunners and Rivals of Christianity* (Cambridge, 1915), Vol. I, Chaps. iii-vi.

half-Jewish sects of Hypsistians, Sabbatists or Saba-
ziens, who share the same hope, that of eternal salvation,
of a beatific life without end, beyond the grave, obtained
through the intercession of a *Sôter,* a Divine Savior.
The communion between the members of these sects is
sealed by their participation in a liturgical and mystic
repast which perhaps already has the virtue of a sacrament. I mean a repast which confers upon those who
partake of it a divine grace, or a special aptitude for
receiving such a grace.[8]

Similar combinations occur elsewhere—in Egypt, and
above all in Syria, where we shall shortly note their
formative influence upon the religious education of St.
Paul.

The syncretistic and gnostic sects based on Judaism
therefore spread gradually outside Palestine; it is even
quite possible that before the birth of Jesus they had
already gained some ground in Judea proper, by means
of the frequent pilgrimages to Jerusalem undertaken by
the Jews of the Dispersion on the occasion of the great
festivals of the liturgical year. St. Epiphanus, a
Christian writer of the fourth century, although he does
not always prove trustworthy, has furnished us with
abundant information respecting these Eastern "heresies." He describes in some detail one among them,
named the Nazoreans,[9] which had obtained some vogue
in the district beyond the Jordan, in Perea, before the
beginning of the Christian era. Its partisans reject the
Temple worship, but adhere to other Jewish customs;
nevertheless they betray the effect of the foreign influence
they have undergone by refusing to acknowledge the
sacredness of the Law. Compared to other men, they
consider themselves "saints" (as the first Christians

---

[8] *Cf.* Cumont, *Les religions orientales dans le paganisme romain*
(Paris, 1909), pp. 94 *et seq.*

[9] Epiphanus *Haeres*, xix. 1, xxix. 9. For various reasons, however,
the testimony of Epiphanus has encountered opponents. It is quite
possible that the old bishop's information was based upon a chronological error. Epiphanus' critical faculty was somewhat weak. If
this were so, the sect we consider the best known to us would disappear
entirely from the purview of history.

also do), and their name, like the epithet Nazarene applied to Jesus, is no doubt to be explained by the Hebrew *nazir*, which the Greeks translated *hagios, i.e.,* saintly. These Nazoreans were very probably ardent Messianists, and possibly they addressed their worship to the future Messiah as the more profoundly pagan syncretistic sects do to their Redeeming God.

Our information, which is unfortunately still very incomplete, does not allow of our being assertive upon all points regarding these syncretistic Jewish sects. But the very fact of their existence is enough to prove that the distance between Judaism proper and the various religions of Western Asia could be bridged, for all have one feature in common, namely, the expectation of a Messiah, under one form or another, or even the adoration of a Divine Savior. It is not an improbable inference that a revival of Messianic speculation, Palestinian in origin, but extending beyond the confines of Palestine, is in full debate in many synagogues of the Diaspora immediately around them, and even in congregations more remote than those of the "proselytes of the gate." The existence of these sects further proves that the orthodoxy of the Jews of the Diaspora was much more readily subject to encroachment than that of the Palestinian community. At a distance from the Temple and its priests, rigid legalism sometimes gave way for these expatriated Jews to more spontaneous forms of expressing religious sentiment, or forms more in harmony with the general religious trend of the milieu in which they dwelt. In the end they filtered through. In other words, the Jews, especially the semi-Jews of the Dispersion, seemed disposed to accept the Apostolic statements respecting Jesus much more readily than the Jerusalem Jews or those throughout Palestine. But yet it has to be feared that the faith in Christ Jesus would only add a new element, a more or less powerful component, to a syncretism which was already fairly complex in many cases.

III

The transfer of the Apostolic hope to the domain of the Diaspora came about in the most natural way, and almost inevitably. In the Book of the Acts we are told that the Apostles gained as adherents a certain number of "Grecian Jews" [10] (*i.e.*, Jews living in Greek and Grecianized districts) who had come to Jerusalem for the Feast of Pentecost. Some of them returned home at once, others remained in the city; and it was not long before the latter had formed themselves into a group apart from the one which gathered round the Twelve. They elected as their leaders a kind of council or committee of seven men. These Hellenists, accustomed to spread their doctrine around the synagogues of the Diaspora, by force of habit tried to impose their new faith, that is, their conviction that the Messiah promised to Israel by the prophets was none other than Jesus the Nazarene, crucified by Pilate, and undertook disputations on its behalf in the synagogues which the great Jewish communities of the Grecian world maintained in the Holy City. There they encountered opposition and resistance which drew the attention of the Sanhedrin to them, and the most ardent of the Seven, a young man named Stephen, fell a victim to his zeal (Acts vi, 9 *et seq.*). Deeming that a longer stay in Jerusalem would now be of no avail to their faith, and dangerous for themselves, the Hellenists gave up the idea of making converts there and went to Phenicia, Cyprus and Antioch, where they began to preach in the synagogues (Acts xi, 19 *et seq.*). "They spake unto the Greeks also" (*i.e.*, to the "God-fearers") and many of these Greeks "turned unto the Lord." The Twelve had neither prompted nor even anticipated this initiative on their part; when they heard what was going on they sent to Antioch a member who could be trusted, named Barnabas,

---

[10] Acts ix. 29. The marginal note gives "Hellenists," and this alternative term will henceforth be adopted.

to conduct an inquiry into a situation which certainly made them uneasy. The enthusiasm of the new converts won over Barnabas; he recognized the "grace of God" in it and plunged himself at once into the good work which had been so well begun. He went on to Tarsus, where Paul was then living, and brought him to Antioch to associate him also with his work. He had found there one of the greatest workers of the future.

Neither the Twelve nor the direct disciples of Jesus could, as we know, do more than mark time, as their Master had done, running the same risks as those he had encountered. Instead of proclaiming, like him, "The Kingdom is at hand," they said: "The Lord will come again," but prolonged waiting for that coming could not fail to diminish the effect of their message. It would thus be difficult to state precisely what the immediate companions of Jesus actually accomplished. Grouped around Peter and John—whom the brothers of the Lord who grew up with him in the same household seem soon to have joined, since Paul himself places one of them, James the Less, beside Peter in the congregation at Jerusalem—they evidently linger there and scarcely ever go far from the Holy City. Later legends show us Andrew among the Scythians, James the Elder in Spain, his brother John in Asia Minor, Thomas in the Indies and even in China, Peter at Corinth and in Rome. All these accounts are not equally improbable, but it is to be feared that not one of them is true, and, in fact, apart from the earlier chapters of the Acts of the Apostles (which we possess only in the form of a second-hand adaptation of the first edition), there exists no information really worthy of credence about the life and work of the immediate Apostles of Jesus.

Such a silence does not predispose us to believe that they did anything very extraordinary and, as a matter of fact, it is hardly probable. We think we know that Peter, the two Jameses and, probably, John the son of Zebedee, suffered violent deaths, and through the writings

of some of the heresiologians [11] we can discern traces of
the petty Judaizing communities they founded and which,
from the time of the great Jewish revolt in 66 A.D., took
refuge on the other side of the Jordan. They are soon left
very far behind, as to doctrine, by their fellow-Christian
communities on Greek soil, and in the second century
after Christ they already are accounted "wrong-think-
ing"; their immediate and direct influence upon the history of Christianity is practically negligible. The quick-
ening leaven is to be found elsewhere.

---

[11] *I.e.*, Christians who wrote upon the various heresies, such as St.
Ireneus in the second century, the author of the *Philosophumena* in the
third, St. Epiphanus in the fourth, etc.

CHAPTER IV

THE PAULINE MILIEU

St. Paul has already been mentioned. He was born of a Jewish family established at Tarsus in Cilicia. It was a very bustling town, situated at the outlet of the Portae Ciliciae, by which travelers descend from the plateau of Asia Minor into Syria. It was also at the junction of important trade routes which brought it within the zone of ideas and influences alike from Greece and Italy, Phrygia and Cappadocia, Syria and Cyprus, Phenicia and Egypt.[1] In spite of a fairly recent attempt of the kings of Syria, in particular that of Antiochus Epiphanus, in 171 B.C. to Grecianize it, it still remained in essentials an Oriental city, at least as far as its principal beliefs were concerned; but it possessed flourishing Greek schools and what we should call a university which, according to Strabo, had an established reputation throughout the Greco-Roman world, especially with respect to philosophical studies.

The masters who direct this university of Tarsus are attached to the doctrine of the Stoics and they are appar-

[1] Upon Tarsus, considered from the point of view that interests us here, consult especially one chapter of Ramsay's book, *The Cities of St. Paul* (London, 1907), pp. 85-244, and Böhlig's *Die Geisteskultur von Tarsos im augustinischen Zeitalter* (Göttingen, 1913). Upon the question of religion, Frazer's *Adonis, Attis, Osiris* (New York, 1914), Chap. vi, pp. 22, 1 and 3; 117 *et seq.* should also be studied. Unfortunately these authors have frequently been obliged to content themselves with faint indications, assumptions and probabilities, since the documents they have at their disposal are few in number and by no means definite. The old town lies beneath about twenty feet of sediment which has been silted up by its river, the Cydnus, and upon this the modern town has been built. For this reason proper excavations have yet to be made. All that we have at our disposal is a small amount of coinage, occasionally very difficult to account for, a few inscriptions and some passages from the geographer Strabo, who died about 20 A.D., and of the rhetorician Dion Chrysostom, who died in 117 A.D.

ently not content with explaining its tenets to the students who attend their lectures; they cast its essential principles and its leading affirmations, its most striking formulas and almost its spirit, into a veritable exhortation or homily adapted to the common people. This explains the fact, so important to our study, how Paul, apparently without having attended the university of his native city, or studied the Stoic philosophy, simply because he has passed his early years in a milieu which intellectually had been Grecianized by these philosophers who were also rhetoricians, is not ignorant of the commonplaces of Stoicism nor of the current methods of Greek rhetoric.

The Acts of the Apostles (xxii. 3) would have us believe that he was brought up at Jerusalem "at the feet of Gamaliel," *i.e.*, in one of the most celebrated of the rabbinical schools of that period. While it is of course impossible for us to assert that this is not true, in any case it is very unlikely, for it is hard to understand how a pupil of the rabbis of Palestine should have come to disown and repudiate his masters as Paul did later. Instead on the contrary he perfectly expresses the kind of Jewish spirit which seems so far as we know, to be that of the Hellenistic synagogues.[2] It is probable that he did receive sound instruction "in the Law," that his religious teaching went far, but it was not received at Jerusalem. Not only in Palestine were there Jewish doctors, but we know that there were also some in Alexandria; at Antioch, the mighty capital of Syria, they were to be found too, and there is reason to believe that it was in this city that Paul completed his studies.

Born upon Grecian soil, speaking and writing Greek, he was the son of a family that was well fixed, since he was a Roman citizen and inherited the privilege from

[2] Upon this important question see C. G. Montefiore's *Judaism and St. Paul* (London, 1914). It seems to me likely that the desire of the author of the Acts to convince his readers that Paul had received a sound rabbinical education placed him under the guidance of Gamaliel, whose name was renowned in the Jewish schools of the Apostolic age. With equal improbability and with the same intention he has put into the mouth of Gamaliel (Acts v. 34) a speech in favor of the Apostles.

his father. Thus he was admirably prepared to grasp and comprehend the religious aspirations of the Jews of the Dispersion who would come to believe in Jesus as he did himself, and also their proselytes.

Violently hostile to the Christians at the outset, he ranged himself on their side after a crisis of which, for the moment, I shall only say that it was the conclusion of a long obscure period of introspective travail. It culminated in a decisive vision: he was convinced that upon a certain day when he was journeying to Damascus he had seen or heard the glorified Christ, and had received from him the status of an Apostle. It must be added that he had not known Jesus in the flesh and that any observations he may make about his personality or his doctrine will not be confined, like those of the Twelve, to actual recollections. Let us add, moreover, that he possessed a soul both ardent and mystic, an argumentative mind, and that at the same time he displayed ready common sense and indomitable energy in getting his mission accepted and imposing his ideas on others.

The originality of these ideas appears striking when they are compared with those to which the faith of the Twelve was limited, even after its early expansion. To convince ourselves that this is so it is only necessary to reread the first few chapters of the Acts, and right afterward the Epistle to the Romans. But we must take care not to fall into a certain delusion. While Paul's religious genius is unquestionable, note should be taken that just as in the work of Philo of Alexandria the results of Jewish speculative thought prior to his own are combined, so in St. Paul's thought, ideas and sentiments take shape which did not originate with him, and the only credit due him is the merit of having expounded them to us. A close study of the greater Pauline Epistles [3] reveals a combination, at the first glance both bold and strange, composed (a) of the fundamental affirmations of the

[3] I refer to the Epistles to the Galatians, I and II Corinthians, and Romans, which critics at the present day are fairly unanimous in considering as substantially authentic.

faith voiced by the Twelve; (b) of Jewish ideas—some borrowed directly from the Old Testament, others the product of much more recent religious thought; (c) of conceptions which were familiar to his Hellenistic and pagan milieu; and (d) of memories of Gospel ideas and of Eastern myths.

It is necessary to lay some little stress upon this point because here we sink a plummet into the depths of the most serious problem set the student by the history of Christian beliefs. It is that of the process by which the mission, such as we have shown it to be undertaken by Jesus, was transformed into a religion of universal salvation.

II

At the first glance that is cast upon the religious life of the East, from the Aegean Sea to Mesopotamia, it is clear that at the beginning of the Christian era a certain number of divinities, so closely resembling each other that they are occasionally confused, occupy the first rank. These are Attis in Phrygia, Adonis in Syria, Melkart in Phenicia, Tammuz and Marduk in Mesopotamia, Osiris in Egypt, Dionysos on Grecian soil, to mention the chief ones only. The Persian god Mithra, then beginning to exercise sway in the Roman Empire ought, however, to be added to their number.[*] Men who travel from one country to another take their religious beliefs with them, and implant them without difficulty elsewhere because in this world of Asia Minor they everywhere encounter religious trends which are not only similar to their own, but which also express themselves in myths of the same nature and seek satisfaction in rites and ceremonies

---

[*] *Cf.* Cumont, *Les religions orientales dans l'Empire romain;* M. Brückner, *Der sterbende und auferstehende Gottheiland in den orientalischen Religionen und ihr Verhältniss zum Christentum* (Tübingen, 1908) ; A. Loisy, *Les Mystères païens et le Mystère chrétien* (Paris, 1919), *ibid.,* "Religions nationales et Cultes de mystères," in the *Revue d'histoire et de littérature religieuses*, Jan., 1913 ; S. J. Case, *The Evolution of Early Christianity* (which gives an extensive bibliography), Chap. ix; P. Wendland, *Die Hellenistisch-römische Kultur* (Tübingen, 1912), pp. 163 *et seq.*

which are closely akin. It is not probable that the myths and rites really spring from different sources, but rather that they resemble each other because they are all traceable to the same fundamental ideas and desires. Their very kinship has been an aid to numerous exchanges between them and their original embodiments. Their mutual interpenetration also favors these interchanges and gives them in the end a very striking family likeness. There still remain, however, very notable differences between the sacred stories which are supposed to support them. This medley of religions, which is called Oriental syncretism, tends to detach from the confused detail of creeds and the practices they involve a certain number of essential ideas and fundamental rites. It is these which stand out at first sight in no matter which of the cults I have just enumerated. As a matter of fact, these same essential ideas and fundamental rites finally seem clearly to constitute the *raison d'être* for them all, which is to offer mankind a hope in and some means of securing a blissful immortality.

The most striking characteristic in the mythological history of their various gods is this: they are all reputed to die at a certain period of the year and be restored to life again shortly after, thus deluging the hearts of their faithful adherents alternately with intense grief and delirious joy. Note should be taken, moreover, that in themselves they are not truly great deities and that, in origin at least, many of them are closely akin to mortals, since they too die. Some, such as Attis, a shepherd, and Adonis, the product of an incestuous union, are even men whom the will of the gods has deified. Only the importance of the function which they seem to exercise with regard to human beings gradually raises them high above their original state and turns them into really sovereign divinities. We shall shortly explain how.

Upon the origin of these various deities and upon the principle, so to speak, underlying the myths they personify, there has been long and profound discussion. Today there is need to hesitate between two explanations only, which, however, are not mutually exclusive. Nothing else than the regular succession of the seasons, considered either with regard to the apparent progress of the sun, or with regard to vegetation, has given birth to the myth of a god who dies upon the arrival of the winter to be reborn at the beginning of spring. Some of these gods, therefore, were originally astral divinities, others agricultural divinities. In the end this occasioned a fairly natural confusion which does not allow us always to ascertain exactly either the true origin of, or the earliest character borne by any particular one of them.

Clearly Mithra is a solar deity, and his birth occurs upon the twenty-fifth of December, *i.e.*, the winter solstice; Osiris now appears to be a lunar deity, but perhaps he was not originally. Tammuz, on the contrary, is a god of vegetation, for the heat of the summer causes him to perish and the first breath of spring revives him. It is the same with Adonis and, apparently, with most of these gods who die and rise again; the evident relation between the sun's course and the processes of vegetable life upon the earth explains how it is that they could finally be represented as solar deities. Most of them, moreover, seem to be closely connected with a goddess, mother of the gods, the personification of the Earth or the fecundity of Nature, who gives them birth or makes them the object of her love. Thus does the Great Mother Cybele treat Attis, Belti-Aphrodite act toward Adonis, Istar toward Tammuz, Isis toward Osiris. And this is also why these gods are paired with and adored at the same time as these goddesses and practically dwell with them in their temples. While the problem of the original characteristic of a particular divinity may be of the utmost importance for a historian of religions, that which interests us still more is the form of representation and, above all, the interpretation of the myth of his death and resurrection. Our clearest information is generally derived from a study of his festival. This festival is of the nature of a drama which enacts a characteristic form of the death and resurrection of the god. Occasionally it is duplicated; by this I mean that there are two festivals occurring at appropriate seasons of the year. In such a case, one of the two takes precedence over the other: thus, in the case of Tammuz, the celebration of his death in the summer solstice appears to be the chief one, and the same is true of Adonis, who is so easily mistaken for him. For Marduk and for Mithra and for the other gods who are plainly solar deities, the festival either of their triumph or of their rebirth is the main one. Sometimes, on the other hand, the two festivals are united in a single ceremony, which takes place either in the spring or in the autumn. In the beginning the death of the god is deplored, and then immediately afterward his resurrection celebrated. Such is the custom at the festival for Attis, which takes place in the latter fortnight of the month of March, at the time of the spring equinox.

III

By an evolution of religious sentiment which we can but mention here since to explain it, even to a limited extent would take us too far from our subject, this myth of the death and resurrection of the god ceased to be regarded as only a dramatic and touching story. It came to be commonly looked upon as the visible expression of the great mystery of human destiny. Upon earth mankind appears to be subjected to living conditions that are usually wretched. Even in the rare cases where common opinion declares that life to be a happy one, it seems so frail and so brief that he can scarcely believe that his being is really limited in duration to the phase in which appearances are present to his senses. He has therefore imagined for that indefinitely extended period which follows his corporeal death another existence, blessed and eternal, which his soul, *i.e.*, his non-material portion, is destined to enjoy. But he believes that since he is incapable of qualifying for this better life by his own powers alone, to attain it he needs an intercessor,

a divine mediator. And this is the office which has fallen
to the lot of the god who dies and is restored to life
again.

Here is the way in which that mission is imagined to
have been fulfilled. The god has suffered, as man may
suffer; he has died, as man dies; but his restoration to life
again is a sign of his triumph over suffering and death.
And if his faithful followers do symbolize and renew in
some ritual each year the drama of his terrestrial existence, their belief has not changed that from the hour of
the real occurrence of resurrection he himself is enjoying
the beatific life appropriate to divine immortality. For
mankind, already closely associated with his sufferings
and death through the very conditions of their humanity,
the problem of salvation amounts to carrying out the
last link in this association that would involve for them,
too, resurrection and survival in unending bliss. The
solution of the problem of salvation so stated is found
in a kind of ceremonious and mystic make-believe fiction
in which the believer is supposed to identify himself with
the god in a series of ritual practices deemed efficacious.
Symbolically he goes through the various stages of the
ordeals through which the god has passed, outward signs
of an assimilation with the god which transforms his own
being, and constitutes a guarantee that his future will be
like that of the god and that, beyond the trials of this
life and beyond death, immortality awaits him. The
destiny of the Divine Savior (for that is the quality
with which the god who dies and is restored to life again
is invested) is both the prototype and the guarantee of
the same destiny for his followers. A Christian author
of the fourth century, Firmicus Maternus,[5] describes for
us a nocturnal ceremony in the worship of one of these
gods that shows the way to salvation. Those who are
present are weeping, a prey to anxiety as to the fate that
awaits them in a future without end, and a priest, passing in front of each, anoints his throat with holy oil,
slowly uttering the sacramental words the while: "Take

[5] *De errore profan. relig.* xxii. 1.

confidence from the fact that the God is saved; you shall be, you also, saved at the end of your trials.''

We do not indeed know all the forms of worship of the various gods that show the way to salvation by which this assimilation of the believers to the Sôter was materially accomplished. But we are assured that in them all certain rites were so designed. At least two of these claim our attention: the baptism in blood and the communion meal.

In the Phrygian cult of Cybele and Attis, but not in that alone, for we find it in various other Asiatic cults and in that of Mithra, a singular ceremony, called the *taurobolium*,° took place. It formed part of the mysterious initiatory rites exclusively reserved for believers. A deep pit was sunk in the precincts of the temple into which the initiated descended and it was then covered over with a grating upon which a bull was solemnly sacrificed; its blood flowed like red rain into the pit and fell on the naked person of the novitiate, endeavoring to bathe all parts of his body in it. This baptism accomplished, the genital organs of the animal sacrificed were deposited in a sacred vessel to be presented as an offering to the goddess, after which they were buried beneath a memorial altar.

Originally these singular rites certainly were not supposed to have anything to do with the immortal future of the initiate; their aim was to obtain the coöperation of Cybele and Attis who, it was believed, governed nature, just as the Dionysiac initiatory rites, equally bizarre from our point of view, were deemed to draw the bacchanals of both sexes into partnership with the fertilizing work of Dionysos. But by the beginning of the Christian era, under influences which are difficult to define and determine, an evolution had apparently occurred

---

° Sometimes called *criobolium*, when the animal sacrificed was a he-goat. *Cf.* Hepding, *Attis, seine Mythen und sein Kult* (Giessen, 1903); Graillot, *Le culte de Cybèle, mère des Dieux, à Rome et dans l'Empire romain* (Paris, (1912), especially Chap. iv; Loisy, "Cybèle et Attis," *Rev. d'hist. et de litt. rel.* (July, 1913); *Les Mystères païens*, Chap. iv; S. Angus, *The Mystery—Religions and Christianity* (London, 1925), p. 91 *et seq.*

which converted the taurobolium into an efficient means by which to secure a blissful immortality. And this is how that use of it was explained. The pit signifies the kingdom of the dead, and the mystic, in descending into it, is thought to die; the bull is Attis, and the blood that is shed is the divine life-principle that issues from him; the initiate receives it and, as it were, absorbs it; when he leaves the pit he is said to be "born again,"[7] and milk, as in the case of a new-born infant, is given him to drink. But he is not born the mere man again he was before; he has absorbed the very essence of the god and, if we understand the mystery aright, he has in his turn become an Attis and is saluted as one. Then, in order to follow in the footsteps of the sacred history the further stage which makes Attis the lover of Cybele, he must also effect a union with the goddess. The offering of the genitals of the bull of Attis of whom he is now a colleague symbolizes this union, which is carried out in mystic fashion in the nuptial chamber of the Great Mother. The mutilation of the bull also recalls the similar acts of Attis who, it is said, castrated himself under a pine tree and died as a result.

The initiate is assured, at any rate for a considerable period of time,[8] that his fate will be the same as that of Attis at his inevitable death and a happy resurrection and survival among the gods his portion. In many of the cults of these savior and interceding gods, such as those of Cybele, Mithra, the Syrian Baals, and still others, the beneficial union obtained by means of initiation is renewed, or at any rate revived, by sacred repasts which the members, assembled at the table of the god, ate. This ritual banquet is often undoubtedly simply a token of the brotherhood existing between the initiates, a mere symbol, but "sometimes also other effects of the food

[7] The words *Taurobolio criboliogue in aeternum renatus* are to be read, on an inscription rather late, it is true, certainly of the fourth century A.D., but they clearly show the ultimate aim of the taurobolic sacrifice.

[8] It seems as if the taurobolium were repeated after a lapse of twenty years; at any rate this was so toward the end of the Roman Empire.

partaken of in common are expected; the flesh of an animal regarded as divine is eaten because in this way it is believed that a union can be effected with the god himself, and participation thus secured in his substance and his characteristics." [9] Unfortunately we have only too few details concerning the food and the ritual of these sacred repasts, but their meaning hardly admits of doubt. We know, however, that in the Mysteries of Mithra there is a ceremony in which the initiate is presented with bread and a cup, accompanied (as a Christian apologist of the second century tells us) by "certain formulas which you know or which you can know." [10]

In the Mysteries of Cybele and Attis, we learn, on textual authority, that the initiate takes part in a mystic repast. Its conclusion enables him to say: "I have eaten of that which the dulcimer contained, I have drunk of that which was in the cymbal; I have become a *myste* (initiate) of Attis." The dulcimer was the attribute and instrument of Cybele, the cymbal that of Attis, and there is reason to believe that the sacred sustenance placed therein was bread probably or the flesh of sacred fishes, and wine. Now, if it be recalled that the name of Attis is currently linked with "corn," *i.e.*, the food grains in general, we are justified in thinking that not only by sitting down at the table of the god and consuming the viands he is reputed to offer to his followers is communion here effected, but the act performed is the act of *eating the god himself* and thus becoming fully impregnated with his immortalizing essence.

Is there any need to draw attention to the striking points of resemblance between these various rites, even if regarded superficially, and the baptism and the eucharist of the Christians? The Fathers of the Church did not fail to note these resemblances. From the first to the fifth centuries, from St. Paul to St. Augustine, there is abundant testimony to prove that they were struck by them. They explained them in their own way,

[9] Cumont, *Les religions orientales dans l'Empire romain*, p. 104.
[10] Justin *I Apol.* 66, 4.

however. They said that the devil had sought to imitate the Christ, and that the practices of the Church had served as model for the Mysteries. This cannot now be maintained. It is highly probable that in more than one case the reaction of Christianity led to changes in pagan cults which also were intent to secure for men eternal salvation by means of the intercession of a divine being. But the essential myths, the main liturgical ceremonies, the symbols and rites of these cults for effecting salvation are prior to the birth of Christianity, and in St. Paul's day, in the Hellenistic world which was his milieu, a large number of forms of worship were practiced which expressed them.

And we must remember, too, that it is not merely a question of rites; the issue here concerns a certain idea of human destiny and of salvation, of trustful confidence in a divine *Lord,* the intermediary between man and the supreme divinity, who has consented to live and suffer like a man, so that man *may* sufficiently resemble him to be able to effect a union with him and be saved by casting in his lot with him, as it were. And this is exactly St. Paul's doctrine concerning the mission and rôle of the Lord Jesus. Not even the weighty moral element implied in Paul's teaching—I mean the injunction to live a life not merely pious, but pure, charitable and lofty—is peculiar to him, for the Mysteries, too, though to a lesser degree, made demands of the same nature upon their initiates.

IV

But—this is the question that at once occurs to us: Was Paul in a position to get acquainted with the essential principles and fundamental rites of the Mysteries, and could it be that he was influenced by them?[11]

[11] Reitzenstein, *Die hellenistischen Mysterienreligionen* (Leipzig, 1910), especially pp. 43 *et seq.,* 160 *et seq.; Poimandres* (Leipzig, 1904), pp. 79 *et seq.,* 287 *et seq.;* Loisy, *Rev. d'hist. et de litt. relig.* (Sept.—Oct., 1913), *Les Mystères païens,* Chap. viii; also C. Clemen, *Der Einfluss der Mysterien religionen auf das älteste Christentum* (Giessen, 1913), pp. 23-61; Case, *The Evolution,* etc.

We are by no means fully informed about the religious
life of Tarsus, his native city, at the time he lived there,
but we do know that two gods were held in especial reverence. The one was called Baal-Tarz, *i.e.*, the Lord of
Tarsus, and the Greeks identified him with Zeus; the
other was known as Sandan and the Greeks compared
him to Heracles.

According to all appearances, Baal-Tarz was an ancient
rural divinity, presiding over the earth's fertility. In
the course of becoming urban and being gradually confused with Zeus, his rank became more exalted and he
assumed the appearance and characteristics of a celestial
deity who rules over gods and men, enthroned so high
above his followers that to them he seemed well-nigh
inaccessible.

Sandan, on the contrary, remains very near them and
almost within reach of men. From the few documents
we possess concerning him and the discussions and
hypotheses to which these have given rise, we get certain
information which helps us. This Sandan originally was
also a god of fertility and, in a wider sense, of vegetation; every year there was celebrated in his honor a
festival in which he was reputed to die upon a funeral
pyre and then ascend to heaven. Thus he is regarded in
Tarsus the same as Attis is in Phrygia, Adonis in Syria,
Osiris in Egypt, Tammuz in Babylon, and many similar
deities elsewhere at the same period. It is even very
probable that he has already done some borrowing from
one or another of them.

Did he borrow from their mysterious initiatory rites
and their hermetic doctrine of salvation, however? Is he
himself treated as a savior? Here we have a twofold
question which can as yet be answered by hypotheses
only. No document gives us positive information about
the Mysteries of Sandan or describes him as savior;
but since the other gods of vegetation that die and are
restored to life again have their Mysteries and are
regarded by their followers as mediators between the
supreme deity and men, *i.e.*, as intercessors and saviors,

the way is open to think that it would be the same in the case of Sandan. Besides, the mere fact that Sandan afforded Paul the annual spectacle of the apotheosis of the dying god would of itself possess much significance.

Were there no other mystery-religions in existence in Tarsus at the beginning of the Christian era? Probably. The very position of the city at the intersection of the commercial routes makes it likely that the traders circulated the ideas and beliefs as freely as they did the merchandise of the various countries, but it would not be wise to dogmatize upon this point. Nevertheless, the nearness of Phrygia and Syria and the relations constantly kept up with Phenicia and Egypt almost force the conviction upon us that the people of Tarsus were quite alive to the spirit of the Mysteries which flourished in these various countries and well acquainted with their principal myths and their fundamental hopes, and that they themselves practiced more or less their chief rites on their own account. The ancient world was the scene of constantly repeated exchanges of this kind in the domain of religion.

Moreover, another ascertainable fact forms the basis of yet another inference of the same kind, that is, the knowledge that the syncretistic tendency which mingles, confuses, or combines deities whose appearance or functions seem more or less similar had been clearly apparent in Tarsus for some time past. Indeed, we may perhaps declare it to be the most outstanding and established manifestation of the religious life of the city. Now we are aware that upon syncretism the Mysteries are nourished, so to speak.

It seems therefore very probable, if not quite certain, that Paul's childhood was spent in a milieu thoroughly impregnated with the idea of a salvation obtained by the intercession or mediatorship of a god who died and rose again, whose followers share his destiny by means of a mystic union of themselves with him, shown not only by a steadfast faith and confidence in him, but also, and one might almost say, *above all,* by symbolic and potent rites and ceremonies. There was no need to be initiated, any outsider could become acquainted with these religious conceptions and their ritual embodiment; I mean, know that they existed, and what they meant. That which the initiated kept secret was the commanding and arresting mystery which, as he believed, had altered his being—not his belief nor his hope.

So, too, in Tarsus at that time, it was not necessary to become a student at the school of philosophy to know something of its doctrine. Under Augustus, Tarsus is literally a town governed by its university, and this circumstance lends peculiar importance to all that the professors of this university do, in the view of the townspeople. Now these professors seem above all to be philosophers, and Stoic philosophers to boot. As I have already said, everything tends to the belief that many of them were already giving courses of instruction in the form of popular lectures, in which their chief moral precepts and many of their technical terms would find utterance. When we read the Pauline Epistles and find there, sometimes in their very fundamentals and very often in their form, traces of the influence of the Stoics, we must not lose sight of these circumstances. Formerly, on encountering them, writers imagined that the Apostle had entered into relations with Seneca, even exchanging letters with him. This open invention is far less likely to account for the matter at issue than the fact just mentioned concerning the importance and the characteristic features of philosophic life in Tarsus. Paul lived in a milieu entirely engrossed with the matter and terminology of Stoicism. And this second instance of the effect upon him of the sphere in which his childhood and, at least, his early youth also were passed, throws all the light needed upon our first questions, and equips us to understand how it was that this Jew of the Dispersion could almost unconsciously receive and retain in the depths of his mind ideas which would only ripen and reveal their full harvest to him at a much later period.

One question, however, still remains open, and the

answer to it would perhaps put into our hands very important information concerning the somewhat obscure preparation Paul received for his future religious life. Were the Jews of Tarsus all strict legalists or, on the contrary, were their synagogues more or less open to the influences of their surroundings? Were there none among them who slipped into the syncretism of which we have already spoken, that seems sometimes to have had a tendency to convert the national expectation of the Messiah into a doctrine of salvation? If this were so— we do not *know*, but I am inclined to think it probable—it would not be necessary to assume that Paul in these younger days should have felt in sympathy with these perverted Jews. We may even, relying upon the early orthodoxy attributed to him, as well as to his family, by the Acts of the Apostles, believe, if we choose, that he detested them. He was not ignorant of them, however; he knew thus early in life what they thought of salvation and of the Savior, and if we could be sure that he had really received these impressions in his youth, we should undoubtedly consider them the essential factor, or if you prefer it, the earliest germ of his life's religious evolution.

However the decision may go with regard to this last point, it is at any rate true that if Tarsus gave birth to the Apostle of the Gentiles, the man who contributed so largely to spreading abroad, under the name of the Lord Jesus, a new religion of salvation, the conjunction was not an accident, but one thoroughly accountable.

Let us remember how from another point of view—that of his general aptitude to do propaganda work for a doctrine of Jewish origin in the Greco-Roman world— he was particularly advantageously fitted because he could offer the triple qualification of Greek, Jew and Roman.

When I call him a Greek, I mean that with his native air of Tarsus he breathed in something of the Hellenistic soul, even without taking note of it and, in picking up the Greek tongue, he acquired a most valuable instrument of thought and action, as well as the most convenient vehicle of ideas existing at that period. We must exaggerate nothing, however; Paul was not trained in Greek; he was not a student of the great schools of thought any more than he was of the Mysteries. But he lived in a milieu where Greek was spoken, and in which words like "God," "Spirit," "Lord," "Savior," "reason," "soul," "conscience," assumed a meaning known to him. A certain eloquence, of which he retained some of the most striking methods, was practiced and a philosophy which left the impress of some of its maxims and not a few of its technicalities embedded in his memory was studied there. A certain expectation of survival, not unknown to him, was the general belief that men hoped to realize by certain means, of which he, at any rate, knew the fundamentals. Undoubtedly critics are right in maintaining that Paul's Hellenism was not the principal part of his make-up, that he was a Jew rather than a Greek, but only on condition that they do not lose sight of the important fact that he was a Jew of *Tarsus*.

It now seems certain that, if he did not receive the advanced Greek culture to be found in the schools of his native city, he was educated to a high standard of the Jewish culture of those days, which regarded the profound study of the Scriptures as the one thing needful. I have already recalled the fact that in the Acts (xxii. 3) he is quoted as stating that he was brought up at the feet of Gamaliel, *i.e.*, at Jerusalem in the school of the famous Hillel's grandson. I repeat that this statement does not inspire me with confidence and that I even hold it to be incorrect. It is, however, an incontestable fact that Paul's letters seem to display a rabbinical knowledge of the Scriptures—I mean, such knowledge as a rabbi, a doctor, usually possessed—and that in them he manifests a mind molded by Pharisaism; a shrewd, subtle and argumentative mind, attacking the Jewish Law with the very same weapons he had but just employed in its defense. He exhibits in these letters also a stock of ideas upon human nature, sin, the relation between sin and death, all of which are as rabbinical as the dialectic in which he clothes them.

It is moreover noteworthy that it is the Greek translation of the Bible, the Septuagint, which seems to be familiar to him. Doubtless he understood it in the original Hebrew, but I would not vouch for it, and, in any case, it is always, or nearly always, the Alexandrine version that he quotes, and with which he is, as it were, saturated.[12] This fact especially inclines me to the belief that it was in some rabbinical school of the Dispersion that he studied the Scriptures, and not at Jerusalem. Antioch, which was not far from Tarsus, comes to mind, for it formed the great intellectual center of Grecianized Asia, where like and unlike ideas and beliefs met and combined.

Only a Jew could, at that time, interest himself in the initiative put forth by Jesus; only a Greek could enlarge it to the world's measure and render it fertile, and, it goes without saying, only that style of Greek whose mind was not hemmed in by the pride of the schools and their culture. The man required, although belonging to the Hellenistic world, must be one, too, who would rather recognize and share its religious sentiment and its aspirations of faith than follow its intellectual trends. Finally, Paul's qualification as a Roman citizen procured him several distinct advantages. It shielded him from the narrow and malignant nationalism of the Palestinian Jew and inclined him to universalism; by means of it he was to find himself led, even though unconsciously, to raise the hope born in a Jewish guest-chamber to the dignity of a world-religion. And it is for these reasons that I have given him the title of the builder of the future.

[12] The Jews of the Diaspora considered the translation of the Septuagint as much inspired as the Hebrew text; this opinion, which their legalist scruples imposed upon them, was founded on the myth of the identity of the seventy-two versions made by the seventy-two translators. Evidently such unanimity presupposed divine intervention.

CHAPTER V

WE should be wrong, however, in attributing to Paul alone the great work of implanting the Apostolic seedling in Grecian soil. It is true, and I repeat it here, that his originality is not to be denied; indeed it is hardly too much to describe it as almost amounting to genius. Rarely is a man found with a more ardent soul, more strength of passion and sharper drive in action and more potent abilities at transposition and adaptation. At the service of these qualities were gifts of expression, often inadequate and uneven, it is evident, but on the whole both admirable and prolific. Nevertheless, he did not originate all that he uttered; he was subject to influences which determined his conversion and abruptly changed him from a zealot of the Law into an invincible witness for the Lord Jesus; he received a Christian education, and by this I mean that certain people acquainted him with the ideas current in their circle of the personality and the work of Jesus and it was upon this foundation that he erected what he termed "his Gospel." To what extent did he modify that which he had learnt thus in his own teaching? Or did he merely reproduce it? It is difficult to say exactly, but at any rate we can press the problem home and arrive at the probabilities in the case.

No means exist of determining precisely what connection there had been between Paul and the disciples of Jesus before the crisis which made him the most ardent of them all. The question whether he had *seen* Jesus has

[1] V. J. Weiss, *Das Urchristentum*, Chap. viii; Loisy, *Les Mystères*, Chap. x; Goguel, *Introduction au Nouveau Testament*, Vol. IV, Pt. I, Chap. iv; Ed Meyer, *Ursprung und Anfänge des Christentums* (Berlin, 1923). Vol. III. *Cf.* G. B. Smith, *A Guide*, pp. 280 *et seq.*

been long discussed in vain; it does, however, seem certain that he had never *known* Jesus.[2] The most reliable passages are found in his own writings (Gal. i. 13 and I Cor. xv. 9), which present him as a persecutor of the "Church of God," before the occurrence of the miracle on the road to Damascus. The account of his malevolent rage in the Acts (vii. 58; viii. 1-3; ix. 1-2) is to be appraised cautiously, with regard to detail; it is probably influenced by a desire to render the abrupt reversal of his hostile sentiments yet more striking. At any rate, he began by detesting the enthusiastic disciples of the crucified Galilean and demonstrating how he felt toward them to the full.

He detests, but in the process of showing his detestation he forms acquaintance with the first community of Christians. While he may even consider the faith of the men he persecutes absurd, and their hopes vain, nevertheless a tendency to converge is already working in the depths of his mind between the affirmations of these Galilean heretics and those of the pagan or Jewish syncretists of Tarsus or Antioch, in which he did not believe either. Light will dawn for him, when he becomes conscious of this convergence from the interpretation that he, as a Jew, will put upon it.

That which appears certain is that his evolution in the direction of Christianity was not accomplished at Jerusalem, and that the form his doctrine took was not due to any contact with the Twelve. There is good authority for saying: "Paul does not proceed from Jesus across the bridge of the primitive Christian community, but by means of yet another intermediate link in the chain, and the order of succession is: Jesus, the primitive community, Hellenistic Christianity, Paul."[3]

The first Christian community of the Dispersion was not founded by Paul. The Acts (xi. 19) record the establishment of groups of converts in the Jewish colonies in

[2] The whole question turns on II Cor. v. 16: "Even though we have known Christ after the flesh, yet now we know him so no more."
[3] Heitmüller, "Zum Problem Paulus und Jesus" ap. *Zeitschift für Ntl. Wissenschaft* (1912), Vol. XIII, p. 330.

Phenicia, Cyprus and Antioch, which do not owe their origin to him, nor was the first Christian church at Rome the outcome of his initiative. It is possible that Paul's change of front would appear less surprising if we knew more about the state of mind prevailing in these primitive congregations in pagan territory. Their Judaism, always less strict than that of Judea, had probably sometimes dipped fairly deep into syncretism, and it seems unlikely that they would receive the statements of the Apostles concerning Jesus and not put an interpretation of their own upon them. The Hellenists who had brought them from Jerusalem had already begun in the Holy City to interpret them for themselves. Unfortunately we are obliged to try whether something can be divined of the creed of these early Hellenist communities by means of doubtful passages in the Acts and Paul's own allusions —and these are not much guide.

II

The first community of disciples in Jerusalem was purely Jewish. Upon this point we have no reason to doubt the accuracy of the testimony afforded by the Acts. Its members did not separate themselves from other pious Jews save in professing a belief that Jesus the Nazarene had been raised by God to the dignity of the Messiah, and that the promises were fulfilled in him. It is hardly conceivable that they should have had any idea of winning pagans over to this conviction peculiar to themselves; there would really have been no meaning in it for a non-Jew. The utmost that the Jerusalem community could do was to give a welcome to a few Jewish proselytes, and this is the historical meaning of Acts x., in which we read of Peter baptizing Cornelius the centurion, a "God-fearer," unless the whole episode is regarded as pure legend, as it has been suspected of being. But very soon and involuntarily, through force

* Upon this point the book to read is W. Bousset's *Kyrios Christos* (Göttingen, 1913), Chaps. iii. and iv.

of circumstances, this first Apostolic community ceased to be, if not purely Jewish, at any rate purely Palestinian. Almost immediately after its inception an element foreign to its essential character was introduced into it in the person of adherents whom the Acts qualify as "Hellenists," [5] who have already been mentioned.

According to all appearances these are Jews who after a long period of years upon Greek soil have come to end their days in their own country. Included also, and above all, are Jews of the Dispersion, come up to Jerusalem for some important festival. The minds of both these classes work more freely and are more open to new ideas than the minds of the Judeans; it is not very surprising, therefore, that a good many of them should have listened to and believed the Apostles. But in accepting the faith in Christ Jesus they preserved their own mentality, and right here probably must be sought the origin of the disagreements that so soon arose in the newly mixed community.

It is not our purpose to recount these differences; in any case, we know very little about them.[6] However, it is not too rash to say that they are concerned with the laxity which these Hellenists display toward the Law and the worship of the Temple. It is also due to the tendency which, as a natural consequence, developed among them to reason concerning the personality and the mission of Jesus far beyond the point which the Apostles themselves had reached. Apparently we are face to face with an application to the Apostolic statements of that spirit of the Dispersion which we have endeavored previously to portray. The outcome is that the Jewish authorities become incensed against these Hellenists, persecute them and oblige them to leave the city, *while the Apostles remain.* This means that the Apostles do not regard these views as permissible or accept those who hold them.[7]

---

[5] Acts vi. 1 (R. V. marginal note).
[6] Acts vi.
[7] Acts vi. 7; viii, 1. *Cf.* Loisy, *Les Actes des Apôtres, ad locum.*

Now it was these Hellenists, either expelled or escaping from Jerusalem, who were *the first missionaries in heathen lands, i.e.,* in the Jewish communities in pagan territory, which comprise, as we know, born Jews and also proselytes more or less reconciled to Judaism but permanently in social contact with Gentiles. We catch a glimpse of some communities to which this early propaganda gave birth in Phenicia and in Cyprus, but the one of capital importance derived from it was the Church of Antioch. Renan viewed the matter correctly when he wrote: "The starting point of the Church of the Gentiles, the original home of Christian missions, was really Antioch. It was there that for the first time a Christian church, free of ties with Judaism, was formed; there that the mighty propaganda of the Apostolic age got its start, and there that Paul received a definitely Christian education." [8]

From Acts xi. 19-20 we learn that, of all the Hellenists banished from Jerusalem, some traveled as far as Antioch, and there told the Greeks also the gospel of the Lord Jesus.[9] We must understand this to mean that they addressed themselves to the Jews first of all—for we cannot imagine that from the very beginning they should have gone outside the synagogue to work—and then to the proselytes who would be found there in large numbers. It is by no means certain that these first preachers of Jesus deliberately turn with their appeal to the proselytes, but they do not avoid them, and as they certainly find them more ready to give a fair hearing to the Christian hope than the born Jews, they accept and enroll them. I incline to the belief that very soon these "Greeks" constitute the large majority of the Church of Antioch. The name "Christians" given to its members there for the first time by the pagans seems clearly to show that outsiders realize that they have become differentiated by their new enlistment from those who

[8] *Les Apôtres*, p. 226.
[9] Moffatt's rendering is given here, as more closely approaching the Greek.

remain in the ranks of authentic Jewry. Possibly, too, they separate from it fairly soon, forming autonomous congregations, and yet more perhaps by subordinating real Judaism to the Christian ideal, *by making the personality of the Christ the main point of their religion.*

It seems in fact very probable, to put it mildly, that it was in this circle of ideas at Antioch, where so many followers who had not known Jesus pinned all their hopes on him, that an accent begins to be put upon his *deification* and it is accelerated, or, if it be too early yet to use that expression, his glorification begins to be fitted out with particulars. The idea formed there of his personality and his rôle tends to strip him of his Jewish character of Messiah, in favor of another and more general conception, something greater and grander, which is conveyed by the title of "Lord" (*Kyrios*).

Do not forget that in their attempts to communicate their faith to the Jews the Twelve themselves were no doubt from the beginning in a very difficult position. The Scriptures, even with the addition of recent apocalypses, never envisaged a Messiah who would be ignominiously put to death. On the contrary, they contained this formidable passage: "He that is hanged [10] is accursed of God" (Deut. xxi. 23). The disciples had therefore been obliged to explain to their own satisfaction how the death of Jesus could form part of God's Messianic design. They succeeded by starting from the *fact* of the resurrection and arguing thus: That resurrection by God from the dead could only mean that a great part yet remained for him to play, and what could that lofty dignity be but that of the Messiah? The death was a necessary preliminary incident to the resurrection—it was the path designed by God leading to the elevation of Jesus from his humanity to the state of glorification now to be needed by him. And in this way Jesus became identified with the "Son of man" that the prophet Daniel predicted would appear shortly in the clouds of heaven.

[10] The Hebrew text gives "upon the tree."

Now this idea of the "Son of man" is not to be found in Paul's teaching; he has replaced it by another which we shall shortly encounter and one that does not belong to the Judaizing Jerusalem Christian community. Not, therefore, from the doctrine of this community did he borrow the starting point of his Christology. The death of Jesus makes no impression upon the Twelve of an expiatory sacrifice; to Paul, it does: "Christ died for our sins." The Twelve never would have described Jesus as "Son of God," but merely as "Servant of God"; whereas for Paul "Son of God" is the usual title given to Jesus. Certain ideas, therefore, which are essential to the primitive community are unknown, or a matter of indifference, to the Apostle of the Gentiles. Since apparently he did not create, even if he was able to improve upon, those ideas peculiar to himself, the assumption is warranted that he found them outside the Apostolic Christian circle of ideas, and this could be only in a Hellenistic community. It is most probable that Antioch was the one.

There is a significant title applied to Jesus which is peculiar not only to Paul's letters but to all New Testament writings of Hellenistic origin, that of "Lord" (*Kyrios*). We have only to turn the pages of the great Pauline epistles to realize that the Lord dominates the whole life of all the congregations that Paul frequents. Each church forms a "body" of which the Lord is the "head"; or, if the reader prefers, it constitutes a group of worshipers in which he occupies the central place. One noteworthy passage from the Epistle to the Philippians (ii. 9-10) brings this out very clearly: "Wherefore also God highly exalted him, and gave unto him the name which is above every name; that at [11] the name of Jesus every knee should bow, of things in heaven and things on earth and things under the earth, and that every tongue should confess that Jesus Christ is Lord (ὅτι ΚΥΡΙΟΣ ΙΗΣΟΥΣ ΧΡΙΣΤΟΣ) the glory of God the Father." The sacred name in the cult of the Old Testament for Jahveh, the one which dominates all the worship of the

[11] A. V.

Temple in Jerusalem, and, quite certainly, that of the Judaizing Christians still, seems to be transferred and inure to the benefit of this new *Kyrios*. For it is Jahveh himself who once affirmed (Is. xlv. 23): "Unto me every knee shall bow." This makes it seem that he has abdicated from power in favor of Jesus.

It is scarcely likely that Paul should have invented and given such wide currency to this title so charged with meaning, for the extent and intricacy of the process of dissemination involved would be something that surpasses human will. This paves the way for the assumption that long preparation for its acceptance had been going on in the consciousness of those who came to hallow it. Now, setting aside hypotheses which have no solid foundation, designed in attempts to prove that the word *Kyrios* may be of Jewish origin, we find that it is the term by which Greek slaves denote their respect for their master, and that it actually signifies the relation between the slaves of Christ and Christ himself (*cf.* I Cor. vii. 22). It is a title never applied to classic deities—I mean those really Greek, or to Roman either, if its Latin equivalent be rendered by *Dominus*—but which is specially applied to the gods of salvation in Asia Minor, Egypt and Syria, when they are spoken of in Greek. From them its use also extended to sovereigns.[12]

It was in the Syrian atmosphere that the first Hellenistic Christian communities were born and grew. There, around their cradle, the title of *Kyrios* and the cult or worship ritual underlying it by which salvation was obtained spread rapidly. Living neighbor to this circle of ideas, the young Hellenistic Christian community, already tending, almost without suspecting it, to deviate from Judaism, and no longer submitting as rigidly as the Palestinians to the constraint of Old Testament monotheism, installs a similar cult or worship ritual of Christ, or if this other way of putting it be preferred, organizes itself around the worship of Christ.

[12] *Cf.* Deissmann, *Licht vom Osten* (Tübingen, 1909), pp. 263 *et seq.;* consult the index of the Greek words under *Kyrios*, p. 356.

And it is there that it receives the name "Christian" to express the dominating position of the Christ in its rites of worship. It therefore appears natural that this young Hellenistic Christian community should have applied to him whom a pagan would have called its religious hero the characteristic title of "Lord," or *Kyrios,* which was in current use for this purpose all around it.

In settling upon this terrain of Hellenistic piety, that which we call, somewhat prematurely, Christianity, assumes the form of a *faith in Christ as the Lord or Kyrios,* and a *cult or worship ritual of the Christ as the Kyrios,* whilst the Galilean Apostles are still content with faith in Jesus and in what he has said, and still show themselves assiduous in the use of the cult or worship ritual of the Jewish Temple.

Never, it may be said, will Christianity undergo any more important metamorphosis in the future than the one which now concerns us. The "Son of man" of the Judaizing Christian congregations of Palestine may be regarded as constituent of Jewish eschatology. I mean that he finds his true place only in the tableau of the Last Things imagined by Jews, and to which Jews can alone adhere; it is therefore properly to be in point of time and place an *eschatological greatness.* He is to dwell apart in the heavens until the advent of the Messianic Kingdom. On the contrary, the greatness of the Lord or *Kyrios* of the Hellenistic Christian community, both in cult and in worship ritual, is an *actual and present greatness;* the faithful who are gathered together "in his name" feel that he is there in the midst of them, just as the initiates of the Mysteries felt the presence of the deity in the secret ceremonies in which they took part. If, then, we let these two ideas of the Son of man and the Lord confront each other, we shall recognize that the conceptions are so different that they are really opposed to each other. Evidently the future is with the Greek conception, because it undoubtedly emanates from the depths of the religious life of the milieu that has engendered it. The other although older one remains buried away in texts and gradually loses status until it becomes reduced to a formula which is incomprehensible and inoperative for non-Jewish Christian believers.

It is upon this double basis of *faith in the Lord* and *the cult or worship ritual of the Lord Jesus* that Paul's Christology really rests, and the acquisition of the conceptions relating to it forms the major part of his training as a Christian. These conceptions go back beyond his time and he borrowed them from a milieu which, through his general education on Greek soil, was much more intelligible to him than to the Judeo-Christian society of Palestine.

But in this Syrian milieu, as we know, the conception was current also of the god, *i.e.*, the Divine Lord who dies and rises again *for the salvation of his followers.* Can it be that Paul was not the first but that before Paul's day the Hellenistic communities had used it to explain and account for the death of the Lord Jesus? In other words, was it not to his early Christian teachers that Paul owed the fundamental assertion of his soteriology: "Christ died for our sins, according to the Scriptures"? It is at present impossible to prove it, but a whole combination of circumstances renders it probable. Here I shall refer to but one only: The Mysteries clearly make the tempting suggestion that not only the idea of a symbol, a type of the death and resurrection of all his followers, attaches to the death and resurrection of the Christ, but also the force of an example and a guarantee. Pressure also proceeded from the Mysteries in favor of the belief that the salvation of the devoted follower depended upon his union with Christ the Savior, a union which could be brought about by observance of the efficacious rites. In Paul's view these rites are clearly Baptism, the symbol of the death and rebirth in Christ, and the Eucharist the communion meal at the Lord's table. In taking from the rites of Jewish proselytism the practice of the baptism of purification and from the

Galilean Apostles that of the breaking the bread in common, it is indeed difficult to imagine that the Hellenistic Christian community should not from the beginning have charged both ceremonies with profound and mystic significance, inspired by the suggestions of these same Mysteries, in which category this Savior-Lord-Jesus conception seems to have so distinct a place. Paul treats all these ideas as if they presented no difficulties; he broadcasts the mystic formulas which relate to them so freely and spontaneously that we get the impression, to say the least, that he is speaking a language already familiar to the congregations he is addressing. It is not he who has discovered the root ideas which he is exploiting, he has merely probed into them more deeply and enriched them. And lastly, if his own words be taken literally, they confirm this impression: "I delivered unto you . . . that which I also received . . . that Christ died for our sins according to the Scriptures" (I Cor. xv. 3).

III

If we admit the probability that the groundwork of the doctrine we are accustomed to consider Paulinism was communicated to Paul in a Hellenistic Christian community—which is most likely that of Antioch—his conversion becomes much easier to understand than if we set him, the orthodox Jew and Pharisee, face to face with the declarations of no great weight—even after their revision by the first Hellenist converts—of the Judeo-Christians of Jerusalem and say that which he at first detested and combated he had suddenly turned round and adopted. If the fact be that (a) Paul first became acquainted with these fundamental ideas and practices of his mentioned above in a Christian community of Hellenists where they were current coin, and (b) moreover, as I have said I believe to be the case, he was really brought up, not in the Judaism of Palestine, but in the much more yielding, and more or less syncretistic Judaism of the Diaspora at Tarsus or Antioch, and (c), from his childhood, faith in salvation through a God who dies and rises again has met him at every turn and obtained, without his suspecting it, a foothold in his mind, even while he was still rejecting it as a horrible pagan idea; and (d) through the influence of this Savior-God concept, again without his having any idea of it either, his own Messianic hope was already tending to be universalized, and—who knows?—perhaps to put itself forward as more or less of a parallel, like the true and its counterfeit, to the hope expressed through the Mysteries, and (e) his education and the influences of his milieu teach him better than to regard everything in paganism as gross error and absurdity— then it seems to me that we are coming nearer to a natural and logical and satisfactory explanation of his conversion. He was converted from the day upon which he became convinced that the Christians were right in attributing to Jesus the Nazarene the fulfilment of that work of salvation of which the pagans have an inkling. They credit its accomplishment in their blindness to their own devils, but the Scriptures had long ago promised that achievement to Israel. In other words, this conversion is brought about by the sudden meeting in his consciousness, so to speak, between ideas which are profound, yet long familiar, and the Christian rendering of them presented by Hellenists in a form digestible by a Jew brought up on Greek soil. His rabbinic training causes him naturally to proceed to explain and adjust and correlate "that which he has received."

But how could a transaction of this nature which absolutely reversed, in appearance at least, the orientation of his religious consciousness have been possible? He himself looked upon it as a miracle which he conceived actually divided his life into two periods: before, all was gloom; after, dazzling light. The Christ spoke to him on the road to Damascus and told him clearly what he was to do. His entrance accordingly into Christianity, like the mode of entrance upon a Mystery-religion, was not an act based on a calculated and reasoned conclusion, but in obedience to an irresistible impulse.

That Paul believed in the full reality of his vocation there is no manner of doubt; unfortunately neither what he says about it himself nor what we learn from the Acts[13] admits of a near enough approach to the phenomenon for us to be able to analyze it really satisfactorily. This does not imply that in itself it seems very mysterious, for the history of religions, especially those of the Greco-Roman world, abounds in more or less similar cases.[14] Except for that which we do *not* know, that is, the immediate circumstance which led to the decisive shock in Paul's consciousness, we may assert, regarding the matter in the light of modern psychology, that it was an effect prepared for by a fairly long period of travail of soul. The components of this inward distress are, in the first place, the Apostle's own temperament, which predisposed him to sudden shock and to mystic hallucinations; and, in the second place, influences which had been slowly deposited, if I may put it thus, in the depths of his subconscious mind: the Mysteries of Tarsus and Antioch had familiarized him with the idea of Sôter (Savior); his Jewish teachers turned his mind toward the expectation of the Messiah; his childhood's surroundings have accustomed him not to condemn off-hand all that comes from pagan sources; above all a profound anxiety with regard to religious matters, of which we learn from a well-known passage in the Epistle to the Romans (vii. 7 *et seq.*). It would undoubtedly be an error to rely too much on this passage, because its subject is Paul's state of mind before his conversion, but it is interpreted as he saw it afterward, and the language used is the language of a convert. We can nevertheless glean from it that the future Apostle felt himself unable to strive successfully against sin which the Law, as expounded by the learned among the

---

[13] Gal. i. 12-17; I Cor. ix. 1; xv. 8. Acts ix. 3 *et seq.*; xxii. 6 *et seq.*; xxvi. 13 *et seq.*

[14] Special comparison may be made with Apuleius *Metamorphoses* 11, and Acts ix. 10 *et seq.*

Pharisees, shows him present everywhere. This was exactly the state of mind which at that period led to the eager seeking for the Savior, the Divine Mediator, the infallible Guide to Truth and to Life.

Paul, then, feels himself far from God, in a state of imperfection and sin, a condition of mind, to say the least, surprising in a true rabbi, for whom faith is joy and certainty; but—we often have to come back to this point of view—Paul is a Pharisee of the Diaspora. It is scarcely possible but that the gladness and assurance which he finds among the Christians he encounters should have struck him forcibly, from its very contrast with his own state of anxiety. If, as I believe, it is not the simple hope of the Galilean by which he is confronted but by a Christology which has already been somewhat Hellenized and has given to the death of Jesus the meaning of an expiation for our sins, "according to the Scriptures," it is not difficult to surmise that he may have been fascinated by these ideas and the evidence in support of them. He may in them have dimly perceived, before he saw it clearly, a solution satisfactory to himself, of the difficulty that he had long been debating.

This work of preparation doubtless is carried on secretly, outside his active consciousness, each aspect of the future synthesis maturing, as it were, separately in its own way. The synthesis itself when it takes place is effected in a flash of mysticism, by an unexpected stroke of inspiration. Such an abrupt upheaval of a person's entire being is not rare with great mystics, and the vision of Francis of Assisi on the way to Spoleto, or the apparition of the Virgin to Ignatius Loyola, to take two instances only, may be set side by side with the miracle on the road to Damascus. All three proceed from causes more or less similar, and lead to consequences alike in their meaning.

In summing up, I imagine that Paul had undergone a twofold preparation for the crisis which made him a potential Christian and a would-be Apostle: one of them somewhat negative and the other positive. The first in the final analysis can be resolved into two elements: (a) the idea of the Savior. While Paul does not set much store by it in the beginning, it is inseparable from his early impressions and tends at least to resemble the form of expectation of the Messiah held by him as a Jew of the Diaspora. (b) His Pharisaic experience of the Law, which leaves him in anguish of soul through sin that threatens from all sides and makes escape hopeless. The second is to be found in the exhibition of assurance on the part of the Hellenist Christian who counts on liberation from the power of sin and salvation through the Lord Jesus. His conversion, then, may be regarded as the sudden resolution of all these different elements and, even if its actual cause remains a hidden mystery, the process of it is known to us in some other cases.

Moreover, it is the logical outcome of such a process that Paul, with his temperament, is not content, any more than Francis of Assisi or Ignatius Loyola, with mere conversion, but that from a persecutor he must become an Apostle. Let us note carefully that the vision on the road to Damascus has not changed Paul; it has merely impelled him to apply his former principles of thought and action in another direction. He adopts Jesus *nolens volens;* he adds to his information about him, possibly first at Damascus, certainly at Antioch afterward, and there he begins to meditate and speculate about what he "receives" by processes familiar to him as a Jew and a Pharisee of the Dispersion. Even when he is fighting for his new faith against the Law, he still remains a Jew as before. Renan expresses his attitude correctly when he says that Paul had only changed his fanaticism.[15]

Assuredly he was not the man to be satisfied with "receiving." There is no doubt that his Gospel owes much to personal inspiration as well as to suggestions having their origin in his apostolate itself, as we shall

[15] *Les Apôtres*, p. 183; *cf.* Deissmann, *Paulus* (Tübingen, 1911), pp. 67 *et seq.*

see. But he has "received." He says so himself. And
that which he has received is the nucleus of his doctrine,
and also, at least implicitly, of those amplifications
which touched and conquered him and which in his turn
he will spread abroad, expounding them with indomitable
energy: a veritable religion of salvation for all men.

CHAPTER VI

It is from the Acts that we learn that the road to Damascus was the scene of Paul's conversion and that same city the center of his early activities, and we find no difficulty in crediting this statement. The main point for us to note is that it was not in Jerusalem nor in association with the Twelve that he served his apprenticeship as a Christian missionary, nor did he regard himself as subordinate to them. Convinced that Jesus himself, the glorified Christ, had constituted him an Apostle by a special act of his own initiative, he does not allow anyone to question the fact, and it is his conviction that he has no need of counsel or Christian instruction from anyone. Let us recall the bold declarations of the Epistle to the Galatians (i. 10 *et seq.*): "Am I now persuading men, or God? or am I seeking to please men? If I were still pleasing men, I should not be a servant of Christ. For I make known to you, brethren, as touching the gospel which was preached by me, that it is not after men. For neither did I receive it from man, nor was I taught it, but it came to me through revelation of Jesus Christ.

". . . When it was the good pleasure of God, who separated me, even from my mother's womb, and called me through his grace, to reveal his Son in me, that I might preach him among the Gentiles; immediately I conferred not with flesh and blood" (here we understand: with any human authority): "Neither went I up to Jerusalem to them which were apostles before me.

---

[1] V. Deissman, *Paulus;* Goguel, *Introduction au N. T.,* Vol. IV; J. Weiss, *Das Urchristentum,* Chaps. ix-xix; G. B. Smith, *A Guide,* pp. 280 *et seq.*

Then after three years I went up to Jerusalem to visit Cephas.''

Let us note also that the very essence of Christian teaching was undoubtedly contained in a few sentences and that Paul apparently was acquainted with these *before* the vision which decided his conversion, so that he found no difficulty in teaching immediately that which he had now come to espouse. On the other hand, we can understand that while the Christian community in Jerusalem might not question the sincerity of his conversion, it should have reservations in regard to the reality of his vocation and find some difficulty in admitting that he was qualified to speak of Jesus—he who had never known him—with as much authority as they themselves, who had shared his daily life. It was only after the lapse of three years that he did decide to go up to Jerusalem, and then he found a defiant attitude toward him in the little Apostolic world there, and no doubt would have been unable to enter freely among them had it not been for Barnabas, who was so struck by his zeal and his strong convictions that he took him to Peter and to James, and they decided to welcome him and recognize his mission.

From the beginning he certainly differed from them about ''the things concerning Jesus''; that is, he adhered to the Christology of the Hellenists, which went further than theirs. If we may believe Acts ix. 29, the exposition of his beliefs which he undertook in the Hellenizing synagogues of the city, frequented by the Greek-speaking Jews, aroused such a tumult that he was forced to leave Jerusalem. He withdrew to Syria and Cilicia, *i.e.*, to Antioch and Tarsus. On to Tarsus Barnabas went and sought him, after the sight of all that had been done for Christianity in Antioch had served as a clue to this noteworthy man (about whom we should like to know more) to the future of the Christian faith upon Greek soil.

Upon Barnabas' initiative it was, therefore, that Paul undertook to spread the Good Tidings of the Lord Jesus throughout the world, and inaugurated that hard life of missionary labor which he was to lead in Asia Minor and in Greece until the time of his arrest by the Roman authorities at Jerusalem. He used to go from city to city, stopping wherever there were important Jewish communities. First of all he would preach in the synagogues, and usually his Gospel, as he called it, would excite dire anger there among the born Jews. If he was able to delay the date of his expulsion from town, he would try to convince the proselyte Jews, and would preach to them by themselves in some private house. Wherever he succeeded tolerably well he would remain for some months—as he did at Corinth—or he would return there —as he did to Ephesus. In addition, he used to keep up a more or less active correspondence with the churches he had "planted," to sustain them in their new faith, and sometimes he would take them to task for their shortcomings. It is not our purpose to lay stress here upon this busy and troublous, perilous yet fruitful life of Paul, but we must try to understand what it taught him.

II

From the very first he saw clearly a distinction to which the Twelve did not willingly consent and resign themselves nor were they able to comprehend it as he did. I mean the difference between the "God-fearers" who were very ready to believe in the "Lord" and the majority of the born Jews who closed their ears and hardened their hearts if the disciples sought to convince them. Were they, as a consequence, to abandon these born Jews to their folly and deliberately to carry the truth to the people outside of Israel? It was easy to foresee that besides the proselytes who, at any rate, were "Judaizing" pagans who were full Gentiles would adopt the faith; could they be accepted, and promised a share in the Kingdom? Were these strangers, ignorant of the Law of Moses, to be made co-heirs with the people of Jahveh? It is easy to imagine that the Twelve, who were thoroughly imbued with Jesus' own teaching and still so profoundly Jewish, would never accept such conclusions without the very greatest reluctance. Paul imposed these conclusions on them because he knew how to draw up convincing arguments based on the success of his first mission in Asia Minor, and the brethren at Jerusalem believed that the guidance of the Spirit was recognizable in the work of the thirteenth Apostle. While the congregation in Jerusalem was poor, the churches founded by Paul often had some wealthy and generous members among their number, and the Apostle knew how to induce them to aid the Mother Church. And furthermore, why should they not recognize the value of preaching that had spread abroad in so many different places the name of the glorified Christ?

The principle that Gentiles were to be admitted once granted, it was expedient to make the application of it easy. Paul knew that circumcision was displeasing to the Greeks and that most of the "works" of the Law did not suit either their customs or their way of thinking. He was not slow in persuading himself that the Law was superseded by the teaching of Christ, who had come indeed expressly to substitute a new covenant for the former one. The Twelve yielded to him again and consented to absolve Gentile converts from the demands of Jewish legalism. Thus implicitly Christianity was separated from Judaism and an impetus given it to become an original religion.

Paul's Christology, teeming with Hellenistic views, made this result inevitable, by modifying very considerably the significance of both the life and death of Jesus to the Twelve. The Apostle soon perceived that the Messianic hope did not interest the Greeks; it was, as a matter of fact, only intelligible in conjunction with the nationalistic hopes of the Jews. For it to become acceptable to the Gentiles, it was absolutely necessary to enlarge its scope, and by combining with it a conception familiar to the doctrine of the pagan Mysteries, to present a changed Christ. He was no longer to be thought of as a man armed with the power of Jahveh in order to raise the chosen people out of their misery and put their oppressors under their feet, but rather as the messenger of God charged to bring *salvation to all men,* the certainty of a future life of bliss in which the soul, above all, would experience the complete fulfilment of its destiny. Moreover, Paul realized also that the Gentile converts would not readily be reconciled to retaining "the scandal of the Cross." To the ignominious death of Jesus, upon which unbelievers did not fail to lay stress, an explanation would have to be given that would suffice to turn it from a drawback into something more acceptable. The Apostle meditated upon this twofold problem, already propounded and probably well defined in the community of the Dispersion where he found it, and he decided upon a solution of incalculable significance. Wholly indifferent to the Nazarene so dear to the Twelve, he resolved to know the Crucified alone, whom he would portray as a divine personality, in existence before the beginning of the world, a kind of incarnation of the Spirit of God, a "celestial man" long retained in reserve as it were, in heaven beside God, and at last come down to earth to institute a veritably new humanity, of which he would be the Adam.

The necessary links in all this chain of speculation came to the Apostle, probably unsought, by a spontaneous flash of memory or turn of thought, from a certain number of the common ceremonials of the Mysteries. It is the *hermetic* or sealed books, *i.e.,* books produced and carefully guarded by these Mysteries themselves, which throw most light upon the Christological doctrine of Paul as I have just sketched it.

It culminated, if I may say so, in an expression which is somewhat surprising to us: The Lord Jesus is presented to us as the *Son of God.* Now, for Paul, God is a Jewish heritage; it follows, therefore, that the monotheism of the Israelite is impressed upon his mind *a priori* and absolutely. This God is the Most High God, entirely distinct from Nature, and remains indispersed in Nature by any tendency to pantheism. Then how can it be imagined that he should have a son, or, if you will, how are we to understand the relation of son to father which Paul perceives between the Lord and God?

At first the inclination would be to believe that all there is here is a question of figure of speech, a symbol. The Jews gave the name of "Servant of Jahveh" (*Ebed Jahveh*) to every man who might be deemed "inspired" by him. The Greek of the Septuagint often rendered this expression by the words παῖς τοῦ Θεοῦ, the word παῖς meaning, like the Latin *puer*, both "servant" and "child." The transition from παῖς (child) to υἱός (son) creates no difficulty and is, as a matter of fact, effected in Judeo-Christian writings such as the Acts and the Pauline Epistles.[2] But a careful examination of the passages in the Epistles of Paul proves that his thought goes far beyond this paltry verbal ambiguity. To be sure of this the well-known text in the Epistle to the Romans (viii. 32) needs only to be recalled, where it is written that God "spared not his own Son, but delivered him up for us all." Nevertheless, we must not forget that Paul, just because he does not yet suspect the innumerable theological difficulties that this conception of the Son of God holds in reserve for the future, may very possibly not use the expression in its literal sense, but as a roundabout way of denoting, as well as one can, by implication in an analogy taken from humanity, a "superhuman" relation for which he had no adequate terms at his command.

Any confusion of the Lord with God must be avoided at all events; for Paul it would be inconceivable, since he has as yet no inkling of the Trinity. The Lord is dependent upon God (I Cor. iii. 23) and obeys him "even unto death" (Phil. ii. 8), being subject unto him in all things (I Cor. xv. 28). The whole question seems to be regulated by the passage in I Cor. viii. 6, which I subjoin.

[2] *Cf.* Acts iii. 13, 26; iv. 27, 30; Didache, or Teaching of the Twelve Apostles iv. 2; x. 2; I Clem. lvix. 2 *et seq.;* etc. The expression "Son of God" appears in the Acts once only (ix. 20) and there it is given as a characteristic feature of Paul's teaching, which is certainly a noteworthy point.

". . . Yet to us there is one God, the Father, of whom are all things, and we unto him; and one Lord Jesus Christ, through whom are all things, and we through him." Thus, however essential and necessary the coöperation of the Lord in the works of God may be, the Lord is not the equal of God. He is the representative of his Spirit, for in II Cor: iii. 17 it is plainly stated: "The Lord is the Spirit." Paul is not able to put forth any form of words which brings these supreme titles, "Lord" and "God," closer together. The relation in his mind between them is the same intimate relation expressed by him in the language of humanity when he affirms that the Lord is the Son of God, without the expression actually warranting the supposition that a theory in the absolute sense of the analogy is intended.

Strictly speaking, it must be said that for Paul the Lord, by himself, represents *one of the categories of creation,* the nearest of all to God, and one which may be qualified as divine. On the other hand, it is very certain that from this time the dogma of the divinity of Christ is on its way, since the Pauline idea seems too indefinite and incomplete to remain stable. And it is in the direction of the identification of the Lord with God that the piety of the believers, heedless of difficulties, will steadfastly lead the faith on.

Without laying further stress, for it is not in order here, upon theological conceptions, the more complex because on more than one point they are somewhat uncertain, enough has been said to show what Jesus the Nazarene became under the influence of the myths of intercession and of salvation familiar to the Pauline milieu, and what the Apostle made him out to be in the light of his rabbinical theodicy. Behold he is changed into the all-accomplishing agent of God, prior to time and to the world, the incarnation of the Holy Spirit—who, if we may put it thus, constitutes the divine principle of his being—charged with the execution of God's great design for the regeneration and the salvation of humanity.

His death in this way became clearly intelligible: all men had crumpled under the weight of their sins. They were unable to right themselves and face the divine light. Christ had been willing to offer them the required means; he took their guilt upon him and expiated their sins through his death of ignominy. Then, that they might share in his accomplishment and find grace in the day of judgment, it was expedient first of all for them to effect a union with himself through faith and love. Thus this pretense of a stumbling block became the great mystery, the supreme end and aim of the mission of Jesus, and Paul was right in saying that all there was to his preaching was "Christ crucified." [3] The Greeks understood and were moved by it, and, in itself it insisted on nothing that could not be accepted by the Twelve. While it left them the full delight of their living memories of him, it exalted the glory of their Master yet higher than they had done. Even so, it entirely changed the perspective and the purport of his commission. At the same time, it laid the foundations of a boundless doctrinal speculation, more than foreign, antipathetic even to the Palestine milieu in which Christ had lived. Less verbose and complicated and, in a word, less extravagant than the great syncretistic systems with which, in the second century A.D., Basilides' and Valentinus' names will be connected, Paul's doctrine opened the way to these; it was already a syncretistic *gnosis,* a composite *revelation.*

III

The pagans who came to the Christian faith by way of the synagogues, or those who directly exchanged their former beliefs for it, lived in a milieu in which a religion without rites could scarcely be conceived. The most moving of these rites centered about the idea of purification and the notion of sacrifice: (a) the sacrificial expiation designed to appease the divine wrath; (b) the sacri-

---

[3] I Cor. 1, 23. *Cf.* I Cor. 1, 18; 'Ο λόγος γὰρ ὁ τοῦ σταυροῦ.

ficial offering, intended to secure the favor of the god; or (c) the sacrificial communion, through which the followers of a divinity could effect a union with it and indicate that they formed one body in its sight. The Twelve, devout Jews as they were, showed themselves assiduous in the Temple service and certainly did not deem any other form of worship necessary; they did, however, attach peculiar importance to baptismal purification, the acceptance of which, in the Gentile congregations, became the sign of conversion. At the same time, when they assembled in the house of one or another of the brethren, they "broke bread together." This act, usual at meals in Israel and probably performed by Jesus at such times as he ate with the Apostles, was already assuming in their eyes the significance of a symbol of union; union among themselves and union with Christ. But everything inclines to the belief that they had not yet established any relationship between this "breaking of bread" and the death of Christ; neither did they attribute any degree of sacramental value to it, nor relate the institution or the repetition of it to a request of their Master.

Paul felt the necessity of discovering the deep underlying significance of this custom. He found what he sought by linking it indissolubly with the drama of the redeeming Passion, and sowing in its prepared soil the fertile concept—seeds of a sacrifice of atonement and of communion—he turned it into the accomplishment of a great mystery, the memorial and the living symbol, longed for by Jesus himself, of the work of the cross. In I Cor. xi. 23 and the following verses we are told: "The Lord Jesus in the night in which he was betrayed took bread: and when he had given thanks, he brake it, and said, This is my body, which is for you; this do in remembrance of me. In like manner also the cup, after supper, saying, This cup is the new covenant in my blood: this do, as oft as ye drink it, in remembrance of me. For as often as ye eat this bread, and drink the cup, ye proclaim the Lord's death till he come." Never had any rite of the pagan Mysteries been charged with more significance,

nor with more seductive hopes than the Pauline Eucharist, but it belonged to their species, and not in any way
to the Jewish spirit; it introduced into the Apostolic
Church "a bit of paganism." Again, however, the Christians accepted it, because its consequence to their faith
was a considerable inflation and it proved the primary
basis of a vast theological speculation, the mother of
many important dogmas.

At the same time the rite of baptism assumes an
equally profound significance. "For as many of you as
were baptized unto Christ," writes Paul (Gal. iii. 27)
"did put on Christ," which means that by baptism the
Christian becomes conformed to Christ. I stress these
words because Paul has never ventured to say that
baptism makes of the Christian a *Christ,* as the taurobolium made the devotee of Cybele an *Attis.* But the
idea upheld by this baptism really moves in principle
on the same plane as that which makes good the pretensions of the taurobolium. By baptism the Christian
"puts on Christ," a sacred garment, as it were, of salvation; his descent into death is symbolized by his plunge
into the river or into the baptismal pool; he rises up
out of it after three immersions, as Christ rose from the
tomb on the third day, and is henceforth assured that he,
too, one day shall be glorified, God willing, as Christ has
been.

I cannot repeat too often that all this did not originate
with Paul. The Hellenist Churches preceding his conversion, and before them, perhaps, groups of Jewish
syncretists and gnostics, had prepared his materials and
stated the main themes covered by his speculations. This
is why it is an exaggeration to maintain that he was
the real founder of Christianity. The real founders of
Christianity were the men who established the Church
of Antioch, and we scarcely know the names of any of
them. But, not only was Paul's share in these beginnings far more ample and well defined, but he also has
the undoubted advantage over them that he was fully
conscious of his share and of its import. He did not

found Christianity, if by founding the adaptation of Jewish messianism to Hellenist salvationism is meant, but he seems to have contributed more than anyone else toward determining the metes and bounds of this adaptation. While guarding against the too favorable opinions that he would give us of his own part in the matter, therefore, we may yet believe that, without him, Christianity would have been something other than its historical self.

CHAPTER VII

CHRISTIANITY AS AN AUTONOMOUS RELIGION[1]

In yielding to the force of circumstances Paul rendered it pliable to his speculative genius. Accepting in advance the cleavage between Christianity and Judaism which circumstances showed him to be inevitable, he had a doctrine all made to explain and account for it. But in any case the reactions of the Grecian milieu upon its thought and practice could not be avoided by the Christian faith as soon as it emigrated from Palestine, and this, as we have learned, had already occurred before Paul's day. It was particularly fatal that there should be applied to it in the Greek world the exegetical processes by which the Jews of Alexandria reconciled the Law of Moses with current philosophy. He was of the line of Philo, this unknown Asian who made the statement in the prologue to the Fourth Gospel, that Jesus the Messiah had been an earthly incarnation of the Logos, the Word of God, the executive agency of Jahveh, according to Alexandrine exegetics, and coeternal with Him.[2] This was a staggering proposition, for nothing less would content it than to identify the Crucified with a direct manifestation of God, i.e., in sound logic, with God Himself. It was also blasphemous to a Jew, who could not even conceive that the Divine Infinity, which he dared not name lest he should seem to be putting

[1] R. Knopf, *Das nachapostolische Zeitalter* (Tübingen, 1905); G. Hoennicke, *Das Judenchristentum* (Berlin, 1908). There is a copious general bibliography given in G. B. Smith's *A Guide*, pp. 324 *et seq.*
[2] John i. 14: "And the Word became flesh, and dwelt among us, and we beheld his glory, glory such as an only son enjoys from his father." We give Moffatt's rendering as more nearly approaching the Greek. The Greek *Logos* is translated in the New Testament by the "Word," or the "Saying."

restrictions on it, should be enclosed within the narrow confines of a human body. But it was a proposition easy to reconcile with Paul's Christology, or, rather, closely allied to it, when the Apostle's fundamental declaration is recalled that "the Lord is the Spirit." Moreover, it was very seductive to a Greek and very much in accord with the profound longing of a faith which, through its persistent tendency to exalt the personality of Jesus, felt forced, almost unbeknowing to itself, to bring God and him nearer and nearer together.

Without yet foreseeing all the consequences these blendings and inflations would have upon the faith of the Twelve, the Jewish Christians did not accept them all with a good grace. First they were discontented, because by passing it around so freely the precious privilege of being "heirs of the Kingdom," which they believed peculiarly theirs was becoming depreciated, and ceasing almost to be a distinction. They disliked these changes because they were Jews and intended to remain so, as they knew their Master had been. They therefore opposed Paul stoutly, even in the congregations he himself established. Even after the Twelve had fellowshiped him as an Apostle side by side with themselves and had apparently given in to the concessions he demanded for his own converts, they assumed the right to withdraw some of them which occasionally caused him embarrassment. Powerful invectives were hurled at him from the ranks of the legalists, and his letters to the Corinthians and the Galatians, however obscure their contents remain to us in detail, at least afford a clear impression of the hostility of these men who, had they been able, would have had him branded a heretic and an impostor. Much later specimens of Christian literature—such as the writings attributed to Clement Romanus, who lived toward the end of the first century A.D.—still bear traces of these polemics.

The theology of the Johannine prologue was also the object of stubborn protests. Nevertheless, toward the end of the Apostolic age it would certainly have been possible to foresee clearly which tendency would obtain in the future.

From that time, in fact, the Christians were obliged to admit that the return of the Lord, the *parousia*, which was certainly long delayed, might not take place for some years yet. Although they continued to refer to his return, they no longer lived upon the expectation of it, and little by little it ceased to occupy the central place in the Christian faith which had at first been given to it. Moreover, the eschatological cataclysm with which it was entwined did not appeal to the imagination of the Greco-Romans in the same way as it did to the Jews. Their former philosophical dualism and their leaning toward spiritualism made impossible for them complete sympathy with a belief in the resurrection of the flesh, or the material aspects of the Messianic Kingdom, upon which Jewish thought loved to dwell. Since the Gentile converts formed by far the majority of the membership, and Christian propaganda had no chance of success save among the Gentile nations, that which was shortly to be known as the "rule of faith" had to be formulated and developed in conformity with their aspirations. Since St. Paul's propositions, or those of the Fourth Evangelist,[3] corresponded with their unconscious wishes, Christological speculation, it can readily be imagined, which already had passed the bounds set by the tenets of the Twelve, would but be amplified still further and henceforward retain the chief place in the Christian creed.

At the same time, too, the break between the Church and the Synagogue was actually effected, and the followers of Jesus began to speak of the Jews in terms which would certainly have surprised the Master. Soon they will deny them all knowledge of the Truth and even

[3] The kinship between Johannism and Paulinism is evident, so much so that it has been possible to maintain that if we possessed the Gospel according to Paul, it would certainly closely resemble the fourth Gospel. *Cf.* B. W. Bacon, *The Fourth Gospel in Research and Debate* (1910).

of the Mosaic Law.[4] The Christian congregations that look up to the Apostles and their Jewish disciples (themselves recruited from among men who practiced Judaism) remain small and poor. They still exist in Syria, in Egypt, and possibly in Rome, but they are swamped by the great churches filled with deserters from paganism. In their effort to keep loyal to the teaching which they have received from those who have known the Lord, they expose themselves to the accusation from the opposite camp of thinking meanly about him, and the hour draws near in which the majority party of Christians will refuse them the right to claim any share in salvation. Toward 160 A.D. St. Justin writes that Christians who continue to observe Jewish practices will, in his opinion, be saved, on condition that they do not seek to impose their practices on others, but he adds that many Christians would not brush shoulders with them.[5] In reality, the Greco-Roman Christians no longer feel themselves allied to Israel; and to that Law, of which Christ had said that he would not change a jot or tittle, they give a purely symbolical interpretation.

Still, in this same period, the Christian congregations, now that they have definitely separated from the synagogues, have already begun to organize their community life. First of all they choose temporal administrators, deputized to watch over their material interests and maintain order within the fold, whilst the Holy Spirit raises up inspired men to sustain and spread the faith. Later, when they begin to feel the need of more stabilized practices, and take exception more or less to the initiative of these inspired members, they try to regularize the administration of these spiritual interests. And when the generation which has known the Apostles becomes extinct, possibly the monarchic episcopate is born: in any case, it will be born soon.

[4] The epistle known as The Epistle of Barnabas, violently anti-Jewish, is apparently a brief Alexandrine writing of 117-130 A.D.; but, possibly more than fifty years earlier, to the Syrian author of the Teaching of the Twelve Apostles, the Jews are already the "hypocrites."
[5] *Dialogue with Trypho* 47.

In other words, at the beginning of the second century after Christ, Christianity already presents itself to its world as an independent religion, lacking cohesion certainly, and with its rites, dogmas and institutions still in a very elementary state, yet nevertheless perfectly conscious that it is not to be confused any longer with Judaism. It has already traveled very far from the ideas both of Jesus and of the Twelve. From now onward it will claim to offer all men, without distinction of race or condition, the Life Eternal.

II

We know that the Greco-Roman terrain, at the time when the Christian hope was transplanted thither, by no means resembled a blank tablet. It was already producing a conception of religion, somewhat incoherent, it is true—since it varied with the individual in the objects to which it was related, or, on the other hand, sought to bring into juxtaposition many dissimilar objects—but at any rate alive, and by no means inclined to allow itself to be uprooted without protest. Among the ignorant, by whom it was very often confounded with superstition, this conception of religion succeeded in resting firmly upon a multitude of customs and prejudices almost impossible to dislodge. In more enlightened spheres, it could also count upon the force of habit, and in addition it received strong support from the intellectual training in vogue. From one end of the Empire to the other, children were subject to the same formative influences in the schools; there they were taught the same reasoning processes, given the same general culture, and their religious conceptions were necessarily molded in relation to these.

Let us notice at the start, for this is a point of capital importance, that culture at the time of the Caesars was almost exclusively literary. Rhetoric, one of the two courses of study which a well-educated young man would pursue to complete his mental equipment, claimed but to teach him the art of putting ideas and words together.

Philosophy, the other of the two, which aimed to unveil the world to him, give him the meaning of life and establish the principles and rules of morality, was not supported by any exact science. The import of experimental demonstration which the Greek mind had formerly possessed had been lost. So men would repeat as proved truths numerous absurdities which a moment's careful examination would at once have overthrown. On the one hand, an inchoate empiricism, and, on the other, pseudo-doctrines of physics, absolutely in the air—such was, in sum, the natural science of those days. This explains why philosophy, rich in moral ideas that were correct, ingenious, even eloquent, but having no roots in reality, was broken up into various systems of metaphysics, interesting as intellectual combinations, but purely arbitrary. Moreover, since they had been long established by Greek thinkers, they were now reduced to scarcely more than themes upon which the "masters" executed more or less individual variations. Fairly enough *because* they remained aloof from experimentally verified facts these themes could easily be transposed and in this way take on developments which were quite foreign to the thought of their original authors. Philo, for instance, had mated them with the main postulates of the Jewish Law; in time the Neoplatonists will draw from them a species of revealed religion; again, the Christian doctors of Alexandria will combine them with the assertions of their faith, and a fresh system of dogmatics will arise out of the mixture. In themselves they proved incapable of successful defense against such attempts; but, on the other hand, they were so deeply intrenched in the minds of educated men, and so universally accepted as truths, even by the grossly ignorant, that every interpretation of the world or of human life and destiny, and every religion, had to reckon with them.

Let us note also that Christianity, though introduced to the Greco-Roman world in the first century after Christ, had not taken firm root there until the second, nor did it show signs of extensive growth until the third.

Now, that which we call public opinion had not stood
still and remained in the same position with regard to
philosophical and religious matters during all that time;
while still continuing to be different in the *honestiores*
and in the *humiliores*, it was modified in both spheres.
If Christianity made such strides in the third century,
there is reason to think that the modification to which
public opinion was subjected was in line with its own
interests.

At the time when the Empire succeeds the Republic,
the official religion of the Greco-Romans is already a syncretism, or a combination which was made after the conquest by Rome of the Grecianized East, and composed
of the gods of the conquerors and of the conquered.
Educated men no longer have any faith in it, but they
respect it in public and, when forced, take part in its
rites.   They do this because they continue to believe
religion obligatory upon the common people, whose dangerous appetites and instincts it holds in check.   They
uphold it also because they do not forget that the ancient
City formerly relied upon it and that the fruitful efforts
of their predecessors were sustained by it.   In so far as
it is peculiarly Roman, they regard it as the visible bond
which unites Roman citizens with each other.   According
to their individual tastes, their more or less pronounced
scepticism demands from the doctrines of the various
schools of philosophy a supply of the metaphysical sustenance they cannot do without: usually they favor
Stoicism or Epicureanism.   As for those of humbler condition, they remain devoted to the lesser deities and to
sorcerers.   The mysterious, mystic and voluptuous religions of the East, however, already implanted in the
Empire, slowly thrive there.   In his scheme for the
restoration of the State, Augustus contemplated the complete reëstablishment of the Roman religion.   But if he
believed it possible at the same time to oblige people
who still possessed any religious feeling to confine it
within the forms of the past, or to restore the faith of
those who had lost it, he was the victim of a singular

illusion. Whatever he thought about it, he only succeeded in reëstablishing in their entirety the temple rites and the temples; and equally he enhanced the *civic* value of the official rites. True patriotism, or even bare loyalty, henceforward implied reverent devotion to the divinity of the Emperor (*numen Augusti*) and to the goddess *Rome*.

Such a religion consisted of simply a few ceremonies; it was devoid of any theology or any real dogma, and could not pretend to afford sustenance to religious sentiment possessing a fair amount of vigor. Now, it happened that the impulse of the East, which the paucity of scientific knowledge favored, and the influence of the ills of all kinds which tested and perturbed mankind from the time of Tiberius to that of Nerva, against which Stoicism protected but a select few, restored sentiment to an increasingly large place in the Greco-Roman consciousness. Its scope enlarged and it became much more imperious than in the past. Even among the enlightened, scepticism was not long in experiencing inundation by profound aspirations toward a deeply religious life, and Stoicism rapidly gave way before Platonism, which was more plastic and could be more easily charged with religiousness. If it is somewhat of an exaggeration to say that Marcus Aurelius was the last of the Stoics, it is true that the end of his reign marks the complete decadence of the doctrine upon which the noble emperor had just shed supreme luster; henceforward the pagan world is ripe for devotion. The advent, with Septimus Severus and his family, of African and Syrian princes, and the dominion of women imbued with the mystic piety of the East, favored the prompt development of fervor, and the third century experienced all forms of it, from the most grossly material, closely allied to pure superstition, to the most refined, the creations of philosophical reflection henceforward inclining toward the divine. The state religions, following the formula known throughout antiquity, were reduced to the single religion of the emperor, now that the nationalities, formerly autonomous occupants of the territory now conquered by Rome, have been absorbed by her; the most vital religious sentiment henceforward gave itself up solely to the salvation of the individual.

All the creeds and all the cults then had their adherents, who molded them to their intense desire for a future of eternal bliss in a mysterious hereafter. From this conglomerate of religious material, each man's piety carved out for itself a religion that fitted it; and usually, in constructing its creed and its form of worship, combined its statement of belief with rites of varied origin.

From the first century Christianity was labeled an Eastern religion, at once mystic and practical, since on the one hand it rested upon divine revelation and promised eternal salvation through an all-powerful Mediator, and on the other it claimed to establish upon earth a new life, wholly loving and virtuous. Its chance, therefore, was a likely one of pleasing men who passionately cherished the very desires of which it promised the realization. Nevertheless its exclusiveness must have been an obstacle to its success before it rendered it secure. It was apparently hostile to all forms of syncretism. However, its dogma and its practice were still very simple, and therefore very plastic, and it could accept and assimilate, almost unconsciously, the most essential of the religious aspirations and ritual observances which it would encounter upon Grecian soil. I will go further: it was unable to avoid them, and in the third century it could meet and overcome the entire pagan syncretism, because *it had itself become a syncretism* in which all the fertile ideas and the essential rites of pagan religiousness were blended. It combined and harmonized them in a way that enabled it to stand alone, facing all the inchoate beliefs and practices of its adversaries without appearing their inferior on any vital point.

This extensive work of absorption, which helps us to understand that a moment came when Christianity was able to arouse favorable attention to itself on the part of the manifold sympathies active in the Greco-Roman world, was accomplished slowly. It went on always in connection with the ascent of the faith through the various stràta of pagan society, in which, as we have just said, the religious mentality never everywhere bore the same stamp at the same time. The Christian faith will acquire something from each of the social grades, and to all she will owe that kind of hierarchy which in fact still exists in the Church. It is observable from the very moment that Christian dogma began to establish itself, and leads by an imperceptibly easy ascent from the simplest faith of the ignorant classes to the philosophical belief of the intellectuals.

Themselves men of the lower orders, it was to Gentiles of the lower orders that the first Christian preachers addressed themselves. To tell the truth, it was among them that the consoling, fraternal and all-leveling doctrine of the humble brethren had the best chance to be well received. We must not exaggerate, however: Paul and his disciples preached to the Jewish proselytes, and they were not all *humiliores;* in their ranks were included many women of the upper classes and certainly, too, some men; we have reason to believe that several were won over to the faith. It remains no less true that until the time of the Antonines the *honestiores* never formed more than an infinitesimal minority in the Church: slaves and day-laborers constituted her main force. In those days every new convert became one more unit on the roll of Christian missionaries, Christianity continued to find its recruits especially among the *humiliores.* But by means of the slaves it reached free women, their mistresses, and it accidentally attracted the attention of some of the learned men engaged in the quest for divine truth. Thanks to the former it crept into the higher classes, and thanks to the latter it came in contact with philosophy, in the course of the second century, and the ramifications of that encounter were incalculable.

Men like Justin, Tatian and Tertullian came to embrace Christianity because their conversion was the logical outcome of an inner crisis. They housed within themselves aspirations which philosophy alone could not satisfy, problems which it could not solve; and the Christian faith answered these problems and abundantly fulfilled these aspirations. Nevertheless, even if such men from the day upon which they became Christians renounced all their former opinions, they could not rid themselves of their education, their ways of thinking, their methods of reasoning, their intellectual and philosophical acquirements. Whether they realized it clearly or only perceived it dimly, the religion of their adoption seemed to lack something, not in its substance, which they deemed as unfathomable as Infinity, but in its formulations. So when it came their turn to speak for it, they were irresistibly drawn toward endowing it with the attractions of a revealed philosophy. Its apologetics or propaganda they strengthened, so to speak, by putting the methods of their schools at its service, and its dogmatics were reënforced with reflections and interpretations suggested by their previous metaphysical convictions when they began to turn the postulates of Christianity over in their minds.

Naturally, however, open as the Christianity of the post-Apostolic age would be to influences of such a nature through the fluidness of its dogmatics, and flexible as it would have been rendered by the Pauline and Johannine speculative thought, it had not foreseen these developments nor did it possess any means of sifting and more sharply defining them. For this reason their first efforts to work them over were marked as much by disorder as by intenseness. Some time necessarily elapsed before the main body of the membership, always tardy in arriving at a clear consciousness of the real situation, sensed the fact that they were driving the faith in two very different directions.

III

The one movement tended to borrow from Hellenist culture all of its ideas that were capable of rendering the early Christian doctrine at once more profound and more beautiful. It is evident that this process of assimilation cared little about scrupulous exactitude, and neither did it always find itself in complete accord with logic or reality. The same was true of its documents. At any rate, its intention was reassuring. It only sought to establish a working agreement between the demands of its fundamental postulates and the most important principles of Greek thought. If the one modified the other to such an extent that they shortly became unrecognizable, the blending proceeded slowly enough to prevent shock. Moreover, it was effected in conformity with the more or less conscious aspirations of the mass of believers. Had anyone come and told the Twelve that Jesus was an incarnation of God, at first they would have failed to catch his meaning; then they would have cried out against it with horror. But they probably accepted what Paul told them concerning him, *i.e.*, that he had been a celestial man and even the incarnation of the Spirit, the *Pneuma* of God. This was the first stage of an inflation that the faith ardently desired, which would gradually in the end bring about complete assimilation of the Christ with God. This movement, of which orthodox belief was the outcome, did not pursue a direct and well-defined path; it wavered, and often lost its way in speculations which the faith of the ordinary man did not accept; it did not readily find the exact idea or formula which suited it, but—and this is the main point—it never deliberately attempted to settle upon a combination between any pagan ideas whatsoever and the Christian postulates. To put it differently, and perhaps preferably, the inflations borrowed from Hellenist culture that it selected and fitted into the system were treated as properties of these postulates even in that wonderful School of Alexandria of which Origen was the pride, which completed the masterpiece: the metamorphosis of Christianity into a revealed and perfect philosophy.

The other movement, known to Christianity from the second century and possibly even earlier, sets out from a different starting point. It, too, seeks to inflate the too simple confession of faith of the early days and to excavate deeper foundations for it. It can accomplish this purpose only by combining it with beliefs and theories borrowed from its surroundings. But, in the first place, it shows no discrimination in its choice, which settles upon numerous features widely different in nature: the Olympic paganism, Orphism, diverse Oriental religions, systems of philosophy—everything is gathered into its net. In the second place, it takes no interest in reconciling what it borrows with the historical data, or even with the traditions of the faith. Instead it pretends to possess a special revelation of its own which it uses to justify most anomalous combinations of ideas that constitute real syncretistic systems, in which true Christianity appears as only one more element. It becomes almost unrecognizable as part of a complicated cosmogony and an abstruse system of metaphysics, neither of which owes anything of value to it. Obviously these various *gnoses* which flourished in the second century A.D., appalled the ignorant, and no likelihood existed that they would endure, even though converted, as in many cases they were, into magic practices more fascinating to the vulgar than the arguments of a mystic and symbolic system of metaphysics. They had their logical place, however, in the evolution of Christianity. By this I mean that the aspect of its evolution which they represent corresponds with what we know of the spirit of the times which gave them birth, and that they help us to understand them.

It is not a matter of indifference either that these various *gnoses* should have appeared, or the other heresies with which the faith had to struggle before it found its rightful place. In most cases, heresies are only matters of opinion which have not been accepted, neither more nor less strange than those which have established themselves. The disputes and discussions which they all have provoked have little by little raised and settled all points of the orthodox doctrine. They have afforded believers an opportunity of scrutinizing and more closely

determining their own opinions and aspirations. They
have defined the problems and emphasized the contradictions which it has been the office of the theologians to
unravel. These disputes and discussions have done still
more: they demonstrated the need and an urgent desire
for a discipline of the faith, *a regula fidei,* and an authority which would defend, as well as represent it. In this
sense the disputes and discussions constitute the most
influential factor in the formation of the ecclesiastical
organization and the clerical authority established in the
second century of the Christian era.

The other factor must be sought also in the reaction
of the Greco-Roman milieu upon primitive Christianity,
a reaction which tends to introduce part or all of the
pagan ritualism into a worship which was wholly "in
spirit and in truth," from the very moment when the
brethren deserted the Jewish Temple. The ritual development of Christianity advances step by step with the
dogmatic, and by the same process. It began with very
simple practices, all taken from Judaism: baptism, the
breaking of bread, the imposition of hands, prayer and
fasting. Then a meaning more and more profound and
mysterious was assigned to them. They were amplified,
and gestures familiar to the pagans added; they were
loaded with the large interests, for example, embraced in the rites of the Greek and Oriental Mysteries, and thus charged, as it were, with the ancient
formidable power of magic. This work was initiated as
soon as the Apostolic faith was transported from Palestine to Greek soil. We have found that it was already
greatly advanced, in Paulinism. It was in process unin-
terruptedly during the whole time that the new religion
was struggling with its rivals.

It is sometimes very difficult to tell exactly from which
pagan rite a particular Christian rite is derived, but it
remains certain that the spirit of pagan ritualism became
by degrees impressed upon Christianity, to such an extent
that at last the whole of it might be found distributed
through its ceremonies. The necessity for uprooting

some of these ancient and very tenacious customs accelerated the assimilation of the remainder which went on in the fourth century. Moreover, the power of the clergy was singularly enhanced by the almost exclusive right which they very early acquired, despite some faltering objections, of ordering and dispensing the magic power inherent in the rites known as *sacraments*.

IV

Contemplate the Christian Church at the beginning of the fourth century, therefore, and some difficulty will be experienced in recognizing in her the community of Apostolic times, or rather, we shall not be able to recognize it at all. Instead of a small group of Jews separated from the majority of their fellows only by a special hope and a more indulgent reception of proselytes than was accorded to them by the ordinary Israelitish nationalism, a vast religious organization now confronts the observer, into which enter, without distinction of race or social condition, all men of good will, who are together conscious of forming a body, the elect people and the Church of Christ. She has rejected Israel, of whom she says offhand that as a nation it has left the way of the Lord and wanders in wretchedness far from the truth; she has found out how to get rid of the practices of the Jewish Law and yet preserve the character of the Old Testament as a sacred Book.[*] Upon the tenets of the faith of Israel as a foundation she has constructed a new and very complicated system of dogmatics, in which the central speculation excels about the person of the Christ, now elevated even to the point of identification with God. The component elements of this system have been drawn partly from the work of inflation done by her own reflec-

---

[*] It seems as if Christianity would have gained by shaking itself free of the Jewish Law, and some noteworthy Christians, such as Marcion, tried to bring this about; they did not succeed because early Christian apologetics, by relying constantly upon the reputation of the Biblical text as prophetical, had strengthened the Judeo-Christian veneration for the Book and authenticated its divine character.

tions upon the earlier data of her faith, and partly from the philosophical and religious doctrines of the Greco-Roman milieu. This system of dogmatics as expressed in a rule of faith which rests upon the opinion of the majority, as interpreted by competent authorities, asks to be received as the revealed and perfected system of philosophy, the *ne varietur* explanation of the world, life and destiny, and theologians devote themselves with ardor to fathom and make it self-consistent.

From another point of view, the Christian Church presents herself to us as an established institution; little by little she has been organized in private churches modeled upon the Jewish synagogues or the pagan associations. Her administrative and spiritual functions are centered in the hands of a body of clergy of hierarchic order. The chief of these have adopted a custom of deliberating together over all matters concerning faith, morals and discipline, and expressing the majority opinion in concerted public statements. This order of clergy presides over rites which are more or less directly borrowed from Judaism or the pagan Mysteries, though entirely readapted to Christian uses and reinvested— the chief of them, at any rate—with the magic mysterious power which the secret cults of Greece and the Orient had rendered familiar to the men of those days. In other words, Christianity has become a real religion, the most complete of them all, because it has taken the best they possessed from all of them; the most kindly, the most comforting and the most human as well. The ignorant man has only uncomprehendingly to believe and unreasoningly to obey the authorities to be assured of eternal salvation, and yet the philosopher finds in its dogmas ample matter on which to speculate.

This religion, however, although so profoundly syncretistic, declares itself invulnerably exclusive; it will not share its converts with any other religion; it tolerates no rivals and, until its victory has been assured, this fundamental tendency of its nature has been the occasion of the most perilous difficulties; it has especially aroused the animosity of the State as well as that of the whole civil community.

But before attempting to account for the nature, development, extent and issue of this overconfident challenge, we must examine more closely and in the *light* of the facts themselves two essential matters which have just been presented, as it were, *in abstracto:* the religion of Christ. I mean the religion which regards Christ as its own peculiar God and has, in the secular society in which it organized itself, created the *Christian Church,* and, from the method of life that it originally was, has become *a body of doctrine* and *a system of dogmatics.*

CHAPTER VIII

THE FOUNDATION AND THE ORGANIZATION OF THE CHURCH [1]

CHRIST had neither founded nor desired the Church. Perhaps this is the most obvious truth forced upon whoever studies the text of the Gospels without prejudice, and indeed the contrary position is an absurdity from the historical point of view; the utmost ingenuity of theologians cannot alter the fact. However incomplete our knowledge of Jesus' teaching, it appears primarily as a reaction against a rigid legalism and an engrossing ritualism. Now it cannot be denied that these are the indispensable accompaniment and foundation of all truly ecclesiastical systems. Next it appears to be a vigorous encouragement to *personal effort*. The individual believer is to mount up to his Father who is in heaven, on the ladder of love and faith, no doubt, but also of *repentance,* a sharp and complete break of his evil ways and, so to speak, the purging of his conscience as well as the stimulation of his will; and all this is the exact opposite of ecclesiastical psychasthenia. Moreover, bear in mind that Jesus awaited the realization of the Kingdom as imminent, and that this hope ought to dismiss from his mind all idea of organizing a future *upon this present earth* for his disciples. Finally do not forget that he was a Jew who was entirely devoted to the religious Law of Israel. When he apparently was opposing it he meant only in reality to extend its scope according to that which he deemed its true spirit. Whoever recalls these things will readily understand why it was that his mind never

---

[1] Edwin Hatch, *The Organization of the Early Christian Churches* (6th ed., London and New York, 1901) ; A. Harn~·k, *Entstehung und Entwickelung der Kirchenverfassung und des Kirchenrechts in den Zwei ersten Jahrhunderten* (Leipzig, 1910) ; R. Knopf, *Das nachapostolische Zeitalter;* A. V. G. Allen, *Christian Institutions* (Edinburgh, 1898), Chaps. i-vii.

paused for an instant upon the idea of an organization like that which we call the Church.

If we admit that he gave the Twelve authority—and this is still a debatable point—it could have been no more than an appointment, in a fashion, of them to preach, as he had done, the Kingdom and repentance. He did not make *priests* of them, for truly he had no need of priests. Moreover, view these Apostles in action, after the death of their Master, and it is plain that none of them had any idea either of founding a Church. They remained attached to the Jewish faith and practiced its forms of worship very devoutly; for them, too, the future meant the *Kingdom,* not the *Church.*

The Gospel text never puts into the mouth of Jesus the expression "my Church," or even the "Church of the Father," except in one passage only, which reads: "Thou art Peter and upon this rock I will build my Church. . ." (Matt. xvi. 18). But a claim to authenticity for this well-known and widely exploited verse would seem to be absolutely untenable unless we are prepared to admit that Christ, in a moment of prophetic frenzy, should have denied his teaching, his labor, his mission and his very self.[2] Gospel passages and relevant facts both prove, up to the hilt, that no such primacy of the Apostle Peter, which Jesus is reputed to have proclaimed in the text of Matthew's Gospel, ever existed. The disciples grouped around him and John and "James, the Lord's brother" (Gal. i. 19), simply honored and listened to him as a man raised in their esteem by the confidence and friendship which they had seen shown him by the Master.

Nevertheless, without desiring it and unknown to themselves, the Apostles laid the foundations of the Church. Later, when *Apostolic tradition* becomes the supreme and infallible test of every ecclesiastical verity, that outcome will undoubtedly be due somewhat to exaggeration, but it will not be pure fiction. This statement requires explanation.

[2] Ch. Guignebert, *La primauté de Pierre et la venue de Pierre à Rome* (Paris, 1909), the first three chapters.

It can be said that the transplantation of the Christian hope from Palestine to Greek soil and, if you will, its universalization, gave birth to *the idea of the Church*. It is impossible even for men who look on life as precarious not to feel themselves drawn together and more or less one solid body the moment they espouse the same hope in regard to their destiny and are obliged in order to do so to step out of their previous into a different religious setting. Now, the converts of the synagogues of the Dispersion are very soon expelled by the Jews "whose hearts are hardened," and it is the same with the converts among the proselytes. Then the pagans who join the faith abandon their old temples and all unite in the cult or rites of worship offered to the *Lord Jesus*. While it is certainly a very simple form of worship, yet it already includes fraternal gatherings (the faithful are known among themselves as "brethren"), prayer in common, an initiatory rite called baptism, and a rite of communion, both between the initiates (in this connection the faithful are known as "saints," a very informative term) and with the Lord at his table. Now all men who "call upon the name of our Lord Jesus Christ" term themselves his "saints" and through him are "brethren," wherever they may dwell—all these form part of the *Church of God*. However they may be dispersed about the world it means that in his eyes they are the assembly of his elect.

Paul expresses this idea with the greatest clearness. When he is speaking of "the Church of God which is in Corinth," for instance, we must not understand him to refer to an organized congregation, an ecclesiastical community established in Corinth, but merely, if I may put it thus, *the increment* belonging to the *universal Church of God* which dwells in that city. I believe I shall make myself perfectly understood if I say that the mystic idea of the Church as a union *in* God arises, in the mind of a man like Paul, out of the *fact* that all have experienced the same initiation. And just as inevitably, it arises even before any question has come up of a special ecclesiastical organization. At the very time the Apostle is able already to speak of the Church of God, his letters testify that the Christian community in Corinth is still living in the anarchy of full dependence upon direct divine guidance: I mean that it is self-governing and controlled by the hazardous suggestions of the inspired. And we know that the directly inspired are the natural enemies of all ecclesiastical orders; it has as yet no clergy.

Such a life can readily be understood during that quite early period of enthusiasm and self-deception when Saturday evenings the "saints" hope that the dawn of the morrow will bring the great day of the *return,* so ardently desired, of the Lord. By degrees, however, as weeks, months and years go by without this blessed manifestation (*parousia*), the disadvantages of the lack of a governing body appear. At the same time, the fraternal union among the saints undergoes consolidation, and their separation from the rest of the religious world raises their hope as believers to the dignity of an autonomous religion. When the time comes that such a local group feels obliged to think about organizing its community, work on it begins on a plan which is the converse of that wrought out in Paul's mind. Each local group of brethren gets formed into a church, and the Church of God becomes the sum total of these independent churches, which all exchange correspondence, and encourage and sustain each other. Therefore, the Church tends, *first of all,* to be no longer only a mystic expression of reality, but also a fact which might be termed corporeal; then too, although in a more remote but inevitable future, she tends, in so far as she is this kind of general fact, to seek for herself a corporeal realization and an organization to consecrate it.

Take a stand, for instance, at the beginning of the second century, and we shall perceive that the Pauline conception of the union of all Christians in God is well established. It is upheld by the conviction that there is indeed only one true doctrine of salvation common to them all, and its unassailable foundation is to be sought in the "Apostolic tradition." It is generally admitted that the depositories of this tradition are the "Apostolic churches," *i.e.*, those which are reputed to trace their history back to the initiative of an Apostle. As a matter of fact the Church is still but the *fraternity* dispersed among the separate churches; but it is averred that the Christians do not like men who live in isolation. As much for the consolidation of their doctrine as for the offering of a united front to the enemies who menace them, they possess a group mind. Accordingly, they cannot conceive how any local church, entirely independent and mistress of her own destiny though she may be, should live and prosper in a state of isolation with regard to the rest of the churches, any more than they could understand why a "brother" should separate himself from the congregation of the city in which he dwells. The Christian fraternity, the Church of God, has not yet been subjected to the organization which is to materialize her, however, and an outside observer, a pagan, would still perceive only local churches.

II

The origin of these local "churches" themselves is also somewhat obscure. To obtain as accurate an idea of it as possible, we must first rid our minds of the Catholic conception of uniformity, regularity, fixity. Between one congregation and another there were for some long time fairly important differences, and although they did finally all evolve in the same direction, their progress was not uniform.

There is no need to look very far for causes which bring men together who are attached to the same faith: religious fraternities were of the very spirit and practice of antiquity. The necessity of presenting a united front to Jewish hostility, which very soon showed itself active, and the difficulty of making a living, which was very pressing among the numerous poor whom the Christian hope first attracted, suffice to account for the organization of the communities. The danger arising from lack of all authority and the scarcely less serious one of full dependence upon the direct action of the Spirit, the troublesome and inevitable disorders attendant upon the absence of organized discipline, all combined to urge these primitive fraternities to provide themselves with some form of government.

There was no lack of models: in both the Greek and the Latin sections of the Roman Empire religious associations or corporations had long been in existence, brought together for some common pious or charitable work, *thiasoi and eranoi,* they were called in the one case, and in the other, *collegia,* especially the *collegia tenuiorum, i.e.,* societies of the humbler folk. They had their elected officials and their own funds, supplied by subscriptions and supervised by special trustees. Moreover, the Jews of the Dispersion, wherever they met, were they but a handful, as we have learned, were grouped in synagogues,[3] regularly constituted and organized, even if they varied somewhat in these respects. The Christians, therefore, whether of Gentile or Jewish origin, knew how to set about governing themselves.

It is probable that both the pagan associations and the Jewish colleges exercised an influence upon them at the same time, now the one and now the other more decisively, according to locality and circumstances. The duties of their officials naturally are prescribed by necessity and their names as naturally borrowed from the language current at the time. This is the case with words like *presbyteros,* which meant "elder," *episcopos,* which signified "overseer," and *diaconos,* the term used for a "server," before these same words came to signify respectively "priest," "bishop," or "deacon." Thus do they make provision with more or less zeal and success to meet the need of converts for instruction, for

---

[3] The word *synagogé* has, in the main, the same connotation as the word *ecclesia,* and it often happens that the former in the second century is still used to denote the Christian gathering.

the maintenance of order and morals and the sound traditions of the faith, for regularity in worship and, finally, to feed their poor.

Whoever will read through the Acts, the Pauline Epistles and the three pseudo-Pauline letters, called the Pastoral Letters,[4] which appeared shortly after Paul's day, will comprehend how rapidly this process of organization, once begun, proceeded. By the end of the first century, in some churches at least, there is a single "bishop," the general "overseer" of the whole community, who consequently is in a fair way to keep the upper hand in all matters; and, at his side "presbyters," specially charged with the exercise of spiritual offices; and "deacons," mainly concerned with material affairs.

That which gives firmness and precision to all this regularly appointed administrative machinery is, first, the growing (and probably justifiable) distrust felt with regard to the inspired persons who, as Apostles, prophets or *didascaloi*,[5] wander from place to place, apparently exercising paramount influence over the communities during their early days. Another factor was the lessening of the authority of the inspired persons who were residents of the locality. People weary of what is extraordinary and incoherent; the faith of most ordinary men naturally aims at stability, which is a synonym to them for truth. The gifts which the Spirit had been scattering at will upon a larger or smaller number of the brethren do not disappear, however; they pass to the bishop and strengthen him in his authority. Again, there is the wish for and the beginning of ritual rendered almost compulsory by their surroundings and that calls for specialists. Lastly, there is the idea which is promptly emphasized, that the shepherds are responsible

[4] I and II Tim. and the Epistle to Titus.
[5] The functions of these various types of inspired persons do not seem to be very clearly differentiated. Perhaps it is not too much to assume that the *apostle* brings the faith to men; that the *prophet* justifies it through his revelations, and that the *didascalos* teaches its doctrine. (The Greek word *didaskein* means "to teach.")

to God for the flock confided to their care, and responsibility implies authority.

These diverse factors agree in a common tendency to make the same people responsible for the originally distinct functions of instruction, edification and administration, or at least to place in highest authority over them all a single person who is referred to as the "ruling bishop." The advent and the triumph of the monarchic episcopate constitutes the first great stage in the organization of the Church, and it has exercised upon her life for many centuries an influence which is incalculable in its consequences.[6]

III

The word "bishop" (*episcopos*) means, as we have already said, "overseer," and in this sense it was occasionally used in the pagan associations as the equivalent of *epimeletes,* which signifies "commissary," or "steward," and in some cases, "director," but it always carries the idea of oversight. In the beginning the bishops (for each congregation had several of them) did not trouble either to teach or to edify in any other way than by their good example. They occupied themselves in maintaining and confirming the Church in the practice of morality and of the precepts of the true faith, and exercised the upper hand in all matters relating to the temporal concerns of the congregation. The oldest texts group them with the deacons and not with the presbyters, and this is a small but significant fact with regard to the origin and nature of their earlier functions.

Their authority developed very fast as soon as the practice of several bishops in the one congregation had disappeared; we do not know exactly how this change was accomplished, but we can easily perceive the causes that made such a step necessary. At a time when the symbol of the faith was still comparatively free from dogma, and the formidable tendency to inflation known

[6] J. Reville, *Les origines de l'épiscopat* (Paris, 1894).

to most religions was operating with excessive energy, owing to the flood of suggestions proceeding from the surrounding syncretistic milieu, it was necessary to organize a vigilant defense for the flock against the "wolves" without the fold, and also those within, namely, the heretics.[7] The work of defense proves to be more ready and vigilant when placed in charge of a single person. Where one man alone is responsible, the authority required to sustain good order and assure good management in the administration of the charities seems more effective. Moreover, the pagan institutions and the Jewish communities are as a rule inclined to choose a presiding officer or chairman in order to secure unity of action on the part of the whole group, and to symbolize, as it were, its union. Among the Christian brethren the belief soon spreads that the Apostles foresaw the difficulties the churches would encounter and that they are the ones who have provided episcopacy for the purpose of dealing properly with them. Each congregation, it is claimed, is a kind of microcosm of the great Church of the Lord, with a bishop as its legitimate head, as Christ is the head of his Church. Finally, as soon as the ritual is developed, the bishop, by a parallel somewhat forced, yet inevitable, drawn between him and the Jewish High Priest, becomes the president or master of the liturgical ceremonies.

Many considerations, it is now clear, different enough in their origin and their trend, concur in lodging the episcopal authority in the hands of a single bishop. However, even after he shares his power with none, but performs his functions alone, he is not necessarily an absolute master in his church. For a time, varying in length with the locality, he appears as the president of the "presbyterion," i.e., the council formed of the presbyters, but this is only one stage, and certain of the churches in Asia have already passed it at the beginning

---

[7] The word "heretic" appears for the first time in the Epistle to Titus iii. 10: αἱρετικὸν ἄνθρωπον. Etymologically, the heretic is "he who chooses," but, as a matter of fact, at the time of which we are writing, it means rather, "he who adds" unthinkingly.

of the second century. At that time Ignatius of Antioch proclaims that the bishop is God's representative in the Church, that no one ought to do anything at all without him, and that to act otherwise is to further the devil's work. Of course it is tacitly understood that the bishop himself always acts in accordance with the presbyters and deacons. In the end, however, Ignatius writes: "Fix your eyes upon the bishop that God may see you," and "It is right to honor God and the bishop" [8] (*sic*). One can hardly go further.

It was between 130 and 150 A.D. or thereabouts that the monarchic episcopate won the day in all the churches, one after another. Its triumph was favored and emphasized by the crises of various kinds which the Church had to undergo from that time on. Persecutions decimated and dispersed the "flock." More especially, they left behind them many apostates anxious to return to the fold, who could not be received without due precautions. Heresies arise which are very dangerous, particularly the syncretistic combinations composed of the fundamental tenets of the Christian faith, ancient Oriental myths and the theories of Greek philosophers. In the first place these captivate the "intellectuals" among the brethren, and in the next they fascinate the mystics and (at the opposite pole) all whom magical operations attract by the appearance of reality displayed by them. Moreover, group contagion soon reduces the resistance which a church here and there may offer to the episcopal movement, and toward the beginning of the third century consent is readily granted by Christians that unity of organization is a direct parallel to unity of belief, and just as essential.

And henceforth the work of justifying the existing situation will proceed energetically. That the monarchic episcopate was instituted by the Apostles themselves, it is soon agreed, and each church produces a list of bishops which runs back to some Apostle who was its founder, or in default of an Apostle, to a disciple of

[8] *Ad Polyc.* vi. 1; *Ad Smyrn.* ix. 1.

an Apostle, or to the deputy of an Apostolic church who is considered to be its founder. The symbol of the bishop's authority is the throne, the *cathedra,* which is reputed to be the seat of all his predecessors. The phrase, for instance, the "throne of Peter," means the "authority of the Bishop of Rome." And the main-spring for this authority, quite as much as for the rule of faith, is in fact the Apostolic tradition. Not until much later did the monarchic episcopate seek justifica-tion for its existence in various passages in the Gospel, and especially in that of Matt. xvi. 19: "I will give unto thee the keys of the kingdom of heaven: and whatsoever thou shalt bind on earth shall be bound in heaven: and whatsoever thou shalt loose on earth shall be loosed in heaven."

IV

The monarchic bishop is elected by the congregation and ordained, *i.e.,* installed in the *ordo sacerdotalis* by the bishops of the neighborhood. In theory, the people choose whom they will, but not counting in the legitimate and usually weighty influence attaching to the sugges-tions which emanate from the presbyters and deacons of the church, it is plain that already efforts are being made to withdraw the power of election from them. Sometimes the bishop himself will name his successor, or again a group of bishops may authorize the nomina-tion to a vacant see, but these are as yet exceptions, justified by the special circumstances of the case.

The conditions of eligibility are still very elastic. The future bishop must be a man of blameless morals, vouched for by marriage or widowerhood, and of a stable faith, hence not too recently acquired. His intellectual qualifications seem to be a secondary consideration, and his age is not yet very important, but it is required—though without extreme insistence on the point—that he should be physically well qualified for the work he has to perform. As yet no strictly ecclesiastical qualification is mandatory, by this I mean that the popular choice may light upon a simple "brother." But the bishops, at any rate, are already tending to demand that he shall previously have held some other ecclesiastical office, and this is good sense.

Even in these remote times, and despite the fact that the position is occasionally a post of some danger, competition and intrigue are frequently at work to obtain it. Moreover, something about it is flattering to the spirit of domination inherent in man, from which Christ himself, if we are to believe the Gospel, was unable to preserve his Apostles. The bishop was deemed responsible to God for the faith, morals and disciplining of his Church; but this formidable responsibility itself enhanced his importance in the eyes of others as well as in his own. As a matter of fact, the religious and moral direction of the community was in his hands, as well as the disciplinary and penance prescribing powers which had originally been vested in the assembly of the brethren. He it was who debarred the sinner whom he deemed a scandal to the Church from communion, that is, practically expelled him from the congregation by excluding him from the Eucharist. He supervised the clergy, administered the finances, regulated the grants of alms and their distribution, and, at need, played the part of justice of the peace in disputes between the members of his flock. Most important, he controlled the distribution of the power that lay in the sacramental rites; he administered baptism and consecrated the Eucharist. Of all his functions this assuredly brought him most prestige; in this respect his dignity will continue to increase in the measure that the magical idea of the mysterious and all-powerful sacrament gains ground. To all this add that it was the duty of the bishop to visit the sick and comfort the afflicted, and the amplitude of his rôle and the varied aspects of his authority may be realized.

This authority had indeed no other limits than those created by his own abuse of it, which would incite the clergy and the congregation to rebel, and might result in a kind of strike which would oblige the rash individual to resign his charge, or the bishops, who had inducted him, to depose him.

However powerful he might be in his own church, moreover, in a neighboring one the bishop is but one of the brethren who is received with due honor, but who cannot preach without the express invitation of the local bishop. From the legal point of view, each church is still entirely independent and free to regulate its faith and its discipline as it thinks proper. Nevertheless, the dangers of isolation involved in this autonomy are clearly visible; if it had continued, the Catholic Church would never have come into existence, but Christians would have dispersed into numerous little sects. Happily, developing practice succeeds in correcting this situation. Each church, in the first place, is concerned to know what its neighbor is doing; the smaller ones, especially, model themselves upon the larger; brethren go back and forth from one to another and often create close ties between them. The bishops visit and also keep up correspondence with each other; in difficult cases they assemble in small groups even at this early date for the purpose of consultation. And thus it comes about that the authority of the monarch-like bishop is, in practice as well as by its claims, the essential basis of the Catholic organization, long before there is any question of a pope.

The bishop achieved an easy triumph over the rank and file of his congregation and dispossessed them of the rights which they had exercised in the primitive community; but victory was a harder matter in the case of the other ecclesiastical officials, the presbyters and the deacons. Proofs are in evidence of cases of stubborn resistance, really useless, however, because in the first place they are unrelated and not acting in concert, but more particularly because they nowhere find firm footing in the way of principles or reasons comparable to those which sustain the monarchic episcopate.

After the bishop's decisive victory, the other ecclesiastical functionaries—the "clergy," as they are called,

beginning with the third century—form side by side
with him an "order," a special class within the body
of the faithful. Entrance into this order is by "ordination," which rests entirely with the bishop as ruler, and
is yet but an installation into an office with special functions. Little by little a special ceremonial will become
attached to this installation in the case of each set of
duties, infused with the idea of a mysterious conferring
of qualifications which will become the sacrament of
"Holy Orders"; but in the second century this is still
far in the future.

In this clergy order (*ordo clericalis*), deacons must
still be named after the bishop, who takes precedence
because they are his assistants—eyes, as it were, to look
around and report to him, and arms to carry out his
decisions. Later on [9] Moses and Aaron will serve as the
type of this relation between bishop and deacons. Very
early in the important churches one of the officials is a
head deacon, called the "archdeacon." As late as the
fourth century, the deacons refuse to accept a place lower
in the hierarchy than the priests, and theoretically they
are in the right, for their official functions were in no
degree inferior at first to those of the presbyters. They
were then more of another kind, which makes it more
suitable to speak of them as equals than of superior
and inferior. But, little by little, time effaced these
original fundamental distinctions so much that the
Councils of the fourth century render a decision that the
attitude of deacons who will not remain standing in the
presence of the priests, or communicate after them, is
frankly reprehensible and indeed somewhat scandalous.

The priests (presbyters) seem to be patterned after the
council of the elders—the Sanhedrin—of the Jewish synagogue. At first they function as the council or board
of the congregation, and, in fact, govern it; then their
functions slowly become restricted to the spiritual
domain, and after the advent of the monarchic episcopate, they become the deputies and, if need be, the

[9] *Const. Apost.* ii. 30.

bishop's substitutes in all his functions in the spiritual realm. So that is why they consider themselves the superiors of the deacons, who are at first engaged almost exclusively in the task of ministering to material needs.

Ritual and ecclesiastical life, as their growth proceeds, gradually add to the clergy order (*ordo clericalis*), and besides the deacons and priests various special and subordinate functionaries appear: exorcists, acolytes, readers, doorkeepers, who all hold office from the beginning of the third century or thereabouts. The bishop selects them, and by degrees use and wont come to regard these auxiliary functions as designed to test and confirm vocations which will ultimately find their true sphere in the diaconate, the priesthood, or even in the episcopate. These clerics must of course be of irreproachable morals, but they may marry, even after their ordination.

The clergy of those days comprised women also. They are known as "deaconesses," "widows," or "virgins," but it is by no means easy to distinguish the particular functions corresponding with these three titles, nor to define any one of them precisely. All that can be made out is that the women attached to the Church are not to teach, but to serve. They seem to be of the bishop's assistants on the occasions he has to deal with the "sisters" of the congregation. Distrust with respect to the temptations of sex seems to have been very highly developed among Christians at that time. It was founded upon experience; precautions, occasionally somewhat puerile, seem to have been taken to preserve the clergy from such temptations.

Theoretically, all the clergy live "of the altar," that is, they live upon the offerings and the gifts of the faithful, but many of them follow the example of the Apostle Paul, and also work at some respectable trade.

The Christian community remains for a long time a little group or unit, like the Jewish "associations" upon pagan soil. All its members are, if I may put it thus, religious equals, and, therefore, the difference which the possession of office makes between those who do, and those who do not, hold office is not one of kind. By degrees this changes. As long as the idea of the sovereignty of the Spirit which "breatheth where it listeth" still holds, no way exists of establishing a lasting distinction between the cleric and the inspired believer, and, I repeat, that *ordinatio* had not yet acquired this meaning. By rights a simple believer may, upon occasion, baptize, preach, consecrate the Eucharist and impose penance. The clergy naturally endeavor to restrict and even to suppress these privileges and powers which circumscribe their own importance. The development of ordination in the sense of a sacrament deemed to confer upon the recipient permanent gifts of the Spirit for the exercise of this and that function, proceeds step by step with the practical disappearance of inspired individuals in the assemblies of the brethren, and gradually places the ordinary believer, the layman,[10] in a subordinate position, playing a passive part in comparison to the clergy.

In the second half of the second century, a curious pietistic movement, begun in Phrygia at the instance of a certain Montanus, makes a strong endeavor to restore the inspired to first place in the Church, and to relegate the clergy to the mere administration of the affairs of the flock, but the failure of this Montanism hastens the result it had arisen to combat. Montanus had, in truth, committed an anachronism.

V

It is observable that the evolution within the Christian communities of the first two centuries leads to the conception of and a measure of realization, in principle at least, of the *idea of the Catholic Church*. The Catholic is something altogether different from the Pauline idea of the Church of God; it is indeed no longer limited to

---

[10] The Greek word λαός means "people"; the λαιχός therefore, means "one reckoned among the Christian people."

a question of the union of hearts between brethren who share the same hope, a hope symbolized, or rather, expressed by the common invocation in use everywhere of "the same divine name," at which the whole creation is to bow the knee. The Catholic idea of the Church includes unity in belief, rites, practices, spirit, discipline, and also in principle a common, general policy—pending the formation of the organism which henceforth will be required to declare and apply a consensus of opinion officially.

The Catholic idea appears, upon the whole, to embrace two main components, one of which has to do with practice and the other with theory, if I may express it thus.

At the end of the second century Tertullian expresses the general conviction when he says that "Christians form a body," the members of which ought to remain united for the good of all and the reënforcement of the truth. Moreover, this fraternal union rests as yet upon no other foundation than the idea that it *ought* to be and the voluntary good will of all in its favor. Still the question has not been raised of the subordination of such and such churches to this other, a course by which, if taken, at least the problem would be simplified. I need only cite as proof the attitude of St. Cyprian, bishop of Carthage in the third century—great advocate though he was of the necessity for agreement. Against Stephen, bishop of Rome, he stirs up the entire African episcopate upon a question of discipline, affirming the inalienable right of each church to remain her own mistress. The origin of the idea of the *Christian body* may be traced, in fact, to the repeated contacts of the different communities with each other, to the discussions between the bishops, the exchanges of letters concerning the solution of questions which are pressing and momentous to them all, such as the fixing of one date for Easter, or the right attitude to adopt toward a new doctrine that is making headway in the Church.

This is the first component spoken of above; the other

is the *idea of the Catholic faith*. The phrase means primarily the common, general faith, opposed to the faith exceptional and particular, and on that account, heretical. I have already said that this *normal* faith, in the opinion of the day, was quite simply esteemed to be that of the Apostles, preserved by an inviolable tradition in the churches they founded. And as an inevitable corollary, the churches maintain that apart from this faith there is no hope of salvation. St. Ireneus, bishop of Lyons in the last quarter of the second century, develops the content of this idea. Its practical consequence is that honorary preëminence is given, for the present, to the Apostolic churches. This means that what one might call the determining of the future administrative framework of Catholic organization has begun. Although the *metropolitans* do not appear as officials before the beginning of the fourth century, they exist in substance for some time prior. To express it differently, the big churches in the large towns gradually exert upon the smaller communities in their neighborhood an influence which resembles those pertaining to the headship of a hegemony. When the time comes for the Councils of the fourth century to recognize the authority of the *metropolitan* bishops, they are scarcely doing more than sanctioning and regulating a state of things already in existence.

Think for a moment of the favorable conditions which the church of Rome had at call for the purpose of acquiring supremacy in the West, and no surprise need be felt that she should one day accomplish her end.

She was considered the daughter church of the Apostle Peter, and believed she possessed his episcopal throne and his tomb. The Apostle Paul, by visiting her and yielding up his life to the executioner's axe near one of the gates of the city, seemed, as it were, to have made her as the church of Peter doubly apostolic. Its congregation early became both numerous and rich, as its catacombs bear witness, and the generosity of its alms to other churches led Ignatius to call the church in Rome "the president of charity." [11] The reflected luster of the capital of the Empire shines upon her. Long before she thinks of exploiting to her own advantage various Gospel passages by making them the basis of her primacy of jurisdiction, the other Western churches (she is probably the eldest of them, and, in many cases, the mother) find no difficulty in according her an honorary primacy, which was her due.

Thus, from the beginning of the third century, the churches already possess an organization, of which they will preserve the framework, at any rate, and they promise to endure. So, too, the universal Church begins its journey from the domain of the abstract and of the dream to seek realization in the union and confederation of the special churches. The future has only to develop logically the premises already laid down.

Let us note at once that this organization which has come to pass of Christians in closed and disciplined communities, combined with the tendency to catholicity, seems to favor Christian exclusiveness, to accentuate the appearance of opposition shown by the believer to the unbeliever and the hostile attitude of Christian society with respect to pagan society. When the matter is more closely examined, it is plain that the churches are not, as they like to think themselves, severed and apart from their milieu, but that on the contrary they live in and are part and parcel of it. Indeed, they constitute wonderful mediums for the extracting and the syncretistic absorption of all religious sustenance in the surrounding religions that has been kept from spoiling. The tendency to Catholicism on the other hand, favors the well-balanced combination in a coherent whole of special and dissimilar acquisitions. And from this time forward it is possible to catch a glimpse of the deep motive forces in the Church which will account for the *volte-face* of the State and of society in the fourth century.

[11] In the address of his Epistle to the Roman προκαθημένη τῆς ἀγάπης.

CHAPTER IX

THE ESTABLISHMENT OF CHURCH DOCTRINE AND DISCIPLINE[1]

WE know, at the time that its separation from Judaism sanctioned the autonomy of the form which Christianity assumed in the Greco-Roman world, a religion without rites was inconceivable. Since the Christian belief naturally gave itself out as a revelation, it was also inconceivable that it should not draw up a series of the settled metaphysical statements which are called dogmas. Note has been taken of the way that Christianity secured a foothold and acquired the apparatus of practical existence during the first two centuries; now an account will be given of the methods it followed and the results it attained with regard to ritual and dogma in the same period.

If a stand be taken at the end of the Apostolic age, toward the close of the first century after Christ, it will be found very easy to become a Christian. It is enough to confess that Jesus Christ is the Messiah promised by God to men, that he died for their sins, and will shortly come again to judge both the living and the dead and inaugurate the Kingdom of God, in which the righteous with their risen and glorified bodies will live in bliss with him. This is about all. Whoever makes this confession receives baptism, a Jewish rite which the Christians have adopted. In the Pauline Mystery, fully charged with a symbolism—and realism—syncretistic in

---

[1] Upon the early form of worship read: Dom F. Cabrol, *Le livre de la prière antique* (Paris, 1903); F. E. Warren, *The Liturgy and Ritual of the Ante-Nicene Church* (London, 1912); J. H. Snawley, *The Early History of the Liturgy* (Cambridge, 1913); V. Thalhofer & L. Eisenhofer, *Handbuch der katholischen Liturgik* (Friburg, 1912). Upon the Creed: A. Harnack, *Lehrbuch der Dogmengeschichte*, Vol. I (Tübingen, 1909); Loofs, *Leitfaden zum Studium der Dogmengeschichte* (Halle, 1906); G. B. Fisher, *History of Christian Doctrine* (Edinburgh, 1902). *Cf.* Guignebert, *L'évolution des dogmes* (Paris, 1909).

origin, it signifies and somehow puts in force afresh, for the neophyte, the death and resurrection of the Lord. For ordinary converts, at the least it symbolizes, and is a ratification of, repentance, the change of life, and a pledge of the blotting out of all sin. Baptism is regarded as stamping the seal of the Lord upon the Christian, and it is accompanied by an *illumination,* which is a gift of the Holy Spirit. The admission is generally that this baptism is necessary as a consecration of conversion, and at first no great ceremony is required. It may be administered by any Christian and received without much previous preparation; it is, so to speak, an act of faith, and the works of the Holy Spirit transpire rapidly. Possibly the baptized person even at this early day recites a brief formula setting forth the main articles of his belief.

We know that these relate to statements that are fairly simple. As soon as the neophyte, however, has entered the Church speculations pounce upon him which certainly are not acceptable to everyone, but which do arouse a passionate interest. The person of Christ is naturally their central theme. Once the little Apostolic band which has known him "in the flesh" has passed away, no veto of history impedes or limits the experiences or inflations put forth by the faith. Summed up, these develop by delving into three initial ideas of the Lord which lend themselves to that process. First of these is the *Pauline* idea, and its main characteristics are: Jesus was a celestial man, *i.e.,* a man who existed in respect to the elements of his spiritual person in heaven previous to his incarnation. His life-principle, if the expression be permissible, is the Holy Spirit himself, for "the Lord is the Spirit." [2] He descended to earth to institute a new humanity, of which he is the Adam, a humanity which he has freed from the yoke of sin by accepting, for the purpose of redeeming it, the wretched life of man and death by an infamous form of torment. "He . . . is the image of the invisible God,

[2] II Cor. iii. 17.

the firstborn of all creation; for in him were all things created, in the heavens and upon the earth, things visible and things invisible . . . all things have been created through him and unto him; and he is before all things, and in him all things consist" (Col. i. 15-18). His person, therefore, as Sabatier so aptly puts it, is "the metaphysical point in which God effects a union with the whole of creation"; his resurrection and his glorification in God assure the believer of his own victory over death. I have already remarked that this Christology betrays the influences of its syncretistic milieu at work and so becomes the first of the Christian *gnoses*. It did not bear all its fruits at once; it was not properly understood and, even in the churches founded by the Apostle, it dropped into the background at first. Nevertheless, it lived on in his Epistles. In the end it was sought out there, deemed inspired when rediscovered, and became one of the foundations upon which the Helleno-Christian speculative thought was reared.

The second of these constructions put upon the person of Christ is the *Johannine* Christology. It rests upon an affirmation of identity between the Lord and the Logos, which at first sight, seems akin to the Pauline formula, "The Lord (Jesus) is the Spirit." In reality it embraces a much deeper metaphysical meaning, since the Logos in its character of an emanation from God is God in the final analysis, and to say "The Lord is the Logos" is almost equivalent to saying "The Lord (Jesus) is God." A Jew, I repeat, would find this a shocking and blasphemous proposition. On the other hand, it would be quite acceptable to a Greek, for Greek thought readily admits grades in this matter of divinity, and certainly its acceptance would be in line with the direction whither the living faith is tending, which is instinctively to exalt the Lord more and more.

The third of these constructions put upon the person of Christ is the *Docetic* Christology (so called from the Greek word δόκησις,"appearance") which maintains that the Lord was man in appearance only, and that he appeared only to suffer and die. On this basis Docetism sought to avoid the necessity of imposing upon the Divine Being a degrading association with the flesh and its works, but it found itself drawn into the necessity of imagining a process of redemption quite different from that current in the common faith. Moreover, notable differences occur in the conception of this process of redemption itself, according to the various gnostic systems which adopted it.

Notwithstanding the differences in their point of departure and, if you will, in their spirit, it is evident that these three Christologies are tending to the same result, that is, to remove Christ from ranking with humanity by bringing him closer to God. This was in itself an exceedingly difficult thing, because from its basic underlying Judaism Christianity had derived an uncompromising monotheism. While accepting the Lord to be really a divine being, it found it impossible, apparently, to do aught else than subordinate him to God, just as the Sôter (savior) of the Mysteries is subordinate to the Supreme Divinity. Long before Christian thought had been directed toward the idea of a Trinity of divine persons, united in a single essence within the Divine Being itself, many different solutions had been essayed, of most of which only vague and confused traces remain. While this was going on the generality of the faithful were not yet obliged to profess adherence to any of them, nor did that which they were asked *to believe* demand a very great effort of thought on their part.

That which was laid upon them *to do* was to live aright, that is, to preserve themselves with the utmost circumspectness from all the moral weaknesses which men by common consent consider sins; to struggle untiringly against the evil instincts of the flesh, supported by absolute confidence in the grace of the Heavenly Father and in the intercession of the Lord Jesus Christ. Frequent prayers and fastings were practices taken over from Judaism and kept up. The entire ritual life is still confined to the Eucharistic reunion—the assembly for worship which takes places on the Saturday evening and lasts until the dawn of Sunday—in which they consecrate and consume ritually the sacred elements, bread and wine. It is not probable, however, that all the communities had yet given their consent to the same idea of the Eucharist. Most of them see in it merely a memorial of the Passion and a repast of brotherhood; others regard it as supplying an effective means of associating themselves with their Lord in the essential act of his ministry on earth, a kind of supplement that puts new life into the gifts received in baptism. We dimly perceive or divine some other practices, such as the anointing with oil, accompanied by the laying-on of hands, which the writer of the Epistle ascribed to James advises to be applied to the sick, and that again is an essentially Jewish custom.

These, then, constitute, toward the beginning of the second century the initiation, the prevailing doctrine and the worship of the Christians. As a whole, it is all very simple and at the same time very plastic. Upon its distinctly recognizable Jewish groundwork, influences from the Hellenistic religions and (indirectly, certainly, but also visibly) Greek philosophic ideas which have filtered down to the public have begun to take effect. Let us therefore try to observe how, as soon as these effects are avowed, they complicate at once the form of initation or entrance into the Church, her beliefs and her practices, all three.

II

Entrance into the Church is pronouncedly complicated through the tendency to elaborate the ritual which develops in nearly all religious camps as soon as a religion begins to be systematically propagated, and seems, moreover, to inhere in the very existence of a true clergy class. We must take into account also the fear of the unsound brother who might misuse the Mystery if he were admitted to it without due formalities. Precautions are accordingly taken to avoid its profanation. For a long time it was believed that this had been finally cared for by organizing them into a system called the "discipline of the arcanum," *i.e.*, of the secret. Under it the instruction and the initiation of the future Christian was arranged in stages, and it was not till the final one had been reached and after very searching tests that the last word of the Mystery was revealed. Something of this kind may be seen in practice following the institution of the catechumenate, *i.e.*, succeeding the organizing of a regular course of instruction in the Christian faith for the use of the candidates for baptism. After all, however, the arcanum can be no more than second hand and a piece of mere ritual dramatization, for the sufficient reason that the last word of the Mystery is the starting point and the *raison d'être* of the conversion. "Progressive revelation" is at that time a mere symbol, for on the very first day the convert knows what will be said to him on the last one, or at any rate, something closely aproaching it. Before the institution of the catechumenate, the arcanum would have been void of meaning, and afterward it never attains much practical importance.

However, the mere intention of taking precautions to protect from profanation, if not the beliefs that cannot be withheld from those who ask for an explanation, at least those rites which I shall henceforth call the sacraments, is a step toward the establishment of a probationary stage for Christian novices. This is exactly what the catechumenate is (the word is derived from κατηχέω, "I teach"). The first evidence of it in operation is found in Tertullian [3] and it seems to have become generally established toward the end of the second century, without, however, attaining uniformity of content everywhere. Always and everywhere, however, it does represent the education and the oversight of the faith of the neophyte by the authorities of the community. By inscribing his name on the roll and submitting to certain preparatory rites, of

[3] *De praescriptione* 41. 2.

which the chief is the exorcism of the devils within him, the candidate becomes a catechumen. Then, after a period of instruction varying in length, and of examination, he enters the ranks of *competentes,* the aspirants for baptism, which is administered by the bishop on some great festival such as Easter or Whitsuntide.

Baptism itself has now become a complicated ceremonial embracing at least a course of special instructions and exorcisms, a threefold immersion, the laying on of hands, accompanied by an anointing with holy oil and the first communion. Henceforth it is understood that if the believer in the catechumen stage is qualified for salvation, only the baptized participate in the *fulness* of the Christian gifts and graces—*charisma.* Baptism alone creates between the believer and his Lord the mysterious bonds which make the full Christian his peculiar own. And it is by no means difficult to recognize echoes of the spirit of the Hellenistic Mysteries in these progressive stages of initiation, these all-powerful rites and the opinion held as to their significance. Such emphasis is laid on the rigor of the engagements entered into in baptism and of the peril involved in their violation, that many men who are perfectly good Christians at heart consider it both more comfortable and more prudent to ask for baptism only when at the point of death. This custom of postponing baptism, although its extension was stoutly resisted by the clergy, seems to have grown very common at the end of the third and the beginning of the fourth centuries, especially among Christians of the aristocratic classes.

III

As to creed, that has been fostered and amplified by the faith. In a milieu which we know from other sources to be thoroughly saturated with dogma, the creed developed under a twofold influence. In the first place, it was the work of ignorant folk, who obviously can scarcely take in anything above very ordinary inventions and inflations. So while they desire ardently that the truth or creed shall remain immutable, they are unable to protect it from changes. In the very beginning, they are the ones who accept and impose the most compromising additions to Christology, because they contribute to the inflation of their Lord's greatness. At bottom, the converts won from the ranks of Hellenism, who come with minds full of the tenets of Orphism or the Mysteries, do not willingly renounce these in becoming Christians. On the contrary, they seek, and desire to find, them in Christianity, and even unconsciously—though irresistibly—they introduce them into it. In the second place, it was the work of the philosophers. I mean the educated men equipped by their training to argue about the faith and to become theologians. There is no room for doubt that from the very beginning Christianity professes to be in possession of the whole gamut of truth; consequently the philosophy whose business it is to search for it no longer has a *raison d'être,* and certain learned doctors, such as Tertullian, Arnobius and Lactantius, do not hesitate to proclaim that its day is done. Nevertheless, the charm of Greek thought continues to exert an influence over most of those who submitted to it before they yielded to the allurement of the Christian faith. These men, too, will not, or at least cannot, however honestly they may try, renounce the fundamental data and particularly the speculative methods of the Greek schools. Accordingly they apply them to the premises of the faith and to the suggestions which they draw from the religious sentiment of the ignorant. Complicated dogmas, such as that of the Trinity, or subtle ones like the doctrine of Transubstantiation, owe their first form and their later developments to the inflations and the lines of arguments of the *philosophers,* pressed to them ofttimes by the contradictory positions taken by the ignorant.[4]

[4] It is especially the Christian doctors of Alexandria who favor this *fertilizing* influence of Greek philosophy upon the data of the faith. The most illustrious among them, Origen (in the third century), goes so far as to explain the "Apostolic truths" in the language of Plato, that is, to regard Christianity through a Platonic and, to a lesser extent, Stoic, interpretation, a task earlier undertaken by Philo with respect to Judaism. *Cf.* the preface to his *De principiis.*

In the one case as in the other, and in the final analysis, it is always faith which exalts and inflates doctrine, and it is ever from her former religious surroundings that faith borrows the fresh elements which she mixes with the old by changed formulas, and thus secures her new belief.

In leaving behind the primitive epoch when faith was regulated by the promptings of the Spirit only, Christians, as was but natural, perceived mainly the danger which might accrue to it through "subjectivity," by which I mean the mischief which individual vagaries might introduce. On the other hand, they went through the everlasting illusion of all revealed religions: the truth is *one,* and therefore *immutable,* and very early they imagined the whole of it was contained in the Apostolic teaching. To strengthen this conviction, quite as much as to ward off the risk of frittering away their beliefs or of overvaluing some of them for lack of due consideration, a tendency developed to establish a "rule of faith" (*regula fidei*) which was declared unvarying. This tendency is admirably expressed by Tertullian's formula: "Faith is contained in a rule; it is both its law and its salvation to observe law."[5]

There are a few indications in favor of the position that from the first century short rules, which could be learnt by heart and repeated by converts at their baptism, were in existence. That which is still known as the Apostles' Creed is only a rule of faith, a very ancient one, for in its primitive form it seems to have been settled upon in Rome about 150 A.D. and attributed to the Apostles in order that it might be accepted by all the churches. It was not, however, the only one of its kind, and documents of the second and third centuries quote others more or less analogous. These quotations prove that there are some differences between the creeds accepted respectively by the various churches, and even

---

[5] *Fides in regula posita est; habet legem et salutem de observatione legis* (*De praescriptione* 14).

that each creed retains a certain elasticity [6] for a long time. But they also bear witness that all the churches now have their rule of faith and their baptismal creed. And this is very important, because the articles of these creeds serve, as it were, as themes for meditation concerning the Christian faith, and in order that dogmas may gush forth it is enough for theologians to delve into them.

Naturally the central point of all this theorizing is questions connected with Christology, and its evolution determines everything else. Without entering here into useless detail, let us note these three main points: (1) in theory the faith did not compromise upon the fundamental point of monotheism; (2) the point of logical climax of all inflations of the faith with regard to the personality and rôle of Christ Jesus was his identification with God; (3) there was a converse tendency to define in three persons, ever more differentiated as to characteristics, *i.e.*, becoming more and more distinct, the three terms laid down in the creed: Father, Son and Spirit. And thus it can be said that the faith clung with increasing firmness to contradictory propositions.

In seeking to escape from this difficulty, common sense could take its choice between two solutions only. The faithful could openly abandon monotheism and resign themselves to *tritheism;* or they could renounce the distinction of persons in the One God and fall into *modalism, i.e.,* regard each of the persons as simply a modality, as *one* of the main aspects of the unique Divine Being. Now the majority of Christians did not wish to choose. Accordingly they tried to maintain, at one and the same time, the indivisible oneness of God and the existence of three distinct persons in him. Out of this paradox innumerable discussions arose, in the course of

---

[6] The Apostles' Creed has been altered many times in order to bar the way to some heresy or other. To get an idea of the *elasticity* of which I have spoken, it is enough to compare three references in Tertullian's *De virginibus velandis* 1; *Adversus Praxeam* 2; *De praescriptione* 13.

which problems and difficulties multiplied thick and fast, which caused enormous trouble in the churches. It was somewhere about the fifth century before these disturbances subsided, engulfed in theological formulas unintelligible to reason.

In the course of the second century it came to be held that Jesus Christ is the Son of God, by special, though direct, generation; that he also is God, and the active agent in the organization of the world by the will of the Father and the assistance of the Holy Spirit. The orthodox view of the relation of the Son to the Father tends to shape itself by repulsing all three of as many different interpretations of this relation. First of these is the *adoptionist* theory, clearly propounded in Rome by Theodosius at the end of the second century. According to it the man Jesus had been, as it were, adopted by God as his son, through a sort of embodiment of the Logos which his peculiar virtues had earned for him. The second, or the *modalist* theory, assumed that God, essentially one, made himself manifest in various characters such as creator, savior, inspirer, whilst remaining himself through it all; so that, strictly speaking, one might say that the Father had suffered the Passion at the same time as the Son and the Holy Spirit. This was taught by a certain Praxeas in Rome about 190 A.D. Thirdly, there was the *Gnostic* theory, which appeared in too many versions to be reduced to a formula, though we may fairly say that it represented Christ as a divine being, an aeon, intermediate between divine perfection and human imperfection. The Gnostic sects usually agree with the Docetics, which means, I repeat, that they considered Christ's human life to be a transit through the flesh, human in appearance only.

The disputes which these Christological differences engender seem confusing to us. They seem so far removed from any reasonably conducted discussions to which we are accustomed that we sometimes find it difficult to take them seriously. We must not stop short at this impression, however; they were of very great importance because they obliged common everyday faith to scrutinize its real possibilities and to define itself more sharply. The fact should not be overlooked that most of the dogmas are formed and fashioned by hammer strokes of negations and anathemas: the opinion which prevails and is avowed is, by definition, that which is not condemned, or the opposite of the one rejected. The reasoning processes employed are borrowed from the sophistry and formal dialectic of Greece; the concepts which by degrees are superimposed upon the earlier beliefs, transforming them into dogmas, are taken from Hellenistic metaphysics and are expressed in formulas fashioned by the help of its vocabulary.

This evolution naturally met with opposition. Some adhere to the older forms of the Apostolic faith and the traditions of primitive Judeo-Christianity. They are probably direct descendants of the first Palestinian converts, for they are still located for some time yet beyond the Jordan, especially in the district in which the Christians who fled from Jerusalem at the time of the great Jewish revolt in 66 A.D. had taken refuge. Very soon the Hellenist churches accuse them of thinking "poorly" of the Lord and despise them, calling them Ebionites (*Ebionim* means "the poor"). We already know that in Justin's time their salvation was called in question, and the day draws near when they will be unanimously considered as heretics in the Church at large. Actually, they are only loiterers who persist in preserving beliefs that are out of date, which cannot be adapted to the Greek milieu. Fairly strong opposition is perceptible also to the theological idea of the Logos, which prepares the way for the dogma of the Trinity and on which it is finally established. But the Alogi (as these reactionaries are called) have no more chance than the Ebionites of stemming the current which is bearing the Christian faith toward the formation of a metaphysical system of dogmatics which becomes more and more complicated and more and more remote from the basic statements of the Apostles.

At the end of the second century this process of dog-
matizing has been only roughly sketched out, but its
tendencies are already very perceptible and will not alter
materially.   From that date the Christian hope has
changed into the Christian religion—the religion of which
Jesus Christ is the real God.   It is definitely dissociated
from Judaism, for which it not only does not profess any
filial feeling but abjures and utters maledictions upon it
as the most intractable enemy of the Truth.

IV

Yet another trait bears witness to the running of
Christianity into the molds of an autonomous and exclusive religion, namely, a higher and ever more momentous
development of ecclesiasticism.   I mean by this that from
the religious point of view the individual tends more and
more to be lost in the community.   He appears to be subject in all the important acts of his life to the direction
or, at any rate, the influence of the persons who are the
constituted authorities of the Church and custodians of
the rites which convey the action exerted by the presence
of the Lord in the midst of his worshipers and effect a
veritable union between them and him.   We must not be
premature or over definite in speaking of a sacrament.
Especially must the term not be applied indiscriminately
to all the customs practiced by the ancient Church
through the mediation of the bishop, for instance, on the
marriage or the death of the faithful.   It is certainly a
true inference, nevertheless, from the mere fact that
there *is* a ritual with regard to them, that these customs
tend to become sacraments, *i.e.*, mysterious operations in
which there is a spontaneous outflow of special graces.

Note has already been taken of how baptism became a
complex ritual and a well-defined sacrament.   Less
rapidly, but yet promptly, two ancient usages that form
part of ecclesiastical practice evolve until they acquire
the same status—the Eucharist and penance.

Changes took place in the Eucharistic reunion as it was

observed by the primitive community, and it became in the course of the second century the *Mass*, *i.e.*, an ordered assemblage of readings, prayers in common, exhortations and hymns, the culminating point of which was marked by the consecration of the Eucharistic elements and the communion. There is still a lack of unanimity as to the consummate significance and the exact formalities which these rites assume in that remote period of Christianity. Only recently there have been long discussions upon the question whether the ecclesiastical block used for the consecration was an altar or merely a table. At any rate it is certain that the Eucharist was henceforth considered a "mystery" which was a means of communion with their Lord for the faithful, in the conception of it which was already paramount in Paul's doctrine. The sacramental elements of bread and wine are regarded as supernatural sustenance which except at great personal peril can be received only by those who come to it in a special spiritual condition.

And since in this rite the ancient root idea of divine communion as a process of absorption of the god is in close alliance with the remembrance of the death of the god, and the belief in the redeeming power of this death, the thought of sacrifice also in its turn inevitably enters into the transaction. This is bound to take place because all the religions of the regions in which Christianity acquired its form are sacrificial, and it is difficult to disabuse men's minds of a notion so universally accepted. The idea of the mystic reënactment of the death of the god in a mode and manner more or less analogous so deeply implanted in the worship of most of the redeeming deities, is another contributing cause. Be it well understood, the point at issue is indeed no longer that the Eucharistic union is a case of *commemorating* the initial redeeming sacrifice carried out on Calvary. If the Eucharist were no more than that, it would have no more value than a mere symbol. The issue drawn now is over the interpretation of it as a sacrifice in which the god becomes the voluntary victim over again, while simultaneously receiving homage through the oblation. The outcome of this sacrifice is the generation of a mysterious and magical dynamic force which becomes the source of mystic benefits of inestimable value to all the participants. It has been rightly said that the acceptance of this idea of the Eucharist was equivalent to the introduction into Christianity of a "bit of paganism"—the paganism of the Mysteries.

Consequences, both for practice and dogma, which are of the highest importance, follow in its wake.

In the Oriental cults of the gods who die and rise again, liturgical stress is sometimes laid in the celebration upon the death and sometimes upon the resurrection of the Sôter, but rarely, as far as we can judge, upon both to the same extent. In the primitive Christianity of the Twelve, first place is given to the resurrection, because it is presented as the guarantee of the great hope: the speedy return of Christ and the inauguration of the Kingdom. Since by degrees the postponement of the *parousia* renders expectation concerning it as a rule less insistent, the significance for the faith of the Lord's resurrection is transposed, as it were. From serving as the guarantee of the near approach of the Kingdom it passes over into an assurance of the resurrection of the faithful when time shall be no more. In Paul's mind this is the part it already plays.[7] On the other hand, the Eucharist takes on deeper significance in proportion as speculation thinks over and amplifies its thought regarding the incarnation and redemption through the cross. Thus it is that Paul, who characterizes all his preaching as "discourse concerning the cross," supplies the primitive tradition concerning the Last Supper with the accretions necessary to make this meal a realization in advance of the mystery made explicit in the Passion, which in its turn the Eucharist is deemed to go on expressing indefinitely. In this way it becomes the central liturgical act of Christian worship and the prime source of the grace of the Lord, placed by him at the

[7] I Cor. xv. 12 *et seq.*

disposal of the community which calls upon his name.

It becomes all this only because implanted in the Christian consciousness is (1) the conviction that the Lord is *in person present* in the Eucharistic assembly, in a contact direct and a communion immediate with his followers, and also (2) a notion of what we call "transubstantiation."[8] The point to be understood is that the consecration pronounced upon them effects an alteration of the bread into the flesh and the wine into the blood of Jesus in such a way that the consumption of the consecrated elements constitutes both a material and spiritual interfusion of Lord and Christian, and in the form which the Lord himself had indicated as appropriate to the fulfilment of the mystery.

These ceremonial enactings of dogma assuredly do not achieve their finished formula in their first efforts, and the passages in which we first find them referred to are by no means free from doubt and ambiguity; it would be surprising if that were not so. However, if the theory in favor of the nature of the Eucharist at the end of the second century has not yet fully won the day, the quarters in general from which the elements of victory will be derived are already definitely perceptible.

V

Penance is evidently in an earlier stage of growth at this same epoch, but its approaching development can be sensed equally plainly.

The matter at issue here is not the penitence which the sinner is able to carry on in private when he begins to repent of his slips, nor of the moral amendment which should be its outcome for him. These several procedures

[8] *Cf.* I Cor. xi. 23 *et seq.* I do not mean to say that Paul himself invented the formula which contains both the affirmation that the consecrated bread is the body "which is given for you" and the cup that of "the New Covenant in my blood," and the order to "do this" (*i.e.*, *repeat* over the elements, bread and wine, the same words and gestures) "in remembrance of me." I believe that the main inflation of the Eucharist which this formula implies was the work of the Hellenistic community in which the Apostle was trained, and that it was transmitted to him as "the word of the Lord."

are obligatory upon all Christians and, ever since the teaching of Jesus himself, they form the core of practical Christian morality. In so far as a man's backslidings are not publicly known and cause no offense, they affect his own conscience alone. It is quite otherwise with failings which may happen to betray to the brethren a lapse which is a source of disquietude over his salvation as well as a bad example to those who are not firmly established in the faith. In very early days, therefore, the community deemed itself bound to a twofold duty when confronted by flagrant offenses: to set the offender right with a brotherly warning, and to take precautions that his sin should not harm others. Thus arose the necessity of settling upon an ecclesiastical discipline to prescribe the atonement for a public lapse, which severs the notorious sinner from the congregation and fellowships him again only when he has made amends. This discipline acquires very soon the appearance of a collection of rites, following out the tendency which affects all the actions of the Church. By reason of the importance (both for the guilty and for the community) of the place acquired by penance in the Christian life, it is inevitable that its administration should acquire the value and the meaning also of a sacrament. It is a sacrament which restores to the penitent upon pardon his capacity to receive afresh the saving graces which are granted to the community of "Saints."

At the end of the second century the ritual regulation of penance has already undergone development to a point of considerable precision, but, to tell the truth, the theology of it as a sacrament does not seem to have been even outlined. It is, however, certain that from that time such a theology appears to be a coming necessity and that it exists potentially in the rites entrusted to the ecclesiastical authorities to *bind* and *unbind*, in earth as in heaven.

If the texts available at the beginning of the third century be examined impartially, not the smallest trace of the existence of the other four sacraments will be found which in the course of time the Church will settle upon—confirmation, orders, matrimony and extreme unction. I do not mean to say that it is impossible for us to perceive germs of them in various practices already used in the liturgy, but I maintain that the Christians in those days had no idea of them.

Henceforth Christianity has settled down into an original religion. It has its own dogmatic system, liturgy, discipline. However simple they still may be, already their main foundations are laid and their chief future trends indicated. These are not the outcome of a kind of spontaneous generation. On the contrary, it is evident that they are the product of a syncretism, of which all the elements have been acquired from the Oriental surroundings—from Israel, from the Mystery-religions and Hellenist philosophy. It is by the same syncretistic method that all three—dogmatic system, liturgy, discipline—will experience the developments which the future has in store for them. Little by little they will absorb and assimilate (certainly not without some hesitation in their choice and twinges of pain in the labor of adaptation, yet without pause) all the religion living and lasting in quality that the Greco-Roman world contains. The *work is proceeding unconsciously,* no doubt, but it will go on without any intermission until the day dawns when the disintegration cannot be disputed of all the religious societies from which the Christian faith and liturgy have drained away their substance.

CHAPTER X

THE success of Christianity was impeded, and even appears for a time to be compromised by the violent hostility which the Roman government and pagan society displayed toward it. This hostility found outlet in what are called the "persecutions."[1]

I

For the quarrels between Christianity and State, each of the opponents share in the responsibility. The earliest Christians not only believed the end of the world to be imminent, but they desired it. Naturally they disengaged themselves from the cares and duties of earthly life, and in their hearts the love of the heavenly Jerusalem seriously infringed upon their loyalty to the Roman state. Military service was hateful to them because it involved concessions to idolatry, and they also loathed warfare. Participation in civic service seemed to them superfluous. Preëminently, they obstinately refused to take part in any of the loyalist demonstrations which the imperial government demanded, because pagan religious ceremonies formed part of them all.

[1] The persecutions have been the subject of frequent studies. *L'histoire des persécutions* of Paul Allard, esteemed in Catholic circles, lacks critical force. The following may be read with profit: Bouché-Leclercq, *L'intolérance religieuse et la politique* (Paris, 1911) ; L. Hardy Canfield, *The Early Persecutions of the Christians* (New York, 1913), which indicates the sources and often gives them in detail; E. T. Merrill, *Essays in Early Christian History* (London, 1914), which deals with both the first and second centuries; A. Manaresi, *L'impero romano e il christianesimo* (Turin, 1914), which treats the problem intelligibly as a whole, and contains all the bibliographical helps necessary. The best general book is Linsenmayer's *Die Bekämpfung des Christentums durch den Römischen Staat bis zum Tode des Kaisers Julian* (Munich, 1905).

Their religious conscience showed itself to be of a very ticklish cast that obliged them frequently to turn their backs with a *non possumus* on the most ordinary requirements of civic life. The pagan state could not allow a group of men to act that way, who constantly increased in number, and whose motto seemed to be the words of Tertullian: *secessi de populo,* "I have withdrawn from society."

All the faithful, it is true, did not manifest such uncompromising nonconformity with regard to the claims of civic life as Tertullian, for that uncouth defender of the faith had to confess that some Christians served in the army and held public offices. In the opinion, however, of the rulers silent surface loyalty of this kind was not enough to counterbalance the embarrassing demonstrations of the fanatics, or, at any rate, the placarding of headstrong resolutions, announcements put out in advance by them. Christians of this stamp inevitably compromised all their fellows, because they were the only ones who came before the magistrates to be examined.

On the other hand, while the State exercised a real and wide tolerance with respect to non-official religions, it nevertheless enforced certain restrictions which it believed indispensable to its own existence. For instance, it demanded a show of deference from all forms of worship to the official cult, and upon occasion it required every citizen to be willing to attest his patriotism by taking an oath "by the genius" (tutelar divinity) of the Emperor, while participating in a sacrifice in honor of the *numen Augusti* (godhead of Augustus). Moreover, the State showed much distrust of the superstitions "which vex the shallow minds of men" so that from its standpoint, the Christian faith, Oriental in its origin and mystic and excitable, was foreign to all that Roman custom regarded as a religion. Since it had neither temples nor the image of any god, it seemed, as Pliny said, to be "a distorted ill mannered superstition" (*superstitionem pravam et immodicam*). Finally, the State had a great dread of secret societies, and its police knew that the Christians held gatherings at night without permission.

The Christians considered there was no misdemeanor involved in frustrating the snares of the demon concealed under the cover of idols, nor in resisting his suggestions, nor in sacrificing everything out of fidelity to God, nor in assembling together to return thanks and make common intercession to him. Their consciences were opposing a victorious vindication to the demands of the State and the obligations of the law. Tertullian was expressing the feelings of the best of them when he wrote: *Legis injustae honor nullus,* "no one is bound to respect an unjust law," and naturally it was Christian scruples which were to pass judgment upon every law. The State cannot countenance such independence.

The incompatibility perceptible between the standards of the State and the Christians made itself manifest, too, between the Christians and society in general. They respected none of its prejudices, none of its customs, and hardly any of its principles. At the end of the second, and the opening of the third, centuries, Tertullian could describe marriage and the procreation of children as a regrettable concession to the claims of the flesh. Spiritual blessings to him were the only true ones; he condemned all the joys and amusements of life. He shattered social conventions by mixing master and slave together in the same religious groups. Upon the whole secular world around him he poured his arrogant contempt.

Naturally Christians were not wanting who were quite ready to fall in with the ordinary life, for they all did not have the spirit of the martyr within them. Nevertheless, the common people usually judged the Church by the individuals who forced themselves upon their attention. The pagans of the patrician class, in their turn, scented danger to themselves, their status and their privileges, from claims so revolutionary in appearance.

It may be imagined that the State and society, unable to understand the elements of nobility underlying Christian nonconformity, were deeply incensed against them. Society held the Christians in abomination, unloading all the anti-Jewish calumnies upon them, and the State persecuted them. At the end of the second century things had reached a point where the clash could be settled only by the overthrow of one of the two adversaries. Christianity does not indeed appear to be in any condition to stand the assault of the public authorities, egged on and supported by quasi-general opinion. The learned despised the Christians, either because they regarded them as backsliding Jews disowned by the Synagogue, or else because they did not deign to inquire into their doctrine. They were hated by the common people because of their strange way of living and the horrible rumors circulated about their gatherings.[2]

Their expression of this hatred in violent outbursts was at first the chief cause of the persecutions. The magistrates intervened in order to allay the uproar and give the blind passion of the populace its sop of gratification; so they proceeded against people whom on their own initiative they would probably have left in peace. They knew perfectly well that they were not very dangerous, and that if their mania for religious uncompromisingness were blameworthy and sometimes even a breach of the law they were not guilty of the practice of ritual murder or the gross immorality which they were taxed with by idle gossip. Nevertheless, the refusal of the Christians to "swear by the *genius* of the Emperor" and to pay homage to his effigy (as to a god) by burning a few grains of incense before it, entailed an accusation of high treason and the death penalty. For this reason the second century had its martyrs, especially in Asia Minor, under Trajan, and in Lyons, under Marcus Aurelius, in 176.[3]

[2] The evil-disposed heaped all the old accusations given currency by anti-Semitism upon them: ritual murders and secret orgies, accompanied by filthy details.

[3] I am not referring at all to what has been called Nero's persecution, for that seems to have been no more than an accidental utilization of the popular prejudice to divert suspicion from the Emperor of having set fire to Rome in 64 A.D.

II

Not until the third century did the State begin seriously to consider the social peril which seemed to be wrapped up in Christianity, but from then on it looked upon it as a species of anarchy. They were the best rulers, most conscious of the duties which their station involved and, as we should say, the most patriotic, who stand out as the most inveterate enemies of the Christian churches. Emperors like Decius, Valerian, Galerius and Diocletian, in the second half of the century, very clearly display an intention to cut short their propaganda, strip them of their clergy and to abet, by the losses due to abjurations obtained by means of threats of torture and death, the total destruction of the new religion. To attain their end, they did not shrink from authorizing the most violent coercive measures, nor even numerous executions. Charges of breaches of the common law were piled up against them to overwhelm the faithful such as these: an illicit religion, a secret society, *lèse majesté* (*crimen majestatis*), a refusal to comply with military regulations, *ignavia, i.e.*, slackness with regard to the duties of public and private life, even magic itself. Those cases, however, where the parties thus accused were Christians present this peculiarity—the charges were quashed the moment the accused consented to say with his tongue that he abjured his faith. This leads us to suppose that it was at bottom the Christian religion itself that was being persecuted for its own sake. Some critics have even wondered whether, from the time of Nero, it had not been by a special law unconditionally forbidden. This point has not been proved, but it is by no means impossible. In practice, everything nevertheless was ordered on the basis that the simple fact of a Christian confession implied misdemeanors and crimes punishable with death on their part. Criminal procedure with the Romans was habitually harsh. In the trials of charges against the Christians it attained its maximum of severity, because with regard to *lese majesté* the magistrate's powers of coercion knew no limits. The most barbarous tortures were put in force to extort an abjuration. Naturally, the personal equation in the case of each particular judge might be a source of mitigation or, on the contrary, of aggravation in this dread form of questioning.

Happily for the Christians, the efforts of the State to exterminate their religion were always disconnected and intermittent; never, even in the worst days of Diocletian, were they carried out to the bitter end; never were they long consecutively maintained, so that in the periods between crises the Church reformed her ranks. The persecutions assuredly did claim their victims, but as far as Christians in the mass were concerned they succeeded only in forcing temporary apostasies, and sometimes, as an offset, in stirring up a contagious enthusiasm. The words hurled by Tertullian as a cry of defiance to the persecutors: *Sanguis martyrum semen christianorum* ("the blood of the martyrs is the seed of the Christians") have often been quoted. On the whole, they have been justified, and the hagiographic documents which are in existence afford some strange examples of psychic contagion. It was above all in the intervals between the crises that the Church derived most advantage from the testimony of blood in her work of propaganda.

At the beginning of the fourth century, after the miscarriage of Diocletian's persecution, the State began to realize that the Christians were too numerous for violent measures henceforth to succeed. Moreover, upon careful reconsideration of the whole matter, the problems raised by them did not seem to present themselves in the same terms as during the second century.

Christianity was no longer to be solely the religion of the under-privileged; it now had adept members in all classes of society. In proportion as the number of believers thus grew, the average of opinion which became established in the Church was wholly reassuring. Christians no longer expected the end of the world from one day to the next; they conformed to current customs and even to current prejudice. Christians joined the army and served in the administration, and the ecclesiastical authorities made no objection. Christian ethics and Christian resignation to the world's continuance had reaffirmed allegiance to all social regulations. Above all, a community of believers, united, disciplined and directed by leaders whom they obeyed, presented to the State a cheering spectacle of order, the product of a well-administered government, which already shows signs of developing a political consciousness. Finally, the prejudices against Christianity which had been so prevalent among the people of the first two centuries had been disappearing step by step with the more open life which the growth of the Church, facilitated by intervals of tolerance, had brought about. It was time for both State and Christianity to think of a compromise.

Circumstances hastened this reconciliation on.[4] In 311, the Emperor Galerian, the most active of its persecutors, recognizing his measures were futile and forced to yield because of the obstacles interposed by the invincible determination of the Church, shortly before his death made up his mind to tolerate her. His edict of toleration very justly gave the Christians the idea that their cause had triumphed. On the other hand, in the struggle to which his death led between many competitors for power, each of the rivals sought to gain as many partisans as possible for himself. The Church embraced the occasion offered to exact compensation for the assistance which her strong position and, above all, her universality, rendered particularly valuable. Now, among these aspirants for the vacant throne was one that had inspired her with confidence who already manifested some signs of good will—Constantine.

[4] P. Batiffol's *La paix constantinienne et le catholicisme* (Paris, 1914), may well be studied, bearing in mind that it is written wholly from the Catholic point of view, and that its author tends to apologetics; also T. de Bacci Venuti, *Dalla grande persecuzione alla vittoria del Cristianesimo* (Milan, 1913); C. Bush Coleman, *Constantine the Great and Christianity* (New York, 1914), a very good study of sources and traditions, with an extensive bibliography; Ed. Schwartz, *Kaiser Constantin und die Christliche Kirche* (Leipzig, 1913), a popular scientific work.

He was not yet a Christian, but the form of syncretism in religion that he practiced was very liberal. Like his father Constantius Chlorus, who, it appears had shuffled out of enforcing the last edicts of persecution during his government of Gaul, he combined respect for the ancient religion with a fear of the God of the Christians. Moreover, his father's court included many of the clergy whom he had known well enough to fathom their true position. He had learnt that, along with the maintenance of the principles which formed the basis of the older Christianity, in practice, they did not refuse to grant the concessions indispensable to the State. He realized that persecution had not only failed, but that it moreover seriously disturbed ordinary life, because the hatred with which the Christians had formerly been regarded by the nation scarcely existed any longer. They had increased in numbers, were better known, and more especially they now lived like everybody else. He knew the Church to be a very active force, and that all the rulers who had fought against her had experienced some misfortune. Finally, he had learnt that his opponent Maxentius, with a large and seasoned army, had taken care to invoke the aid of all the pagan gods by means of prayers, sacrifices and even magic rites. For him, therefore, no alternative remained but to make an appeal to the Christ.

Possibly his resolves and his hopes, when they came to exteriorize themselves, presented themselves to him in the form of a vision to which he supplied the details when relating the story of it later. In any case, he was the victor, and on that account regarded himself as more or less in debt to Christ. Gratitude, faith and policy all combined to suggest the Edict of Milan (313), which made a place, among the divinities worthy of veneration, for the mighty God of the Christians, and intended to establish in the eyes of the State the equality of all religions upon a basis of liberty of conscience. But, to tell the truth, the Church would not tolerate any such solution, and the State was not able to cling to it.

III

Although the Christian Church was thus led by force of circumstances and by a very practical sense of the real issue to accord to the demands of public and social life all essential concessions, she had not, for all that, renounced her principles. As the depository of divine truth, she saw in every pagan an agent of the Evil One, and the mere idea of equality of treatment with paganism for herself was like an outrage which necessity alone could force her to tolerate. Moreover, there was no reason why she should not continue to drain the living sap from the pagan beliefs, as she had already found it profitable to do. On the other hand, the State could hardly cancel its old obligation to maintain a close bond between the City and its religion. The public safety seemed also to require that the government should keep a controlling hand over the disputes to which the antagonism of the two religions could not fail to lead, and its impartiality in that rôle was bound up with a policy of strict neutrality. Nevertheless, the rulers did not remain neutral, for the power of Christianity, increased tenfold by its victory, caught them in its grip and they soon became involved. The clerics entangled the rulers almost in spite of themselves in their own clergy concerns, obtained numerous favors from them, and induced them to take an interest in their ecclesiastical success.

Toward the end of Constantine's reign, the union of Church and State, the absorption of paganism by Christianity, and its total destruction with the connivance and, if necessary, the help of the State, could have been foreseen. This achievement, which was accomplished in the course of the fourth century, was subjected to some delays. These delays did not arise from any move of the Church, who very soon accustomed herself to consider that it was the duty of the State to come to her aid, against heretics and pagans, without foreseeing the state of servitude into which she was herself advancing by this course. They were due to the action of the emperors who, either from hostility, like Julian, or from a sincere desire to maintain a balance between the two religions, like Valentinian, offered a spirited resistance. With Theodosius, through the influence of the first statesman that the Church produced, St. Ambrose, archbishop of Milan, she attained her aim, and the Christian religion acquired the character and status of a State religion, to the exclusion of all others.[5]

Paganism certainly did not vanish all at once, but it offered only a loose and feeble resistance to the methodical attack of the Church and the unrestrained zeal of a few bishops and monks who took it upon themselves to pursue it unrelentingly. Its disintegration was due not only to the loss of the support of the government, which left paganism without any central control and split it up into many different cults, but above all to the fact that its most stubborn adherents looked upon it from such varied points of view that they could scarcely present a united front in its defense.

The aristocrats of the older Roman towns, especially those of Rome itself, clung to their religious customs even more stoutly than to the beliefs of their ancestors, because these customs seemed inseparable from their family traditions. Their admiration and respect for the past felt really at home only in the setting in which that past had been lived, and these sentiments constituted a very tenacious form of religion because it held fast, as a principle of allegiance to a point of honor, as it were, and could not be directly assaulted through its convictions, which were themselves an object of veneration. Thus Toxotius, the husband of Paula, believed himself bound to remain a pagan, because he maintained that he was descended from Eneas.

Many of these aristocrats shared in a very profound and sincere conviction, which has been well expressed by the most celebrated among them, the *praefectus urbis* Symmachus, who in his report in the year 384 demanded the reinstatement, in the hall where the Roman Senate

[5] Consult Boissier, *La fin du paganisme* (Paris, 1894).

held its sittings, of an ancient statue of Victory which the Emperor Gratianus had had removed the preceding year. It was not expedient, they were convinced, for men to discard religious practices which the experience of time had consecrated as of proven efficacy. The Republic, urged Symmachus, prospered as long as it remained faithful to the gods of its ancestors. Only since reverence for the national deities had wavered had it encountered misfortunes and dangers. Critically examined, it was assuredly a feeble argument, but from the point of view of sentiment it had no need to be weighty to appear forcible. When Rome was taken by Alaric in 410, a loud outcry against Christianity arose from the ranks of the pagans who realized their humiliation, and St. Augustine does not think that in writing his great book, *The City of God,* he is taking too great pains to combat it.

Let us add that the fundamental leveling tendency of Christianity toward social distinctions, whatever its compromises in actual practice, called forth little sympathy from men who still retained some of the pride of the great *gentes.* Obedience to clergy, or bishop, no matter what their birth and family station may have been, could not be very agreeable to them.

Little by little, however, this resistance began to yield. To begin with, an aristocracy which does not function at the same time as a political party finds it difficult to withstand growing government disfavor, and undoubtedly tradition capitulates more readily than a stiff religious belief—and this particular faith was now almost the exception among these aristocrats.[6] Then the misfortunes of the age, especially in the fifth century, induced many of them to take up asceticism which, though not exclusively Christian, was much in sympathy, however, with Christianity and at this very time in the form of monachism was spreading inside it. Lastly, the ladies

[6] The most interesting of these exceptions seems to be Praetextatus, an important official of the second half of the century, an ardent theologian and a very pious priest of several cults.

of rank very soon succumbed to the mystic and ascetic Christian faith offered them by eloquent and enthusiastic monks. The most exalted Christian personages in Rome toward the end of the fourth century are Melania, Paula and her daughters. All of them are great ladies, whose zeal urges them to leave the world and lead the life of ascetics. They finally settled in Palestine, the one under the guidance of Rufinus, the others under that of Jerome, both of them monks.

Side by side with the aristocracy of birth, the aristocracy of the intellect for a long time refuses its adhesion to the Christian faith, and often, indeed, it pretends to treat it as beneath its notice. In place of the family traditions of the aristocrats, the intellectuals have a superstitious reverence for Hellenism. I mean by this an admiration of Greek thought and literature which is more sentimental than aesthetic. All Hellenic culture is really steeped in paganism, inseparable indeed from the ancient myths and the gods of old. Moreover, the Neoplatonic philosophy, under the influence of Porphyrius and still more of Jamblichus, became a liberal syncretism or composite in which metaphysics, theurgy or magic, and the doctrine of the Mysteries are all close neighbors. It offers all the required materials for the reinterpretation of the myths and the inflation of the gods. The Mysteries themselves, are still sturdy and add to this powerful composite their sensual emotions, their hopes and consolations. A superabundance of benefits is at times harmful. In the mass they may overwhelm man, who cannot enjoy them unless he can dominate them. When it comes to classification these ideas, doctrines, theories, symbols, customs, traditions form such a confused mixture that no one can combine the whole into a true-born religion. Those who, like the Emperor Julian, attempt to do it, achieve only a pietism which is certainly sincere, but vague, entirely personal and really *incommunicable*. From the "common heap" offered to him each one makes his choice, and carves out a religion that suits him. At the most there are only a few schools of philosophy which have neither the cohesion nor the overflowing vitality of the Christian churches. For this reason the effort to restore the ancient cults, attempted by Julian during his brief occupancy of the imperial throne (360-363), had no chance of success.

The "Apostate" was a thoroughgoing pietist and a fanatical Hellenist. As a philosopher his thinking was obscure, and his syncretism gathered as best he could do so around the central idea of ardent worship of the Sun, could scarcely pass for a creed or doctrine. He himself expressed with emphasis and a certain amount of wit his strong antipathy for the "Nazarenes." All his sophistry, however, was unable to draw up a coherent system of dogmatics which alone might make possible of success an attempt on his part to overthrow their system. So, too, as a part of his policy he endeavored in vain to create one church and one clergy out of the scattered priests and the strange rites of all the cults which he would have liked to unify. Through the force of circumstances, he was reduced to a distant and very middling imitation of Christianity, which henceforward gave expression to the religious sentiments alive in this age and the ritual customs really adapted to their needs. From our point of view, while his campaign commands our respect for its undoubted sincerity, it appears therefore like a somewhat foolish anachronism. His imperial officials made an outward show of following their master's direction. He complained of their lack of zeal. The Christians stood fast. Since Julian had neither the time nor, probably, any disposition to return to the coercive measures of Diocletian, although the Church has never been sparing in her hatred for him, really there were only some trifling annoyances chargeable against him.[7]

Proportionately with the weakening of the pagan culture (both because it produced nothing new that was

[7] J. Geffcken, *Kaiser Julianus* (Leipzig, 1914) ; A. Rostagni, *Guiliano l'Apostate* (Torino, 1920) ; P. Allard's *Julien l'Apostat* (1900-1902) betrays the same faults as the author's *Histoire des Persécutions*, a lack of critical judgment in the treatment of the documents, very dangerous in this case.

really enduring, and lived on the past, and because Christian dogmatics more and more completely absorbed the life and substance remaining in Greek thought), the intellectuals yielded by slow degrees and individually became members of the Christian body. Their attacks, which are of no interest save to scholars, had to be conducted with caution in order not to run counter to public authority. They were powerless to prevail against the contagious religious enthusiasm and the numerous urgent rejoinders of the Christians. During the fourth and fifth centuries, an extensive literature of apologetics was produced which squarely confronted all the arguments of paganism. Its lines of reasoning are not at bottom better than theirs, but neither are they any worse, and at any rate the advantage is theirs that the positions defended are not reactionary. The Christian apologists profess to preserve that which is worthy of being retained in every domain from the traditions of the past, while at the same time they find a place for it in the great current of religious thought and the tendencies of fideistic sentiment which are apparently carrying all men with them in those days.

The most stubborn resistance comes from the country people, the *pagani*,[8] through their attachment to highly specialized minor local deities and to ancient customs intrenched by superstition. Their uncouthness renders the evangelization of them a somewhat dangerous matter, inasmuch as it is difficult to persuade them to adopt different views save by impressing their imagination by a bold attack upon their sanctuaries, their idols, their sacred trees and miraculous springs. As the faith radiates from the towns, it soon finds in the rural monasteries help which is very valuable and well situated to perform good service. In many cases it succeeds in imposing itself upon these men who live off the land by the

---

[8] The word *paganus* means a dweller in the country (*pagus*). It has now been demonstrated that the hostility of the peasantry to Christianity gave the meaning of "pagan" to *paganus*. This seems to date from the first half of the fourth century and it gradually becomes general in the second half.

gradual penetration of daily pressure; in others, it converts with one stroke a village or even an extensive district. The method oftenest used is the method of substitution. Existing legends and superstitions are turned to its own account, which the worship of the saints renders a fairly easy operation. Saints exchange places with the well-known little divinities to whom the peasants are so profoundly attached because they demand from them so many trifling daily services. By this method the country parts are, at any rate in appearance, in the way of becoming Christianized. At the end of the fifth century this work is already far advanced.

Moreover, from the very beginning the issue of the mortal combat begun in the first twenty-five years of the fourth century could have been foreseen. The abiding success of the Christian faith in the great urban centers and in the official world, the organization achieved by the Church in contrast with the inability to act together of her scattered adversaries, and above all the vital energy pulsating within her, compared with the sinking slowly to their deaths of the old pagan religions were all tokens of the coming triumph of Christianity for which they prepared the way.

CHAPTER XI

THIS triumph which is conspicuously attested by the conversion of the Roman Empire, in the fourth century, marks an important stage in the evolution of Christianity. Victory, moreover, had been purchased at so great a cost, that it may be boldly affirmed that believers belonging to the Apostolic era would have regarded it as a catastrophe. The excuse for the Christians of Constantine's day is that no other choice offered itself as far as conditions of settlement were concerned.

At the very first glance we realize that it was not, to discriminate carefully, the disciples of Christ who vanquished the hostility of the State and moderated its opinions, it was those who ruled and acted for them; it was the Church. The advantages which the uneducated laity derived from the Constantinian compromise were one of the results of the agreement reached by two different sets of authorities, two governments, each of them instinctively seeking its own advantage first of all.

The clergy, now secure as to the future, finish the work of Church organization in the fourth century. The establishment of metropolitans (who are, in effect, archbishops) and of primates (corresponding with patriarchs) tightens up and correlates its hierarchy better, carrying it by degrees toward a pontifical monarchy in form. The multiplication of synods and councils imparts firmness and precision to the idea already held by the clergy of the *catholicity* essential to the faith, and at the same time allows them to make their discipline more uniform, and give their dogmatics wider scope. The whole body of Christians is animated by a mighty impulse to put its energy at work, and it seems to attract to itself and make part of its own substance all that the pagan world still preserves of its vital elements. Even the liturgy in which it clothes and adorns itself assumes a more spacious and brilliant aspect; it confiscates to its own uses all the pomp and dignity of the ancient cults which do not clash absolutely with the fundamental tenets of the faith.

From another point of view the Christian Church, which in relation to the State is the personification of the entire Christian population, is inclined to model her administrative organization upon that of the State and to accept its sub-divisions, county and municipal, as the boundaries of its dioceses. She tends to go further and become one of the two great branches of public administration, without relinquishing her own liberties and privileges which if need be she well knows how to defend. Due to the reflex influence of the mingling inevitable with officials of all kinds and of her conquests among the ranks of the aristocracy, a disposition to govern and manage develops within the Christian Church which separates her more and more from the laity and at the same time inclines her more and more to form political alliances. In this way the Church loses her independence; and more: the spirit of the age seeps into her so much that at last the full significance of her *raison d'être* and her mission becomes obscured.

That which strikes the least prejudiced of observers in the triumph of Christianity is first of all the power of sacerdotalism. It seems as if the whole life of the Church of Christ were contained in the consciences of the bishops. Next the huge development of theology is noticeable. The leaven in all this speculative research is always the Greek thought, which reacts upon the faith as the age does upon manners, or the State upon the Church. Christians drink deep at this abundant spring of metaphysical ideas, either directly from the writings of the Neoplatonists, whom they both despise and follow, or indirectly from the works of Origen. They may admire or condemn him, but his learned detractors exploit him almost as much as his admirers do. The fourth and fifth centuries, therefore, witness the most extraordinary conflict between transcendental doctrines, which either clash, and destroy each other or else combine. Under these conditions the thought of a few learned doctors guides the timid and unlearned. For instance, it may be a question (a) of determining the relation of the nature of the Son to the Father in the Trinity, or (b) of deciding in conformity to what modality the human nature and the divine nature that the person of Christ possessed equally act in perfect concord, or (c) if the Virgin Mary has any claim or not to the title of "Mother of God." Orthodoxy is really the opinion on which the majority in the Councils can get together, and that majority is but rarely strong enough to impose definite solutions promptly upon the whole Church. The Church as a rule makes up its mind only after hesitations which are perplexing to the simple, who, as is well known, prefer to believe that the truth is one, eternal and hence immutable.

The fresh element which appears in the doctrinal conflicts of the fifth and sixth centuries is not the disagreements as facts, nor is it the originality of the questions then at issue. In the three previous centuries difference of opinion has been the very condition of the progress of the faith, and like sustenance to it. Many of the questions also which form the subject of the later disputes to which I have alluded were raised long before. That which does surprise us somewhat is the wide range, the rancor, and the endlessness of the battles. Logic propounds problems which arise out of each other in a long succession. In truth, Christian dogma, which the third century left in too unfinished a state to satisfy the normal life of faith, is passing through an inevitable phase of further evolution. Choice must be made on more than one point between several tendencies still ill determined and indefinite. As soon as a desire arises to sift them and get them less loosely defined, discussions start, and the more important the subject, the more acrimonious are the disputes. As the scheme of dog-

matics becomes more complicated, so, too, the greater is
the difficulty experienced in coming to an agreement.
Sometimes the disputants lose all sense of proportion
both in word and gesture, and the spectacle which the
sudden turns and vicissitudes of the Arian or Monophy-
site controversy afford is really something extraordinary.
Men like Eusebius of Nicomedia, the Most Christian
Emperor Constantius, or the three terrible patriarchs of
Alexandria—Theophilus, Cyril and Dioscorus—do not
create the impression that they are very strongly attached
to the great Gospel commandment, which Jesus is
reputed to have said contained all the Law (and, consequently, one would imagine, all the theology)—to love
God and one's neighbor supremely.

It seems as if the Church has turned all those forces
which persecution no longer required to be stretched in
her defense against herself and is tearing her own body
to pieces. In reality, however, she is passing through a
crisis of growth. The outcome of her "growing pains"
will be an orthodoxy which will perpetuate the victory
of the mass over the individual, and will lay the
foundation for the necessity of intolerance in God's
name. Theology, which is the science of subtle distinctions and of conciliation, thrives upon all these
controversies, and through them it becomes in the end
of frightful importance in the Church. It tends to make
religion become scholarly; the formula prescribed settles
down into a tyranny, the initiative native to religious
sentiment grows feeble, and personal enthusiasm renders
one suspect of heresy. Henceforth doctrine will take
control of faith, an event of capital importance in the
history of the Christian life.

It is worthy of note, moreover, that all the great dogmatic controversies which disturb these two centuries
are waged in the East. The Western world does not
understand them. It has no interest of its own in them
and does not take sides unless they seem to menace
Catholic unity or to compromise the "Apostolic tradition." Of its own accord the Western portion of the

Empire fixes its attention only upon practical questions like the following: How is man's moral nature constituted, and how much may be expected from it? What is sin, and how may it be avoided? What succor may be looked for from grace, and to what extent is it necessary to salvation? Is man possessed of freewill, or is he the predestined agent of decisions which God has willed for him? The heresies known as *Priscillianism* (in the fourth century) and *Pelagianism* (in the fifth) sprang from these problems, which deal more with morals than with theology.

Nevertheless, the Catholic idea is acquiring acceptance in a more and more sharply defined form; the conviction that there can be but *one* faith and *one* Church is becoming intrenched. As a corollary the opinion gains ground that outside this one Church there is no salvation, and that she demands not only a free and filial submission ready to comply with her authorized decrees, but also assent which is inner and complete to her doctrine. The proof is still in evidence that the doctrine which is forming through much groping among violent contradictions and little by little becoming fixed continues to be but a theological syncretism or composite. Side by side with the data of the Apostolic faith are fundamentally dissimilar religious and philosophical ideas borrowed from the complex surroundings in which Christianity has been living its life, and a union is effected between them by arguments very similar to those in use by Greek sophistry, concealed beneath more or less ingenious formulas, but, at bottom, empty and deceptive. In this work the influence can be specially traced of the aristocrats of the intellect, the men of letters and the philosophers whom the faith has won over. I must repeat that in adopting Christianity, these men have not divested themselves either of the substance or even more particularly the method and forms of speculation which they had hitherto used. In recent years research has endeavored to prove that most of the Greek Fathers of the fourth century thought, argued, spoke and wrote according to the rules and methods and customs of pagan rhetoric taught in the schools of dialectics, and it has absolutely succeeded. It is even curious to observe the extent to which they have become the slaves of the devices which, openly, they profess to despise. The origin of the material they use in adapting the Christian faith to the needs of their own thinking is the very same as the forms of thought which they cannot discard: both come from the schools of philosophy which they formerly frequented.

It will appear to anyone who will look more closely into these matters that the people at large who seem submissive to their clergy representative and ready to accept their rule of faith at his hands are really far less passive than they seem. Moreover, it is in their religious life that the principle must be sought which is at the bottom of most of the transformations that Christianity has undergone. Such persons neither reflect nor reason; they pay no attention to the contradictions or even the absurdities into which they may fall, but they are quick to divine and they are easily moved. Their faith is intense and spontaneous and its demands for self-expansion are imperious. The objects dear to it must undergo inflation and their number be increased. On the other hand, ignorant people that they are, with no way of giving the suggestions of their surroundings the slip, or of discarding the habits acquired by heredity, their whole existence is still permeated through and through by paganism. Upon paganism, therefore, they will draw to obtain the elements of inflation, upon ancestral customs, time-honored rites almost bred in the bone, upon life-long beliefs and superstitions, which have come to be no longer distinguishable from their own immediate religious thought. Syncretism desired Jesus to be God, and God to remain One, at the same time; this double desire became the source of legends which made the birth and existence of Christ the most marvelous of miracles. With the worship of Mary it reinstates a genuine goddess in its religion and, upon the addition of the worship of the

Saints, this becomes a veritable polytheism, the elements of which are often taken from the legends of the pagan heroes. Naïvely convinced that nothing is too good for God, it desires to find in "the house of the Lord" all the old idolatrous splendor of the pagan ceremonies. With its confidence in the value of gesture and formula, it reintroduces all the magic of the Mysteries, and even worse, that of Orphism, which is the Mystery of the populace. Naturally, this bent of the popular faith puts the theologians to a good deal of embarrassment, but it is their business to extricate themselves by discovering, cost what it may, the compromises or adjustments which may be necessary.

Moreover, from the fourth century onward, means of expression which are very effective are placed at the disposal of the popular religion, because the monks from this time begin to multiply. Not all assuredly are men of the people, for the monastery soon attracts many of the sensitive souls whom the world intimidates or harrows, many high-hearted Christians who more or less clearly understand that the Gospel code of morality, which is dear to them, ill accords with the exigencies of the age, and that the Christianity which suits their world in general is not Christianity according to the mind of Jesus. In the ranks of the monks, however, these form but a minority. Their ardent piety, moreover, in perpetual dread of temptation, is naturally favorably disposed to the inflated conclusions reached by the faith of the simple-minded, and derives fresh comfort from them; it often puts strong props under them, gives them its encouragement and perfects them. A St. Jerome is a prey to the rebelliousness of the flesh which he seeks the means of vanquishing both by mortifications and by meditating upon the mystery of the virginity of Mary. This will lead him not only to accept it at the full scope already accorded it by the popular religion in affirming the perpetual virginity of the Mother of Jesus, but, as it were, to carry it a step beyond by propounding, as a corollary, an affirmation of the perpetual virginity of Joseph. The majority of the monks came from the people. Their common fund of religious passion, its intensive cultivation by them, the authority derived from the saintliness of their lives, the wild stubborn vigor of their asseverations, the genuine moral greatness of the most notable ones, whose glory shed luster upon them all because their rule of life placed them all upon the same footing—all these things redounded greatly to their advantage with ordinary believers. Much against the grain, they also compelled the ecclesiastical authorities to reckon with them. The desires and suggestions of the popular faith reached their culmination in their hands; through their agency they were clarified, sifted, arranged and finally imposed upon the theologians who had to adjust themselves to them as best they might.

Thus, by a sort of unintentional collaboration of influences of somewhat diverse origin, yet convergent in their effect, a religion very different from the Christianity that we caught a glimpse of in the beginning of the third century acquired shape and form in the fourth, and has become practically mistress of the Roman world when the fifth century opens.

When we think of Christianity in the Middle Ages these are the features that stand out: it is universalist in temper and given to warfare; exclusive, violently intolerant, to the Jews especially menacing; bristling with peremptory dogmas which set reason at defiance; marked by complex elaborate rites, mighty in their potency and mysterious; cluttered up with innumerable special "devotions" addressed to a good many Virgins fairly distinguishable from one another, and also to a good many specialized Saints; directed by a clergy in control of the faith and conscience of the laity who already form a strict hierarchy and tend more and more to take their orders from one sole center; kept up to the mark by a formidable army of monks and kept in check by a quibbling troop of acute theologians. If we first look upon the countless magnificent churches in which it has its abode, and the splendid ceremonies carried out therein surrounded by the symbols which inspire them, and then compare it with the religion of the Galilean prophet, humble and gentle, who claimed only to announce to his brethren the Glad Tidings of the coming of the Kingdom and to make them worthy of receiving it, compare it, I repeat, with the religion of this same Jesus, whose simple piety lifted his soul toward the God of his fathers by its childlike confidence, it is difficult to discover what these two have in common. It seems as if it is the philosophical and religious form of paganism, with all its contrarieties and incoherences, that has taken on fresh life under the name of Christ and triumphed over the religion "in spirit and in truth" which the Jewish-born Master had taught and lived. Nevertheless, unlike as they may be, the Christianity of a St. Thomas Aquinas, of a Peter the Hermit, of Jesus or of St. Peter are joined across the course of the ages together by a bond fragile but real. The needs of life, if it was to be preserved, have determined and made subject to inevitable evolution the movement whose starting point was the rise of Jesus. Thomism, as well as the faith of a Crusader, the theology of St. Augustine, the gnosis of Origen or the Gospel of St. Paul are but stages in this history. It is no less true that the *triumph* of the Church in the course of the fourth century was rendered possible only by the failure of the early faith, of that which we may call the faith of the Twelve.

II

It was the misfortune of Christianity to be based from the first upon the great hope of the *parousia.* An admirable and unattainable plan of life is easy to sketch out, given the conviction that all human existence may come to an end at any moment, and that during all eternity fruits will be reaped from the efforts of the remaining few days. Now this great hope was not realized and constant postponement delivered over Christians in general, like other men, to all the temptations of their animal nature and the downward drag of atavistic tendencies. While they did not in practice renounce the ideal of life without which their religion would have lost its meaning, they no longer sought its realization. With them, a belief in dogmatic assertions and a faith in the magic efficacy attached to certain rites took the place of the personal effort which the Gospel demanded. This deterioration did not begin in the fourth century, signs of it appeared some time before—but that triumph gave it fresh impetus, simply because the extremely numerous conversions of that time brought into the Church too hastily prepared believers who for that reason were less capable of keeping in check the basic force of life, so formidable to every religion.

Henceforward the incubus of persecution is no more, and the Christian can lead a normal existence; now his duties as a believer have become more entirely distinct from his needs as a man. His duties consist of certain obligations, of which even the number and especially their exactingness tend to become less hard and fast;[1] his needs, on the other hand, multiply practically without any restriction, in line with the forms which custom has ordained for the ordinary life of the day. In other words, the mystic struggle which primitive Christianity undertook against life had ended in complete defeat. In fact, the Church accepted and acquiesced in it, and was content to transform the ideal which contains the very essence of the primitive faith and indeed constituted her own *raison d'être* into a theme for pious meditation.

The entire Greco-Roman way of living is still there underneath an appearance of Christianity, and goes on side by side with the ideal just referred to which disowns it without inconveniencing it. The chief visible result at the beginning of the fifth century, therefore, from all points of view regarding the triumph of Christianity, is that it was triumph in appearance only. Far from hav-

---

[1] In this way the services performed in the church by degrees grow shorter, and it soon becomes the custom for the ordinary members of the congregation to take no part in them except on Sunday.

ing transformed the Greco-Roman world, Christianity was really absorbed by it and applied to its own atavistic needs and customs in the whole domain of both mind and body. And because in so far as the Church has become a governing power and in that way lent herself to compromise and concession, and because the Church has also *triumphed* on these same lines, although she had previously identified herself with Christianity, it is the Church who is responsible for the consequences which inevitably followed.

She has become one of the different aspects of the Roman State; with its machinery and its gifts of administration, its insistence upon order and regularity, she has also taken over its dread of too original and enthusiastic individuals who agitate and confuse the simple-minded, and interrupt the lilt of the long-hallowed social rhythm. She only pays the old ideal the tribute of maintaining it as the chosen theme for its sermons; it no longer exercises any real or profound influence upon the policies of the "nominal and external Christianity," as Tolstoi calls it, with which little by little the Church learns to be satisfied, as far as the observance of the ordinary layman is concerned.

The fifth century, in bringing about the downfall of the imperial power in the West, will at first seem to elevate that of the Church, since it will make her in some sort the Empire's successor in the political and social domain, as she has already become its substitute in the domain of religion and ethics. In the Roman world overthrown by the barbarians she will remain the sole organization in which there still dwells the old Roman principle of unity and centralization, and very soon she will think of making a really monarchic control for herself a reality. The security afforded by her protection will when that takes place become a very active means of propaganda, and her *catholicity* will gain accordingly. But the fresh temporal power that she will acquire will plunge her deeper into *secularism,* still further alienate her from her primary *idealism,* and tie her more closely to the *realism* of life here below. Yet more, neither her doctrine nor especially her morals will gain anything, and there will arise within the Church that idea of the necessity of "reform" which is destined to be the bugbear of her existence for many centuries.

One special circumstance, however, singularly furthered this capitulation of the Church in practice to the world. Its importance from another point of view has been pointed out, and I return to it here. At all times men were to be found in the Church, or upstanding characters by her side, who did not admit that the Christian doctrine, under whatever aspect it be considered, was only an unrealizable ideal, who made an heroic effort to embody it in their own persons. They protested with splendid vigor against any disavowal of the divine rule of life; they cast a blight upon all capitulation. Tertullian and Commodian were men of this attitude; so also was the Montanist sect and, to a lesser degree, the Novatianists. In the fourth century their breed has not become extinct, and, logically, the excessive amount of the evil ought to increase their zeal. And, indeed, it actually does.

A profound current of asceticism and austerity runs through the entire Christian life of the fourth century, and, as a matter of fact, all the religious life of the time. At first glance surprise may be felt that it should not have more visibly counteracted the movement which swayed the Church in the other direction we have described. The explanation will be found in the fact that organized monasticism has come into being, and that the convent doors stand wide open to Christians who repudiate the disquieting concessions made to the spirit of the age and seek the means of living in genuine conformity to the real Christian code of morals.

There are isolated ascetics who live in the world and become noted for their austerity. They receive a spectator-like admiration from the simple-minded, but they do not influence them very much, because the ecclesiastical authorities keep an oversight upon the sometimes

indiscreet zeal of these extremists in order to prevent
them from disparaging the ordinary life of the world, and
especially from preaching against marriage and the
varieties of food usually cooked and served. The truth
is that it is the works of the flesh and the use of meat and
wine that most offend them. In the fourth century, a
Spanish monk named Priscillianus undertakes to *restore*
the observance of the primitive Christian discipline by
the faithful. Most of the other bishops in his own
country consider him a dangerous fanatic. They become
suspicious and accuse him of Manicheism because that
religion, Persian in its origin, taught strict asceticism,
and they succeed in having him suppressed by the
secular authorities. In Gaul, St. Martin, Bishop of Tours,
the worship of whom was to become so widely extended
some time after his death, spends his life in the isolation
in which his episcopal brethren seclude him because of
the severity of his personal asceticism and the "bad
example" it sets. As soon as the number of hurt, uneasy
and burdened souls increases, the Church brings the
monastery into play as a "safety-valve." I do not mean
to imply that she deliberately removes the faithful who
are an inconvenience from the field of secular life, but
simply that she indicates to those among them whose
hearts are set upon the pursuit of the ideal that the means
of attaining it is to step out of life in a very real sense
without waiting for death. Oftenest she has but to leave
them to themselves and even as early as the fourth century it already sometimes appears wise to thwart hastily
undertaken vocations.

In this way, by a kind of differentiation between
finished and unfinished, the "believers" and the "perfect," such as existed in Buddhism and Manicheism, two
categories of Christians come into being. Both subscribe
to the same doctrine, but it is understood that a curtailed
application of its precepts in practice shall suffice for the
salvation and will agree better with the capacities of the
vast majority of men. The application of them in their
entirety is reserved for a chosen few. Their hardy vir-

tues are deemed to be an offset for the weaknesses shown by the multitude who, moreover, have at their disposal also effective means of "compensating" or making amends on their own account. Included in these means are the exercise of charity in the form of almsgiving and by testamentary dispositions, and "works of piety" of all kinds. It has been very truly said: "The true Christian is the monk." Thanks to the monk also Christianity has been able to adapt itself to the life of the world and yet not quickly become anemic, nor allow itself to be submerged in the inevitable undertow of return to old pagan customs in religious matters, which persist long after the positive faith which justified them has ceased to exist.

III

Such, then, is the account which the triumph gives of itself from the Christian standpoint. From the more general point of view of the history of religions it presents itself differently.

First of all we must remember that primitive Christianity was essentially an *Oriental* religion, an edifice for which Judaism provided the foundation and all the materials of the superstructure were obtained from the Hellenistic world, in which Greek and more accurately Eastern (Asiatic, Syrian, Mesopotamian, Iranian and Egyptian) influences were mingled from the time of Alexander's conquests. The Western world was prepared for Christian permeation by the propaganda work done on their own behalf—along the commercial routes or in the camps—by various Oriental religious Redeeming cults, such as that of Isis, of the Great Mother of Phrygia, of Mithra and others; but it took no part itself in the formation of the new religion. It gulped it down whole, as it were, and after assimilation by it, Christianity became more massive and stricter.

It was unable to grasp, and still more to express, in the undifferentiated Latin at its command, the subtle, fluid qualities of the Greek thought, the foster mother of early theology. The intricacies of the mystic impressions of the East which explain so many of the eddies in the main stream of the faith during the first few centuries altogether escaped it. Nourished altogether upon legal learning as it was, it instinctively tended to encase Christian metaphysics within strictly circumscribed, rigid formulas, and to codify religious ethics with great exactness. It was really this method of procedure, which gave Christianity the physiognomy that it retained in Western Europe, with which we also are most familiar. But it presented another face to the world at the time of its triumph, which it will not actually begin to lose until the fifth century, under the influence of the Roman Church. In the fourth century we are still dealing with a purely Eastern religion.[1]

Our account of the state of religion in the East at the time of Jesus and of St. Paul showed the existence of a vast mass of religious material derived from cults that were either out of date, or abolished. While this material was still largely amorphous, it was in a fair way to be reintegrated around a certain number of crystallizing cores, under the molding influence of tendencies both definite and general. In other words, very urgent religious needs abounded throughout the whole of the East. Dominant among them was a desire for salvation, the certainty that man alone could not compass it, and that the help of a divine mediator was necessary, and also the conviction that by a worthy life and efficacious rites this life-giving aid would be his due. These needs sought means of self-expression by utilizing the ancient cults and inflating the old myths.

To tell the truth, these form too narrow a framework to be an adequate setting for ideas that are constantly growing, and for which they were not designed. More-

[1] I do not mean to say that the transformation of Christianity in a juridical and ritualistic direction had not already been begun in the churches in Italy, Africa and Gaul, but merely that, until the time of the triumph, these churches, that of Rome excepted, have little radiating power with which to penetrate the popular mind and that all doctrinal life still comes from the East.

over, the reappearance of the same identical basic prejudices and theories in one cult after another thereby gave rise to the idea of a reintegration comprehensive enough to include or surpass them all. Men had only to look around them and to reflect a moment upon the facts to realize that the Mysteries of Isis, setting aside the sacred history, were of the same religious substance as those of Adonis or Attis. Now the solution of Apuleius, who sought and obtained initiation into all the great Mysteries in succession, was not within the grasp of everybody. An instinctive syncretism had propounded the problem; during the second and third centuries, a self-conscious syncretism sought the solution of it. Each redeeming cult exalts its god as its solution to the status of a Supreme Divinity, of which the others are but aspects or functions, as it were; he absorbs them all into his composite being. That is an imperfect and inadequate solution, for these reasons: in the first place, too many separate cults as a matter of fact still remain extant; then the syncretistic process leaves too much to individual fancy; finally, when all is said it remains practically incomprehensible and inaccessible to too large a proportion of human beings. This is the explanation, in the second half of the third century, of the necessity which is distinctly felt for a more inclusive and substantial coördination.

In short, Christianity constitutes the first, in order of date, of the attempts made in this direction, and it was also the first to succeed, because its Jewish antecedents gave it the advantage of a fundamental monotheism and of an exclusiveness, intolerant, to be sure, but at that time also salutary. That exclusiveness was a guarantee of individualism which did not prohibit it from borrowing, but obliged it to assimilate these appropriations immediately and convert them into one coherent whole. Undoubtedly there arose, within the body of Christians, differences of opinion which were sometimes very serious over fundamental questions. These differences might even lead to secessions and to the forming of sects. In any case there remained a body of general opinion, the conviction of the majority, which soon reduced dissenters to the position of heretics. In this process of defining its own thought more sharply, it must necessarily strengthen itself against their errors.

It has long been believed that about the time Christianity became well rooted in the Empire, entertained the idea and even had acquired the rudimentary constitution of an orthodox doctrine, *i.e.*, in the course of the third century, the world was halting between giving its allegiance to Christ or to Mithra. This, I believe, is a gross exaggeration of the undeniable influence of Mithraism. Its methods of propaganda are much narrower and more restricted in their operation than those of Christianity. It never gathers any but small and scattered coteries. It deprives itself of the indomitable proselytizing spirit of women by admitting men only to its initiations. It possesses naught of what is needful to make it, or cause it to become, a popular religion in the wide sense of the term. The real enemies of Christianity are to be found elsewhere.

These true antagonists are two religions, Oriental like itself. They originate in the same general trends of thought as itself, are nourished by the same religious sentiments and deal with the same religious matter that has been described. These are known as Neoplatonism and Manicheism. Originating in the same religious crisis as did Christianity, these two take shape and form at the same time, in the second half of the third century. Although at first sight they differ from Christianity and from each other in their forms, their starting point, their mythical setting and sacred stories, the selection and systematic arrangement of their main elements, still they present the same general characteristics.

Thus Neoplatonism preserves the aspect of a philosophy which relies, if I may put it thus, for its *spiritual* foundation, upon Plato's thought, bringing it into line with the speculative ideas of the age, and on its *supernatural* side borrows its conceptions from Olympic polytheism. It is plain at once that philosophic specula-

194

tion here is but an instrument of adaptation which serves to interpret this polytheism by symbols, subordinate it to Oriental *monolatry* (that is, to the worship of the Sun which is at the bottom of all the Oriental religions of Salvation) and to develop into a pantheism.[3]

Manicheism, on the contrary, rests upon Chaldean dualism as its base: the myth fundamental to it is the struggle between light and darkness, good and evil, spirit and matter. Its doctrine originates in the revelation of a prophet, Mani, and not in the reflections of a school of thinkers. Its elements are borrowed from a far wider field of thought than Neoplatonism or even Christianity, since they are derived from Mesopotamian, Persian, Buddhist influences, together with those of Gnosticism, which forms the major portion of its groundwork.

IV

These three religions are mutually antagonistic and clearly marked by a spirit and tendencies which are unlike; but yet, how many points they have in common! All three have broken with the old conception of the national religion; all are universalist; all, obviously, account for the world and life in the same way, or at any rate, by the use of the same method; all three maintain that they can rescue man from his state of misery and lead him to eternal salvation in God; all three are at heart monotheistic, and all desire that man shall obtain life immortal and bliss by submitting to the rites of its cult and the rule of an austere morality.

From the beginning Neoplatonism shows itself to be distinctly inferior: it has no founder, and never succeeds in discovering one; it cannot refer its doctrine to a personal manifestation of a God who authenticates and, so to

[3] The first two great masters of the school, Plotinus and Porphyry, still very much dread the allurement of superstition, and this is one of the reasons for Porphyry's hostility to Christianity; their successors, beginning with the illustrious Jamblichus, give more and more attention to religious questions and to pagan apologetics rather than to really philosophical research; they pose as the defenders of *Hellenism* against the *barbarous* intolerance of the Christians.

speak, lends concreteness to the revelation which it maintains has been committed to it. For this reason it never
loses the appearance of an artificial religion, a kind of
abstract and very personal theory. It is very different
with Manicheism, which has Mani for its objective justification, as Christianity has Jesus.[*]

Christian doctors have usually represented Manicheism
to be a Christian heresy. Nothing appears to be more
inaccurate, for it is but *secondarily* through contact with
Christianity and for reasons of propaganda in a Christian milieu, that the doctrine and history of Manicheism
have acquired a Christian physiognomy. The capacity
for syncretism displayed by Manicheism was not
exhausted by its founder, but it is as an original religion
that it first presents itself. If Mani considers himself a
spiritual descendant of Jesus, whom he counts among
the messengers of God who have preceded him, it is the
Jesus of the Gnostics that he has in mind, for he owes
nothing, or scarcely anything, to the Galilean Gospel.

He preaches a religion of salvation by the path of
renunciation, just as Christianity did in the beginning,
but it is, metaphysically speaking, much simpler and
clearer and more strictly logical than Christianity, and
from the moral point of view more austere and searching. The calumnies which the orthodox Christians once
more revamped and circulated with respect to it have no
more foundation than when they were used earlier (for
the same things were said) with regard to the Christian
gatherings. After a brilliant, rapid success, Manicheism
found its good fortune abruptly brought to an end by
the fierce opposition of the Roman State, which regarded
it as an anarchic movement more to be dreaded even
than Christianity, a sort of extreme Montanism, bound
to lead all its sectaries to abandon all their duties as
citizens and men. Moreover, since it came from Persia,
the hereditary enemy of the Empire, it could not agree
with the Romans. Such was the point of view taken by

[*] Mani, Manes or Manicheus was born in Babylon in 215 or 216, and
was put to death in Persia between 275 and 277 A.D.

the emperor Diocletian when (about 300 A.D.) he issued a terrible edict pronouncing the harshest penalties for the Manicheans, evidently intended to accomplish their total extermination. The hatred of the Church, who regards this rival religion as a renewal of Gnosticism, far more redoubtable than its predecessor of the second century, leads it to concur heartily in the views of the State.

And here we have the true cause of the final failure of Manicheism, in itself a very interesting and potent religious movement. Despite the relentless persecution to which it was subjected for many centuries, it betrayed surprising vitality. Its doctrine, to be sure, was no more rational than the theological metaphysics of Christianity, but it was a little simpler. If its inhumanly strict code of morals could scarcely hope to win the acceptance of the masses, the happy distinction drawn by it between the "elect" and the "hearers" allowed of more than one compromise. To be convinced that this is true we have but to recall the success of Albigensianism in the South of France in the Middle Ages, for that seems to have been essentially a Christian adaptation of Manicheism. As to its chances of success among the intellectuals, to realize that they were considerable it is enough to remember that St. Augustine was won over by it and professed himself satisfied with it for many years. After the illustrious doctor had seen nothing blameworthy in the Manichean gatherings while he belonged to the sect, we are sorry that he should have later betrayed such weakness as to collect, and publish over his name, the unworthy twaddle derogatory to them current in Christian circles.[5]

At the time when Manicheism began to be a cause of disturbance the Church already had the advantage over it that she was fairly organized; her unity and cohesion, which episcopal discipline energetically maintained, were easily able to cope with Manichean local groups which stayed isolated and felt forced to remain secret. In her fight against the asceticism of the Manicheans and

[5] Particularly in his *De moribus manichæorum* 2, 19, 70, and in his *De haeresibus* 46.

their anti-secularism, she had at her disposal the effective weapon which she employed to neutralize her own too ardent zealots: I mean monasticism. Thus Manicheism exerted upon the development of Christian monasticism an influence difficult, it is true, to estimate in these days, but at any rate considerable. Moreover, Manichean tendencies will long remain an object of dread to ecclesiastical authorities, and many a time will furnish an occasion or a pretext for the severest accusations. Priscillianus, the Spanish bishop, perished as the victim of one of these in 385.

While there was little chance that the world would be converted to Neoplatonism, on the other hand, it might very easily have become Manichean in the fourth century. The explanation why it became definitely Christian must be sought particularly in the advance of the Church and the strides taken in the process of her organization and propaganda. She had already adapted her catechetics to the needs, *i.e.,* to the customs of the average person, whilst her theology offered matter in abundance for the intellectuals to theorize upon. We must look for the explanation, too, in the support extended by the State, which persecuted the Manicheans, and in the help given by monasticism, for it opened a way for Christians naturally inclined to Manichean austerity to lead a rigorous life, whilst remaining in the Church to its edification.

In other words, Christianity supplanted Neoplatonism and Manicheism during the decay of the old world because it could express their own tendencies better than they could themselves and also express the one not to the exclusion of the other, but together balancing and harmonizing them. The especial reason for its victory was its ability to regulate them to the actual point of correspondence with the needs of all the various classes of men who were seeking spiritual sustenance for themselves. Three centuries of experience with difficulties of all sorts were the source of a ready tact which enabled it to avoid wild theses and intolerable forms of discipline; it had acquired a sense of *life.* Real life filled its veins and bore it along with itself. Similarly, Christianity blended itself with life in the spiritual domain and did it with such extreme facility that the proof lies on the surface if one good look be taken at the heart of the facts.

Let us note, moreover, that in supplanting Neoplatonism and Manicheism in the fourth century, indirectly Christianity partially absorbed them, taking over the dogmatics of the one and the ethics and discipline of the other; it did not really obliterate them. They will continue to live on by its side. Neoplatonism will pass into the philosophic treatises which will long continue to give direction to the theories of Oriental metaphysics, and be productive all through the Middle Ages of profound infiltrations in Western theology. Manicheism will be prolonged and perpetuated by various widespread sects which at various moments of recovery will put forth formidable, tough-lived heresies which will cause the Catholic Church great uneasiness. Simply by the effort she will make to repress them, if no more, Manicheism will exercise a lasting influence upon her spirit and her institutions.

PART II

THE MIDDLE AGES

THEOLOGY AND THE PAPACY

CHAPTER XII

HENCEFORTH we shall consider the Western Church by itself. The Eastern Church has a history of her own, dependent upon the animating spirit special to her, the language she speaks, the circumstances in which her life evolves. Her influence upon the religious life of the Western world since the beginning of the Middle Ages has been very slight.

From the earliest centuries of the Christian era the Eastern peoples were possessed of a genius for speculative religious thought, a taste and faculty for theological discussion, to which their versatile language with its delicate nuances was moreover well adapted. They were the originators and the fathers of a system of dogmatics which, after many heated discussions, was settled as to its chief outlines at the beginning of the fifth century. But in the end they became engulfed in their own subtlety. In condemning Origen particularly, and his writings and methods, at about the time mentioned, they inadvertently shut themselves off from the main highway for their speculative thought, and the path that it had been following for more than a century. They dissipated their thought upon details and frittered it away in sorry disputes, so that it was not long in reducing its tethers to the measure of their ordinary preoccupations. In the middle of the eighth century, John Damascenus, in whom the spirit of the great doctors of old seems to revive, constitutes an exception as remarkable in this arid age as it is unique. It might therefore be said that from the day the Byzantines lost habitual

[1] See the bibliography in G. Ficker and H. Hermelink's *Das Mittelalter* (Vol. II of Kruger's *Handbuch der Kirchengeschichte*, 1912) ; Taylor, *The Mediœval Mind*, (1920) ; V. Eicken, *Geschichte und System der mittelalterlichen Weltanschauung* (1917).

contact with the practical and well-balanced Latins, they did no more than mill round in a circle. It was certainly not through their own fault that this invigorating contact was lost. The disruption of the Western Empire and its dismemberment by the Teutonic hordes seemed to plunge the Latin world into barbarism once more, and the Western people forgot their Greek; the bishop of Rome himself knew it no better than the rest. The turmoil of the time affected both conquerors and conquered, and regular communications and consecutive negotiations, nay, even intermittent and passing intercourse, between one end of Christendom and the other, became extremely difficult. The outcome was the Teutonizing of the West, by which it acquired a new spirit which did not harmonize with that of the Eastern peoples, but was held in contempt by them. Italy indeed did for some time remain a common ground upon which the two worlds still met, but the Byzantines, by too harsh behavior as masters, made an enemy of the bishop of Rome, who could not rest until they had been expelled.

From the beginning of the eighth century the relations between the two groups of Christians combined to set them at variance. On the one hand, the patriarchs of Constantinople found the pretensions of the Roman Pontiff intolerable. One of them, in the ninth century, by name Photius, broke off relations; in 1054 another, Michael Cerularius, exploiting both doctrinal differences —such as that upon the procession of the Holy Ghost,[2] and differences in liturgical custom—such as the use of ordinary bread (the Eastern custom) for communion as against the use of unleavened bread (the Western custom), made the breach a final one. It is very clear that this rupture with the other half of the Church, which had actually founded and fashioned the faith, could not be accomplished without serious harm to the Western Church. It had never possessed true theological capacity, that fertility of mind and resourcefulness in

[2] Did the Holy Ghost proceed from the Father alone, or from the Father and the Son? The Eastern Church maintained the first, the Western Church the second, assumption.

the expression of dogma at once wide and profound, by means of which the Eastern Church had advanced from the Apostles' Creed in the direction of the Nicene Creed and that of Constantinople. Such a cast of mind was responsible for troubles and disputes, no doubt, but it was also the agency of continual advance, I mean, of uninterrupted readjustments between the faith and the changing needs of men's religious consciousness. The Western Church, thoroughly imbued as it was with the juridical and practical Roman spirit, had taken little interest on her own account in any questions save those relating to morality, ethics, discipline and organization. It may even be said that it was always in their bearing on these main perplexities that she was interested in the doctrinal debates of the East which did reach her. In the future she will not act otherwise, and her thought ventures, except in occasional instances showing real initiative, will rarely carry her beyond the problems to which she has hitherto given the preference. Her main theological effort—which is not to be denied —tends to defense or *apologetics,* and also to the *demonstration* of the truths acquired outside her precincts, much more than to their evolutional development within them. She will make a dogma, as it were, of immobility. If it were actually impossible for her to act otherwise, she could, we may believe, have avoided the imprudence of compromising her future, by continuing to submit to the influence of the progressing thought of the East which proclaimed its immovable adherence to tradition, but kept on modifying it continually. Never could any effort of the Western Church succeed in renewing the broken bond.

On the other hand, the constant friction engendered by the Crusades, the taking of Constantinople in 1204, and the exploiting of the Greek Empire by the Western barons after the fourth Crusade, the recapture of their lands and their cities by the Byzantines less than sixty years later, were all causes of an antipathy which was shared by both sides.

Nevertheless the Greeks, after many evasions, had just decided (December 12, 1452) to proclaim, in the cathedral of St. Sophia, the treaty of union concluded at Florence thirteen years before, when Mahomet II appeared beneath the walls of Constantinople, and the city was taken on the 29th of May, 1453. By the decree of the Sultan (joyfully obeyed upon *that* occasion) the Florentine compromise was soon repudiated, and the Greek Church, divided into racial congregations slightly connected with one another, had henceforth enough to do to maintain her existence under the Turkish rule, without seeking to recover the lost tradition of her former theological activity. As a set-off, however, she gave in to the demands made upon her by the faith of the simple folk whose distresses she consoled and whose hopes she upheld, and grew more and more meticulously ritualistic. In the process, she paganized herself, gave herself to schooling as little as possible and, sunk to the state of religion characteristic of stationary peoples, she lived, like them, without budging an inch, and without doing any thinking. It is not until our own days that she, and the churches in the East born of her, have shown any serious signs of awakening. Throughout the Middle Ages, she scarcely influenced the faith of the West except to act as a source of disturbance if, as it seems reasonable to believe, one at least of her heresies (that of the Paulicians, arising toward the middle of the seventh century out of an Armenian church, which maintained the creed of the ancient heresiarch Marcion) little by little gained a footing in the Western countries, and became one of the sources of Albigensianism.

II

It might be said that the ancient history of Western Christianity came to an end with St. Augustine. The age in which the great doctor lived witnessed the occurrence of decisive events which razed the Roman world of the West to its very foundations and denoted its end.

In his great work, too (the product of an uneasy mind
and a spirit always progressive), the whole Christian
thought of the first four centuries was epitomized and
interpreted, cleared up and put in good order by the
profound, though not always visible, aid of Platonic principles. His mind put all the ideas current in the Church
before his day to the test, and his doctrine constitutes
a landmark, erects a ledge, as it were, in the increasingly
steep climb upwards of the faith. For this reason it can
be said with equal exactness that all the medieval evolution of Christian theology in the West originated with
St. Augustine. He forms the real connecting link between ancient Christian thought and the speculations of the Schoolmen. Moreover, his rôle does not
come to an end with the overthrow of the Schools. He
is the founder of the mysticism of the Reformation as
well as of the Middle Ages, and he is an inspiration to
Protestantism as he was to the medieval Church. This
does not mean that his influence, still so powerful in the
seventeenth century, in which it engenders Jansenism,
is the only one at work for more than twelve centuries,
but it did continue to be the basis of all speculative
thought, even the most syncretistic and the most foreign
to his spirit. In the long and intricate symphony composed of the theological thought of the ages which have
followed him, it constitutes, we might say, the deep
thorough-bass which it is not always necessary to express,
but which does provide a foundation that can confidently be relied upon for the most daring developments
of the melody.

It is not only the most conservative tradition and the
most scrupulous orthodoxy that seek and find props,
throughout the Middle Ages, for themselves in the writings of St. Augustine. His doctrine—except for some
extravagant theses upon predestination which theologians
have disregarded by common consent—is looked up to
as the supreme authority by the doctors of all schools.
Before risking disagreement with him on the smallest
point, they make use of all the tricks of interpretation

known to them to effect a reconciliation. They accord as much respect to explanations which have been given by him merely by the way and as simple hypotheses, as to established truths. Equally with the masters in the art of reasoning, the mystics also revere him and regard him as the mainspring of their meditation. Even the heretics defer to him: in the ninth century, Gottschalk,[3] and afterward, Luther, Calvin and the Jansenists. Nay, more, the two worlds into which Western Christianity is divided today, the Catholic and the Protestant, still meet on common ground in him. Finally, his opinions upon certain essential points of the faith, on grace and on predestination, for instance, or upon the connection between reason and revelation,[4] from his times to our own, have supplied the grist for all the discussions of the theologians. His dread statements also on the necessity of punishing the sacrilegious furnish the justification, in advance, of all the later medieval intolerance and the Inquisition.

Nevertheless, St. Augustine did more than found the Western theology, state the main themes of its speculative thought, orient its mysticism and formulate rules for its public morality. Nobody worked harder than he to strengthen in the Church (I mean in the constituted body of ecclesiastical authorities) the principle of *authority* in matters of faith. No one contributed more than he toward the adoption of the opinion that a decision of the Church is a truth against which human reason is not qualified to rebel, and that the worth of Holy Scripture

---

[3] Gottschalk was a monk who maintained man's absolute predestination, and suffered great persecution from his archbishop, the celebrated Hincmar of Rheims.

[4] Let us note, in passing from the special point of view to which Christian thought has evolved, how Augustine conceived this connection. God, he used to say, has given us our reason in order that we may know him, therefore, it can know him; but of itself, it only conceives of him *negatively; i.e.* it can only say that he is not *this* or *that.* A more direct and more positive knowledge of his nature proceeds entirely from revelation and there reason must limit itself to explaining revelation. Hence the celebrated dicta: "I believe in order that I may understand" (*credo ut intelligam*) and "faith precedes intelligence" (*fides praecedit intellectum*). This is a long way from the Greek rationalism, which was, however, Augustine's starting-point.

itself is due to the guarantee and the interpretation given it by the Church.[5] This impressive stand, which the Reformation rejected (though less entirely than it believed), was during the Middle Ages the corner stone of the Catholic edifice, so that one cannot conceive how it could have been erected without it.

Moreover, this same stand met with substantial support from the popular faith, to which Augustine well knew that he must make such concessions as contenting himself with its assent to the main points of his doctrine, shutting his eyes, when necessary, to its minor errors, and above all, its involuntary reversions to atavistic customs. But he did not understand thoroughly well what an ardent desire for stability lay concealed beneath the apparent mobility of that faith.

Simple folk are doubtless accessible to all forms of suggestion, whether they proceed from the past, or from circumstances or from environment. Their religious sensibility is more quickly stirred and reacts more profoundly when it is under the influence of group contagion, and then they usually show themselves so incapable of regulating it, that they very often put the theologians to embarrassment. Instinctively, too, they feel impelled to multiply the objects of their faith, and to inflate them. As a matter of fact, therefore, they constitute a disturbing element in the Church, more or less in evidence according to the period, but in ferment and always unstable. Nevertheless, nothing frightens them worse than the prospect of change in their belief, and nothing is more logical than such a fear. For a man to accord to any creed whatever his reasoned and well-considered assent, he must experience an ordinary need for reason and reflection; he must also be accustomed to reasoning. Experience proves that this habit is not common, but presupposes an educated mind and a daily schedule which from time immemorial has been the previous privilege of a minority, even smaller in the fifth century than it

[5] He used often to repeat that he would not believe the Gospel if the Church had not guaranteed its truth.

is today. The majority of men may indeed find that they possess within themselves a religious life in principle, but it ferments in their consciousness as a vague yearning; they prove incapable of organizing it, just as they remain impotent to regulate their minds. Of themselves they do not succeed in unifying either their intellectual or their moral ego. The necessary light and direction come to them from without, usually in the form of statements of a metaphysical kind which cannot be verified. It matters little that they are neither very coherent in themselves nor easy of justification, provided they appear to be clear and decisive. But, if they are to be classified with the Truth, they must not vary by a hair and issue from an authority worthy of confidence—or at any rate, deemed so—in which they shall find unwavering support. For this reason simple-minded faithful souls in Augustine's day, and he along with them, willingly believed that the Church represented a divine institution, established to teach unerringly and to preserve intact the eternal truths revealed by Christ and by the Holy Spirit. Do not let us forget, besides, that these fundamental assertions, these essential truths of the faith, regarded as given and not debatable, are never more than a framework. The reality of the religious thought and life enclosed in that setting varies infinitely from age to age and milieu to milieu, for the passage of time modifies the reason of educated men as it does the impressionableness of the ignorant.

III

Now at the beginning of the fifth century, the ignorant and the semi-Christians thronged into the Church in numbers. As Mgr. Duchesne has so well expressed it, "The mass was Christian to the extent that the mass could be, on the surface and according to label; the waters of baptism had touched it, but the spirit of the Gospel had not pierced it." And it could not be otherwise. The clergy had believed it necessary to hasten the conversion of the masses of people whom the imperial government delivered over to their propaganda and, sacrificing quality to quantity, they had joyfully inscribed, as converts to the faith, the names of men who knew little of it save some few formulas. They could not understand these at all well and, in making their acquaintance, they had forgotten none of their pagan customs. It would have needed much time and work to turn these neophytes into real Christians, and to shelter the doctrine, as well as the ethics, of the Christianity set up in the first three centuries from their unintentional raids. But at that time the Roman world was breaking up; everywhere premonitory signs of an approaching cataclysm were apparent and the Church herself was seriously disturbed by heretics and partisans. Accordingly it did not seem to be a favorable hour for undertaking such a long drawn out work, and the bishops of that period had to content themselves with redressing, as best they could, and in experimental fashion, the shocking malformations of the Christian faith which they perceived around them. Very soon the invasions of the barbaric hordes will render their efforts futile.

Had the choice been offered the Church of leaving the invaders to their paganism or trying to win them for Christ, her duty and her material interests alike would have dictated her decision, and would have inclined her to be content with a conversion which she could not hope would be very profound. She was not even free however to decide the matter for herself. To begin with, a good many of the barbarians were already nominal Christians when they entered the Empire. Of such were the Goths, converted in the fourth century by Wulfila, although indeed to Arianism. Most of the others, in their ardent desire to be the equals of the *Romani*, accepted the faith of the Emperor without delay. I should say that they *believed* they accepted it, for what could the clergy do with such a number in such a short time? Instruct them? It was out of the question; they had to be content with teaching them no more than the symbol of baptism and then baptizing them *en masse,* postponing until a later date the task of eradicating their superstitions, which they preserved intact. To tell the truth, this "later date" never arrived, and the Church adapted to herself, as well as she could, them and their customs and beliefs. On their side, they were content to dress their paganism in a Christian cloak.

The invincible opposition of the orthodox clergy to the Arianism of the conquerors preserved the mass of Christian believers over whom they possessed supreme influence, from heretical contamination by it. Even yet, Catholic historians attach great importance to the baptism of Clovis at the hands of St. Remi, because it made the petty kingdom of the Salic Franks a bulwark of the authentic Nicene faith. The Merovingian conquests clearly favored the elimination or the absorption of the independent thinking Burgundians, Visigoths and Ostrogoths and strengthened the authority of the Church, but these two results were not of equal importance. By this I mean that the Christian faith of the newcomers and of the "Romans" of the ordinary sort was not then so delicately differentiated that it could be really altered by a troublesome variation of opinion concerning the nature of the Son and his relation to the Father. It had by no means reached such a pitch, and according to appearances, had Arianism prevailed, there would have been no great change in the after history of the Church. On the other hand, it was by no means an indifferent matter to her for the king to be of the orthodox faith, as, in the Merovingian kingdom, ecclesiastically a model for the others, where the Church became a kind of "national" institution of which the king was the temporal chief. In return, it came to stand for the only principle then existing of social and even political unity, the only organ of union and moral discipline which was not brute force.

The most abandoned rascals now dreaded her supernatural power, by means of which she could open or close the gates of paradise to them. The surest works of merit, and above all the most efficacious form of penitence, in the ordinary opinion of the day, was a handsome donation to a church, or, if possible, to several, so as to make friends among the saints invoked therein. The example set by the princes themselves was so faithfully followed, during the sixth and seventh centuries, and the funded wealth of the clergy grew so fast and so large, that sovereigns were disturbed by it. At the same time Church lands by degrees slipped out from public obligations, taxes and military service.

This privileged position in which the Church entrenches herself is not secured without some disadvantages to her; there is another side to the picture. The barbarian kings come to look upon bishoprics as mere royal offices of which they can dispose as they please without regard to canon law,° and their selection is not always an enlightened one. They may happen to reward with a miter services which are in no sense ecclesiastical.

On the other hand, in the degree that the wealth of the Church increases, and her order and perpetuity give her a better standing, she puts stronger temptations before the very persons responsible for her improved condition. Needy princes, such as Chilperic and Charles Martel, cannot resist them. But to tell the truth, the Church does not lose in the end by these occasional spoliations; from the penitence afterward of the guilty she always exacts handsome compensation. Her staying power enables her to overcome fleeting trials; bad rulers pass away, and she remains to reap the benefits conferred upon her by good ones.

It may indeed happen that the king, with the intention of serving her interest, will compromise and vex her a great deal by interfering in her affairs with the naïve presumption of an ignorant person who is conscious of his own power. Did not one of the grandsons of Clovis, the detestable Chilperic, have the mad fancy to believe himself a theologian and the open audacity to pretend

° An edict of Clothair II in 614 calmly states this pretension as a right.

that he could elucidate in a fashion of his own the mystery of the Trinity?

Nevertheless, given the general conditions imposed upon the life of Christianity by the stifling of all culture consequent upon the fall of the Roman Empire the genuine intellectual apprehension of the Christian religion falls rapidly away into obscurity. The formulas which Churchmen go on repeating without really understanding them themselves, only serve as a mask for an unbridled immorality and a faith really uncouth and incoherent, a gross syncretism in which Teutonic superstitions, mingled with those native to the soil, really count for more than the Christian dogmas.

Then too, in alarming fashion, the cult of saints and relics and images, and a credulous trust in rites and signs, attain increasing vogue and in this way polytheism and magic manage to reëstablish themselves in the Church. These new barbarian converts to the faith brought with them an anthropomorphic idea of the Deity which coincided with and strengthened the primitive thought of God which the peasants of the Roman Empire had never entirely abandoned. The God of the Christian creed must have seemed to them very difficult of access, and the intercession of the saints, who were to them the natural successors of their old specialized and familiar gods, fascinated them far more. They therefore kept developing the cult of the saints, not a very exalted one always, it is quite certain, but a *practical* one and, if I may express it thus, good for everyday use. The saints are implored to perform useful miracles, to effect imperative cures of the sick, and to furnish in difficulties of all kinds a solution which has been sought in vain by human means. The people maintain a constant intercourse with them; they write to them and await their reply; they dread them, yet they sign and seal deeds, and even make bargains with them; they reward them when they are pleased with them, and in the contrary case, they threaten and even punish them, by withholding homage to them or, at times, by inflicting upon their images serious bodily injuries. They are taken to war in the guise of relics and they are borne in long processions as a safeguard from epidemics and other disasters; even in death their protection is sought, by the selection of a burial site as near as possible to their tombs. The ancient Roman law, already inscribed on one of the Twelve Tables, *hominem mortuum in urbe ne sepelito neve urito* ("a dead body shall neither be buried nor burned in the city"), is completely disregarded, in spite of clerical opposition; to await the hour of resurrection *ad sanctos,* and, as it were, in the shadow of the blessed, is the dearest wish of every man.

To obtain favoring relics these men are prepared to run all risks; if need be, they will snatch them by force, or steal them. To undertake a voyage is not a prudent thing for a venerable personage to do if he is in bad health; he can never be sure how far the hope of a neighborhood giving sepulcher to a distinguished corpse may impel zealous persons to go, among whom he may have to linger on the road. It is no longer possible to conceive a church that does not contain the *sepulchrum* of a saint, *i.e.* a tomb with some part of his body, or at any rate an object which has touched it and therefore into which his supernatural power (*vis*) has passed. The sanctuary which has the good fortune to possess the *sepulchrum* of a saint reputed influential and active has its fortune made; pilgrims and offerings pour into it. Thus St. Martin enriched his basilica at Tours with the gifts which fear or gratitude heaped upon his sarcophagus.

It must be understood that while devotion of that kind has little in common with Christian dogma, on the other hand it is closely and intimately bound up with pagan superstitions. Note should be taken that as a rule the Frankish kings, especially the Merovingians, do not seek to impose their beliefs on their subjects; in this connection they very rarely intervene. Nevertheless they are opposed on principle to idols, the destruction of which is imperatively ordered by an edict of Childebert I.

Failing this action by the people, they are to be destroyed by the clergy in the fields where they are still to be found in large numbers. But the disappearance of the images from the landscape was not enough to put an end to the profound superstition still vigorously active as their mere presence had testified. Beneath the Christian practices of those days, or side by side with them, it is by no means difficult to perceive a number of atavistic customs which contradict them that were also common practice.

The worship of trees and springs seems to have been particularly current. Diviners and wizards do a large business. The ancient festivals are kept as holidays and celebrated in the country parts, and the Church can only neutralize their effect by turning them to account for her own profit. There is nothing stranger, from this point of view, than the instructions given by Gregory the Great to the monk Augustine, his missionary to England. He is to transform the temples into churches, after they have been ceremonially cleansed; and to replace the devil-sacrifices by processions in honor of some saint, with an offering of oxen to the glory of God, and the distribution of the flesh among the congregation. Moreover, the king of East Anglia, Redwald, after his baptism and Christian confession, is careful to keep opposite the altar in his church at which mass is celebrated, another altar where the sacrifices demanded by the ancient gods are carried out.

It is instructive, too, to note how very small a place questions of dogma seem to hold in the matters which engage the attention of the Merovingian Councils; it is an exception and a rare exception for them to dwell upon them; all their care seems to be applied to regulating questions of ecclesiastical discipline. It would be a mistake, moreover, to believe that men, so exclusively occupied with liturgical rites and gestures, would prove very close observers of what are still called, in Church language, their religious *duties*. They do not even frequent the "Holy Table" as often as they ought to do, and

215

the Church is greatly exercised over this neglect. A Council of Agda, held in 506, even declares that those who do not communicate at Christmas, Easter, and Whit- suntide, shall not be considered Christians. Such a canon law reveals a good deal!

In those days, too, the large majority of the clergy are miserably ignorant and share in the profligacy of the age. The high standing of Gregory of Tours, a ready but very inexperienced writer, an upright man, yet possessed of a moral sense which demands little of others, serves as a standard by which to measure the depths to which his colleagues had fallen. Scarcely anywhere save in the heart of a few monasteries, the most celebrated of which is Mount Cassin,[7] in the sixth and seventh centuries, does the light of intellectual culture and of theology still even flicker. It is by his industry and his virtue, more than by his learning, that Gregory the Great, who died in 604, is nevertheless able to make a record as a Father of the Church. All creative force seems to be in a state of exhaustion after Boetius (who died about 525), and his friend Cassiodorus, who, at any rate, were scholars; Isidorus of Seville, toward the end of the century, pos- sesses the especial merit of having read a great deal, and compiled as much as possible of it all.

This sorry age, therefore, turned out a religion and a Church that was to its own mind and conformed with its needs. And it succeeded all the more easily in doing this because at the beginning of the Middle Ages there was as yet no official and complete exposition of the faith and of Christian institutions. It was continually urged that both were bound by the closest ties to the

[7] The monastery of Mt. Cassin, founded in Campania in the sixth century by St. Benedict of Norcia, was governed by the rule known as *Benedictine;* it very rapidly spread throughout Western Christendom. The monks who accepted this rule had to take vows of *steadfastness, poverty* and *chastity;* moreover, they had to promise *obedience.* Those are necessary conditions for the constitution of a monastic order, but the monks who followed the Benedictine rule, being grouped in "houses" where they led a communal life, did not at first form an "order." The "houses" were independent and for this reason the prac- tice of their rule very quickly altered. It was by the advice of Cas- siodorus that this rule gave a place to study, side by side with manual labor and devotional exercises, in the life of the monks.

Apostolic tradition and that of the Fathers, but in practice it was in St. Augustine's writings that these were
sought, and in collections of extracts, or *catenæ,* compiled
from the whole range of Patristic literature. The decisions of Councils and Synods had not yet been either
harmonized or codified. It is an easy surmise that doctrine so little set in fixed phrases and so widely dis-
seminated would be very difficult to preserve successfully
from additions and alterations. A good catechism which
the whole Church could accept would have been her best
protection in this case. But who would have been able
to edit it, and secure for it œcumenical approval, when
there was still so much divergence between the theological authorities of the past and the present-day
opinion? With a clergy sunk in ignorance, who possessed even the elementary qualifications? In the sixth
century Cassiodorus, a high official at the court of King
Theodoric, had vainly sought to establish in Rome
schools in which some of the clergy would have been
trained, and the state of affairs elsewhere can be imagined. Until the time of Charlemagne, anyone at all who
can get a bishop to accept him for that office may be a
priest; anyone at all who is elected by a church or chosen
by the king can be a bishop; but there is no regular place
where a man may prepare for his vocation. The least
ignorant of the clergy either come from the cloisters, or
have been brought up in the house of some old priest.
Such men are usually incompetent to give religious
instruction to their flocks. So they content themselves
with performing the customary rites, and that is how
the liturgy, plus certain puzzling formulas, and many
parasites in the way of superstitions which the clergy
can neither recognize nor eradicate, becomes the whole
of religion. By a strange turn of fortune, Christianity
now tends to become actually nothing more than a collection of legends and of *sacra* (acting *ex opere operato,*
like the operations of magic), and consequently to
resemble that ancient Olympic paganism whose poverty
of dogma and morals, lack of teaching capacity and

childish ceremoniousness it had formerly inveighed against so bitterly. This was the foundation, and not the completed Patristic Christian tradition, upon which the popular religion, the religion *practiced* in the Middle Ages, was reared. In the sixteenth century the Reformation will try to uproot it, and will only partially succeed.

IV

This deep humiliation of the Church and general corruption of the faith, however, in so far as they were the result of the relapse into barbarism which held sway, after the death of Theodosius, in the Western world, had not gone beyond hope of recovery. Purgation and restoration were the natural outcome of a transformation in civil life which became observable at the end of the eighth century. Its source must undoubtedly be looked for in the painstaking labors of the relatively learned monks and clerics, because these superior attainments drew them nearer to the kings; but it will be found above all in the personal goodwill of some choice sovereigns, like Charlemagne in the Frankish Empire, and Alfred the Great in England, who looked upon their kingdom as a theocracy and upon their office as priestly in character. The great effort made by Charlemagne to maintain order and justice in his realms somewhat curbed the baser instincts of their peoples. The care he took to choose only pious and zealous bishops conferred moral authority upon these heads of the Church. His diligence in establishing clergy training schools beside the cathedral churches and at the larger monasteries lessened the number of ignorant priests. In giving the bishops a share in the government by delegating to them, conjointly with, as the counts-palatine, the oversight of the provinces, for instance, he armed them with substantial authority and credit which they could use for the good of religion. At the end of the ninth century Alfred the Great followed the same methods, also limiting his ambitions, since he seems to have given his consent that the religious instruction of the body of his subjects might proceed as far as the familiar knowledge of the *Paternoster* and the *Credo*. In the tenth century the three Othos in Germany followed much the same policy in regard to these same matters.

Let us note well that this taste for letters and ardor for study, which contributed so much to establish the renown of Charlemagne and of Alfred, did not proceed from mere intellectual curiosity. As in the older case of Cassiodorus, both were anxious above all to rescue the clergy from their state of ignorance and equip them to instruct the people. That was why Charlemagne ordered the preachers to abandon the use of Latin in their sermons, and to express themselves in the vulgar tongue that they might be understood of all. In truth he was obliged to be satisfied with very little, as little as to show pleasure when a cleric knew how to read the Gospels and the Epistles, and could recite the liturgical prayers correctly.

Knowledge of this kind could not lead very far on the road to improvement and, as a matter of fact, that which is sometimes called "the Carlovingian revival" is of much more interest in its intentions than in its results. The number of monasteries in which studies were held in honor did increase, however, and churchmen at least had the impression that a far-reaching reform in morals and beliefs was involved in any return to Patristic tradition. An example was given and a pattern set for this reform in the time of Louis le Debonnaire and upon the initiative of Benedict of Aniane, in many of the monasteries which followed the rule of St. Benedict of Norcia. Finally, in proof that there was some slight revival of theological activity at that time, various heresies appeared, and doctors arose to refute them. Better still, the age of Charles the Bald produced a true theologian, a profound thinker and, therefore, one inclined to reach heretical conclusions. This was Scotus Erigena, a thinker with a far wider horizon than his contemporaries, not only on account of his own peculiar genius but because he had visited the East and knew Greek.[8]

He is a man worthy of close attention, who will exercise considerable influence, not in his own time, which did not understand him, but later, especially in the thirteenth century. He espoused a pantheistic explanation of the world, in which nature is conceived as coeternal with God, who is all in all, so much so that in all places God's is the sole presence.[9] Although Erigena tries to cover up his venturesome theses in orthodox formulas and quotations from Scripture, none the less the Christian mysteries vanish before explanations rational in character of his devising; he fills in and obliterates the abyss which Christianity acknowledges between nature and God.

It is not however this final conclusion of Scotus Erigena's thought, interesting as it is, which should detain us here for a moment; on the contrary, it is its principle and its starting-point. He derives them both (a) from that Neoplatonic philosophy which we have already seen constituted in the fourth century a rival religion to Christianity, and (b) from Manicheism. Manicheism is soon due to reappear. Long obliged to hide under cover to maintain its existence, the hour of its resurrection will strike in the Middle Ages. Neoplatonism found it more difficult to maintain a foothold in the popular faith, but it survived in the speculative thought of a few sages. It appears in a Christianized version, in the writings of the Confessor Maximus, and in those of the pseudo-Dionysius the Areopagite, and these, with the Neoplatonic treatises of St. Augustine, are exactly the original sources used by Erigena.

Thus nothing of the protective envelope which at the time of the triumph of Constantinian Christianity enfolded the living religious substance is lost or missing. Neoplatonism is going to remain as a powerful leaven

[8] St-René Taillandier, *Scot Erigène et la philosophie scholastique* (Strasbourg, 1843).
[9] *De divisione naturae*, Vol. VIII: *Erit enim Deus omnia in omnibus, quando nihil erit, nisi solus.*

in Christian theology. Besides its contribution to the formation of dogma at the time when the main doctrinal strata are laid down, it will on various occasions, and not in Erigena's case only, evoke a veritable impulse of renewal or revision. In order to give this notice in advance that the Neoplatonic influence is to be one of the profounder elements of the theological life of the Middle Ages, it was necessary to mark, chronologically, the position of the thinker who will often serve as an intermediary and vehicle for it, side by side with Dionysius the Areopagite.

Let us not make the mistake, however, of failing to recognize that the slight renewal of theological activity or at least of theological interest which is the result of the Carlovingian revival in no way denotes an appreciable transformation of the religious spirit of the masses, for they do not change their ideas so quickly. Scotus Erigena indeed took good care to emphasize the difference between his theology, which was, he said, *vera theologia* as well as *vera philosophia,* and the popular belief. As a matter of fact, the doctors who join with Gottschalk, Rabanus Maurus and Hincmar, in the dispute over predestination or the effects of the consecration of the Eucharist, take no interest in the ordinary believers, nor do these ordinary believers take any interest in them. And, although this aristocratic isolation of Christian thinkers with regard to the mass of Christians is nothing new it is none the less very disturbing. Not only will it favor the theological virtuosity which plays with empty words and juggles with abstract ideas, remote from all religious experience and concrete reality, that is so much time lost, but it will also turn the "intellectuals" of the Church aside from their real duty, which is to instruct and enlighten the ignorant, to safeguard them from themselves and the suggestions of their milieu, and to make them better people.

This does not imply that the faith of the body of believers remains fixed, but that it extends its acquisitions in the direction which the need of the hour, or the instinct most spontaneous, or the logic nearest home seems to impose upon them. Is an example necessary? Whilst Paschius Radbertus is busy clearly propounding the doctrine of transubstantiation in the eucharistic offering,[10] and Rabanus Maurus and Ratramnus are raising objections to it, the great body of ordinary believers are becoming more and more firmly attached to the belief that the consecration of the elements renews the sacrifice of the Cross. This is at first sight a very strange similitude, hard to imagine arising as a product of popular *reasoning*, but quite easily explainable through the combination of an atavistic custom with the impression which repetition invariably produces. Ancestral practices very ancient in date had bequeathed to these people the custom of considering sacrifice the essential part of worship, and it is plain to them that in their present religion the eucharistic ceremony is the central point of divine worship. Moreover, tales are told them of miracles which have testified to the supernatural character of the consecrated elements. They are therefore drawn altogether spontaneously to the conviction that the Lamb himself is the occupant of the altar during the Mass, and that the consumption of the bread and wine constitutes a genuine sacrifice: Christ is sacrificed anew at every Mass, as he was upon the Mount of Calvary. While the theories about transubstantiation will fall into perfect agreement with that conclusion, that conclusion did not spring from those theories, nor was it arrived at in order to coincide with them.

V

The political results accomplished by Charlemagne were not lasting. In less than fifty years his Empire was entirely broken up. The jurisdiction of royal authority became so impaired as to be no more than an illusion,

[10] The first use known of the word *transubstantiation* is that of Hildebert, Archbishop of Tours, who died in 1134; its first authorized use in the doctrinal vocabulary dates from the fourth Lateran Council in 1215.

222

for people whom the Emperor thought he had brought under the discipline of law fell back into absolute anarchy. The close of the ninth century and the whole of the tenth, the period in which what is known as the feudal system was set up, possibly exceeded, in violence and disorder, the dread days of the barbarian invasions. This anarchy had a direct reaction on religion, on Churchmanship, and on the Church. To say nothing of the innumerable attacks made by the barons upon churches and monasteries, which reduced the clergy frequently to penury, and always to insecurity, and rendered them unable to fulfil the task of religious instructors, it must be noted that the schools established by Charlemagne have disbanded or else merely vegetate in a few monasteries, still rich and powerful, but isolated, like that at St. Gall, for instance. In most cases it is the feudal lords, do not forget, who hold in their grasp the nomination of ecclesiastical dignitaries, and everywhere turn it into a source of revenue. That gives some idea of the prelates, men less fitted to feed their flock than to fleece it, and more versed in the articles of war than in the writings of the Fathers. With a few exceptions, such as are to be found at all times, the clergy of those days shared the vices of the laity; they were coarse, ignorant and churlish.[11] Nevertheless the poor sought the consolation and hope they so sorely needed in religion; their piety was lacking in delicacy and discernment, but it

[11] This ignorance continued long, and only disappeared, little by little, in the course of the fourteenth century, when the universities began to assert and extend their influence. It was only in the latter half of the twelfth century that the great episcopal schools of Paris and London really began to function. Until that time the best among the clergy had been trained in monastic centers, such as the Abbaye du Bec, in Normandy, St. Victor and St. Geneviève in Paris, St. Denis, St. Alban, of Fulda and Utrecht in the Holy Roman Empire, those of Cambridge and Oxford in England, of the Lateran in Rome. It goes without saying that the pupils in these schools form but an infinitesimal minority among Churchmen. Moreover, they find themselves sadly hampered by reason of the prevailing ignorance, and do not rightly know how to set to work upon it. From the beginning of the twelfth century, we find in circulation the "Bibles of the poor," which are collections of sacred pictures; but these are rare and costly and not sufficiently numerous until after the invention of wood-engraving; to be really useful they require continual exposition, and in any case they move and edify, rather than instruct.

was profound. Unfortunately, their credulity also was unbounded, and they became attached by preference to the most indifferent rites and practices because those best agree with ignorance and thoughtlessness.

I must repeat once more that Christian dogmas had been established and formulated by keen, subtle, Eastern minds. The metaphysics of the ancient Greek masters, as well as the verbal ingenuity of Greek sophists, had been large contributors at their birth. The ideas they contained and the phrases used to express them proved equally incapable of penetrating tenth-century minds. If the veritable core of Christianity dwelt within these dogmas, then the contemporaries of Otho the Great or of Hugh Capet had to content themselves with a semblance of Christianity, composed entirely of a liturgy and a few statements meaningless to them. They were obliged to accept these as truths which could not be verified. But as such enigmas do not form a religion, by which I mean, as religious sentiment, ever so slightly alive, cannot be content with anything so meager, they created a substitute for the Christianity that escaped them, which did accord with their own minds and hearts. Moreover, it proved naturally a sequel to the form it received when the peasantry and, shortly afterwards, the barbarians entered the Church. God and Christ still reigned within it, no doubt, but they did not govern; its substance is found in such particulars as these: (a) the Holy Virgin, whose virtues the monks multiply, and whose worship they develop; saints, whom, in a pinch the people themselves create,[12] specialize according to their needs, and treat their relics and images like real idols; external and showy observances which work upon the feelings and serve as a lure to religious sentiment;

[12] The people spontaneously raise to the dignity of saint, and pay that honor to anyone who appears to them worthy. Naturally, vexatious errors are by no means rare. The ecclesiastical authorities become disturbed about the matter, and in the eighth and ninth centuries we find many capitularies which aim at reserving for the diocesan bishop the right to make canonizations. It was only at the end of the tenth century, after the canonization of Ulrich of Augsburg in 993, that the Pope laid claim to the exclusive right to deal with such matters.

legends, originating none knew where, and embellished as they pass from mouth to mouth, which recall, when given a Christian label and amazing miracles for a setting, familiar conceptions and attachments.

"Philosophy" or, to express it more modestly, thought, found no place in this scheme. To tell the truth, orthodox dogma, which the thoroughgoing pantheism of Scotus Erigena had for a moment threatened, had then nothing more to fear: it soared far above the practical faith, and very few were acquainted with it or gave it a thought. Only—and it is quite understandable—the historian of sacramental theology will be able to glean material of value to him from the practices of those days. Then it was, for instance, that the anointing with oil of those in danger of death became a sacrament, and the custom of giving absolution to the sinner before his fulfilment of the penance imposed, was established. This period also saw begun an extraordinary system of penances that became, and remained, the method preferred by the ecclesiastical authorities for use in the complete subordination of the faithful. In the minds of the body of believers, this system practically confounds the rule of doctrine with a sort of catalogue of interdictions and penalties corresponding to faults and offenses which are of daily occurrence. Everything in everyday life was included, but true piety was deprived of all initiative, and religious guidance reduced to the almost automatic application of a tariff. It is convenient, but genuine religious sentiment, as well as genuine morality, has nothing to gain from it: the triumph all goes to sacramental mechanism.

The excess of the evil supplies the remedy. Just as the intolerable ills engendered by political disorder end in giving birth to an immense longing for peace and stability on the part of the inhabitants of the towns, so the Church came to realize her fallen condition and feel a desire to stand on her feet again. With a keen sense for reality, she was convinced that the deeper cause of her misery lay in the feudal anarchy, the state of perpetual tumult in which men were living. For this reason she supports with all her powers the various efforts made to restrain violence and agitation and where necessary herself took the initiative. This is the reason also that, when she could, especially in France, she placed her influence at the service of the royal authority which, like herself, was interested in securing peace. But whence came to her at this time such an understanding of her interests and of her duties? As might be expected, it came first of all from the monasteries.

They had attracted to themselves in this dread period the best Christian spirits; in them something of the intellectual culture of former days had always survived or, at any rate, a formal respect for "tradition," if not the understanding of it. Now it happened that in the tenth century an innovation of capital importance was imposed upon monasticism. Up to that time each monastery lived an independent existence. While the rule it had accepted might make it resemble many others, it did not establish any link of dependence or association between it and them. In the tenth century, on the contrary, orders were established, *i.e.* large associations of monks submissive to one common rule, peopling the monasteries (in some cases very numerous) scattered throughout Christendom, whose policies were inspired and directed by a single head. Thus the foundation of the order of Cluny in 910 marks an important epoch in the history of the Church. In the twelfth century the order had two thousand houses in France alone, and it will find many imitators; the Camaldoli order founded by St. Romualdo, who are like the Clunisians of Italy, date from 1012; the abbeys of Einsiedeln in Switzerland and Hirschau in Germany show vigorous life in the eleventh century, the one at the beginning, the other at its end, and their rule is modeled upon that of Cluny; St. Bruno founds the Carthusians in 1086; Robert de Molesme, the Cistercians in 1098; St. Bernard, the order of Clairvaux in 1115; Berthold of Calabria, the

Carmelite order in 1156. In other words, the movement which originated in Cluny spread through the Western world for two centuries and a half, and grew there, but it had not to wait for this vast growth to bear fruit.

In the first place, each monastery after undergoing reform according to the Cluny rule becomes a center of active and purified religious life, and at the same time a school in which clergy qualified for the parochial functions of the Church are trained. In the second place, the monks of Cluny, by reason of the extended range of their horizon, have minds hospitable to general ideas. They plumb the depth of the ills from which the Church and the faith are suffering; they seek a remedy for them and, as it were, formulate a theory to get to the bottom of both cause and remedy. They rise above episcopal exclusiveness, do not stop even at the boundary lines of states, but look at everything from the standpoint of the universal Church. Quite naturally, they come to think that its vast body, like their own order, should have a sole and supreme head, who knows the salutary paths for it to take and leads it therein either by consent or by force. They themselves feel the need that this headship for Christendom shall be set up in order to consolidate and maintain their own unity, menaced as it is by feudal anarchy. Not by mere chance does the first great theorist who championed the pontifical omnipotence over the Church and over the rulers, and at the same time the relentless foe of simony and nicolaism,[13] Pope Gregory VII, come from Cluny. For it was among the Clunisian monks that the doctrine of the sovereignty of the Pope was really worked out in detail, and they can be reckoned the most active of the workers who imposed it upon the Christian world of the West. The establishment of pontifical domination is a fact of capital importance which we must now consider by itself.

[13] I must remind readers that by *simony* is meant the trafficking in sacred things, especially ecclesiastical dignities, and by *nicolaism* the incontinence of the clergy, either by marriage or concubinage.

CHAPTER XIII

THE ORIGIN OF PAPACY [1]

CATHOLIC theologians in our days subscribe to a doctrine respecting the origin of the Papacy which might be described as an article of faith, obligatory upon all who desire to be considered orthodox, namely, the doctrine that Christ himself determined the position and functions of the Pontiff in his Church. Consequently the rights and privileges of the Pope owe nothing to the historical development of that Church, any more than to any other circumstance which may have helped to confirm and extend them; they were resident in St. Peter, implicitly, no doubt, but there in their entirety. In short, St. Peter and his successors in the earlier centuries, while not unaware that they possessed them, judged it wiser not to exercise them all in the beginning, and in fact they accommodated their action to circumstances. Use was made of them only on occasions when it was necessary to maintain intact the sacred deposit of faith and morals, or to safeguard the unity of the Church. The fact is that they deemed it wise to act on human considerations of expediency. They would mark time until men's minds were prepared to receive the truth in its fulness, and to comprehend all their rights. Nevertheless, the Church in general, and the most important of its bishops, in particular, never any more than the Popes themselves disowned their supreme authority.

The truth of history is widely different from this decidedly biased theory.

[1] Upon the whole question with which this chapter deals, see the first volume of Döllinger's *The Papacy; Its Medieval Origin and Its Development Down to 1870;* and Turmel's *Histoire du dogme de la papauté* (Paris, 1908). The ancient writings upon which Papacy founds its privileges are collected in Rauschen, *Florilegium patristicum,* Vol. IX (Bonn, 1914), and all the essential documents upon the question will be found in Denzinger's *Enchiridion symbolorum et definitionum* (Friburg, 1908). See the *Index systematicus* in Ficker and Hermelink's *Das Mittelalter,* §§ 7, 8, 15.

That Christ had no intent to found the Catholic, Apostolic and Roman Church is a truth which it is no longer necessary to demonstrate. Consequently, there is no further need to prove that St. Peter did not consider himself Pope and to show that it took a great deal of time—many centuries—for his successors to perceive that they might become Popes. The Papacy is a creation of man, constructed little by little in the course of the Church's existence, by the logic of its development and by a series of historical accidents.

It is quite certain that the claims of the bishop of Rome to the right to conduct the Church do not date from the eleventh century, for long before that period he had gained a distinct preëminence in the hierarchy. This must remain incomplete, precarious and somewhat rudimentary as long as it was not authenticated by a supporting doctrine universally admitted and largely founded upon accepted principles and textual authorities. Now to anyone who reads the documents and interprets the facts without party bias it is clear that during the period preceding the fall of the Roman Empire, no such doctrine existed, *not even in Rome*. Nobody in the Church, during the first four or five centuries of its existence, seems to have been disposed to consent that the bishop of the City has a right to govern other bishops, his brethren and equals. Although his exclusive use of the title of "pope" was finally established and consecrated by custom, it did not so belong to him at that time: all the bishops, the "fathers" of their flocks, are equipped to claim it. Until the episcopate of Celestinus I (422-432) the bishop of Rome gives it to his colleagues, and does not arrogate it to himself. It was only toward the seventh century that its present meaning was determined and settled in the Western Church; and it was in the eighth century that John VII, in 705, first wore a crowned tiara.[2]

---

[2] It was, we are told, Boniface VIII (1294-1303) who added the second crown, and Clement V (1305-1314) or Benedict XII (1334-1342), the third.

Nevertheless, in the early ages of episcopacy, two main considerations had placed the bishop of Rome in an ecclesiastical position which was exceptional and practically unique. In the first place, he supervised the congregation in the capital city and, in the eyes of Romans throughout the Empire, this circumstance invested him with peculiar prestige. Moreover, the size and the wealth of his flock early permitted him to practice, on a large scare too, the duty of fraternal charity for the benefit of other churches, sometimes very distant ones. Thus, in the beginning of the second century Ignatius, bishop of Antioch, praised the Roman church as "the president of charity." Those who contribute largely, it is said, always receive good consideration.

On the other hand, as there was no directing authority installed in power at that time as head of the Church of Christ, the body of believers, in their difficulties and their needs, called up a moral authority, that of the Apostles, out of the past. *Apostolic tradition* was everywhere regarded as the invariable and infallible guide, both for faith and morals. Now this tradition which was not a written one was believed to dwell, so to speak, in the official person of the bishops who occupied *the seats of the apostles*. The bishops thus referred to were those who directed the affairs of the congregations said to have been "planted" by the Apostles, in which the apostolic doctrine was, it was held, preserved in its integrity as a precious deposit. It was to one of these apostolic sees that every Church turned, when it found itself in difficulty over some dispute concerning faith or discipline. Now, nobody denied that the bishop of Rome occupied the chair of St. Peter, prince of the Apostles; he was the chief official of a church which still held the memory of St. Paul, too, in equally vivid remembrance. With the tomb of the two *heads* of the primitive "fraternity" in its possession, did not the Roman community, more conspicuously than any other even of the apostolic communities, also preserve in all its purity the apostolic tradition? Let us add, too, that the Church of Rome was the only congregation throughout the West deemed founded by an Apostle.

A passage from St. Iræneus[3] throws light upon this point of view. He says in it that the truth lies in the apostolic tradition, which is preserved by the bishops of their choosing, whom the author can enumerate; but, as the list would be a long one, he will content himself in answer to the heretics with citing the faith of a single apostolic church, the one founded by the two glorious Apostles Peter and Paul. It readily appears that Iræneus does not imply that the faith of Rome is to be adjudged better than that of any other church which had preserved the deposit of apostolic tradition intact, but merely that he is certain that she, at any rate, has preserved it, and that men may confidently submit their disputes to her decision. This is certainly the view taken, during the early ages, by most of the bishops, and this is why they are glad to consider, not the *power* of Peter, but Peter's *faith,* implanted in his church as the basis in principle of the desired orthodoxy and unity. And this is why, too, that when they try but do not arrive at an understanding unaided they so often turn to the bishop of Rome to ask for a ruling which will settle the matter. This ruling, however, has not in any way the force of law for them; they never feel themselves *obliged* to agree with it.

Nobody therefore, in the early days of the Church, refused to render either deference or respect to the bishop of Rome; nobody was above taking counsel in difficulties with him; no one denied that his opinions carried weight in all cases, and were worth considering; but at the same time, nobody—and this is the *essential* point —regarded them as authoritative pronouncements; they were not accepted except after examination and discussion, and it often happened that they were not followed even after they had been solicited.

It is not to be denied that on several occasions the

---

[3] Bishop of Lyons at the end of the second century: *Adversus omnes haeroses* 3, 3, 2.

bishop of Rome speaks in a tone which might easily mislead us, and incline us to confuse the *fraternal duty* of *counselor,* which he often fulfilled, with the *right* to decide, which he certainly did not possess. Close scrutiny always reveals in such cases that his acting with a synod of bishops and speaking in its name explains the air of authority he assumes, or even that the opinion expressed through him is the opinion of the Western episcopate. He is, as a matter of fact, evidently its primate, although no official organization has ever bestowed this dignity upon him. In no case, and this I cannot too strongly stress, does the reception of his view by the churches constitute an admission of a duty to comply; they scrutinize his opinion carefully, and do not adopt it unless they think it wise. In demonstration that this is the historical fact, I shall recall some incidents which took place in the course of the first six centuries.

In the third century the African churches, when heretics desired to be received into the fold of orthodoxy, were in the habit of rebaptizing them. The Church of Rome, on the contrary, maintained that baptism, provided it had been administered with the intention to make a person a Christian, was valid in itself, however unworthy the officiant might be, or however unorthodox his creed; accordingly, to repeat the ceremony of baptism was contrary to true Church order. This theory, with reason and good sense on its side, prevailed; it was even very properly generalized later, and applied to all the sacraments. Nevertheless, at that period the African churches adhered to their practice, and when Stephen of Rome undertook to force them to abandon it, they resisted. It became the occasion of an exchange of heated correspondence between the Pope and the bishop of Carthage, St. Cyprian, who was supported by the entire episcopate of the province, in his loud demand in behalf of the independence of every bishop. It was not the principle that Stephen was contesting, but only this particuular decision under it which he conceived to be an error. He cut off Cyprian from communion with him, just as Cyprian might have debarred *him* from communion on his side, had he believed it in order to do so, but the African churches did not yield. No one blamed them for it, and they even were warmly commended by Firmilian, bishop of Caesarea in Cappadocia. In the letter he sent express- ing this, we may read such sentences as the following: "For my own part, I am justly incensed at Stephen's open and manifest foolishness. He who boasts so much of his episcopal position, claiming that he is the successor of Peter, upon whom the foundations of the Church rest, he it is who has introduced many other foundation stones and begins building many churches over again, when he persists in authoritatively prohibiting our baptism. For the churches giving it are certainly the majority. . . . And he does not see that he is concealing and, to some extent, doing away with the reality of the Christian foundation, when he betrays and thus abandons its unity." Not therefore upon Stephen's authority, but by the sentiment of the majority, is unity of belief in the Church to be regulated. When at last the matters at issue were settled, under Stephen's successor, it was by a compromise which permitted each party to cling to his own opinion. In the third century, then, the bishop of Rome possessed no recognized right to regulate *doctrine*.

In the fifth century another episode, having its origin in Africa also, leads us to a similar conclusion with regard to *discipline*. A council held at Sardica (Sophia) in 343 seems to have granted the Pope the right to receive appeals, at any rate those of bishops who were dissatis- fied with the reproofs recorded against them by their Provincial Synod, and also the right to designate the judges of appeal from among the bishops of a neighbor- ing province and to decide himself, as a last resort, in cases that still resisted settlement;⁴ but it is probable that this was but a circumstantial case, decided solely in favor of Pope Julius, in order to end a deadlock. In no case did the African bishops more than the Eastern

---

⁴ The authenticity of the canons of Sardica has been disputed, and the matter is not yet entirely settled; it nevertheless seems probable that they are genuine.

ones regard it as dealing with a universal and lasting privilege to which they must necessarily bow. This is the attitude taken toward the bishop of Rome in Africa.

A cleric of the diocese of Sicca, Apiarius by name, had been deposed by his own bishop for various grave breaches of his duty. He appealed from this sentence to osimus, bishop of Rome (417-18), not, it is plain, for a verdict and because he regarded him as the official head of all Christendom, but for an opinion because the importance of the church of Zosimus might effectively serve to get the sentence revoked, if he disapproved of it. Zosimus did, in fact, pronounce himself in favor of Apiarius. Immediately a Provincial Council met at Carthage in 418, and it notified the Pope that, in conformity with canon law, *i.e.* with the rules laid down by the tradition of the Church and sanctioned by the Councils, appeals must first of all be brought before the sees which were neighbors to the one in which the contested decision arose, and then, if need be, before an assembly of all the bishops of the Province. Consequently, whoever were to carry his appeal "beyond the sea" (by which we must understand, *to Rome*) would be dismissed for that act from the African communion. Zosimus insisted; he sent legates, and appealed to pretended canons passed by the Council of Nicaea, which an inquiry on the part of Africa proved to be non-existent. Probably they were only the canons of Sardica, of which we have just spoken. All that came of it was the strengthening of the African churches in their position, and as the matter remained unsettled on the death of Zosimus, a fresh Council of Carthage, held in 424, wrote to the second Pope who had succeeded him, Celestinus, a very firm letter which definitely repudiated his claims, in the name of ecclesiastical custom, and the authentic decisions of the Council of Nicaea, and urged him not to renew them. Could it be possible, inquired the Council ironically, that the Holy Spirit reserves his illumination for a single person, and denies it to a large body of bishops?

No less characteristic, as bearing upon the *authority* in general of the Pope, is the affair in the sixth century, known as the "Three Chapters," of which Pope Vivilius (537-555) was the hero. Three theologians of the preceding century, the illustrious Theodore of Mopsueste, Theodoret of Cyr and Ibas of Edessus, were reputed in the Eastern Church to be Nestorian heretics. This means that they were credited with a refusal to the Virgin Mary of the title of "Mother of God" (*Theotokos*), recognizing her only as "Mother of Christ" (*Christotokos*), and with tending too completely to separate the divine from the human nature in the person of the Savior. For reasons of state the Emperor Justinian condemned them in 543 but, since the Œcumenical Council of Chalcedon, in 451, had already absolved two of the three incriminated, the imperial decision was not accepted in the Western Church, and Vigilius declared the three accused men were perfectly orthodox. In a short time he was summoned to Constantinople, and after imperial pressure had been brought to bear, he revoked his opinion and subscribed to their condemnation (548). Then the bishops of Dalmatia, Illyria, and of Gaul rose up against him and rejected his sentence; the bishops in Africa added excommunication to their censure. Finally he was forced to change his opinion once more, and to reinstate the three theologians.

Such facts cannot be denied; efforts have been made to weaken the conclusions to which they lead by arguing that there was an evident intention to rebel against the legitimate authority of the Pope, or at the very least, that the failure to recognize his rights was temporary. Unfortunately these acts are so often repeated in the course of the first few centuries, that the exception becomes the rule. It must be understood that the examples chosen are characteristic and not unique, and that they might easily be multiplied. For the moment I shall confine myself to mentioning that of the five hundred and six years from the death of Constantine to the end of the dispute regarding images,[5] *i.e.* from 337 to 843,

[5] A grave conflict, developing in two main crises in the Eastern Church in the eighth and ninth centuries, between those who favored the use of images in worship, and in the ornamentation of churches, and those who adhered to the letter of the Biblical prohibition against their use.

two hundred and forty-eight of them, which is nearly half that time, were spent in open and avowed schism between the Eastern churches and Rome. The dissension divides up into seven crises varying in length, the shortest lasting eleven years, and the most protracted, sixty-one. The facts compel us to believe that these Eastern churchmen treat the claim of the Pope to primacy of jurisdiction very lightly, and seem to enjoy living in a state of insubordination. At all events, each time that they broke off communion with Rome, or Rome excommunicated them, it was done because they would not abandon their own point of view on some question of faith or discipline.

And the Eastern churches are not the only ones to show this independence. When Pope Pelagius I, the successor of Vigilius, approves the decisions of the Fifth Œcumenical Council (that held in Constantinople in 553) which condemn the "Three Chapters," the African churches give in only under the pressure of imperial force. Those of Aquila, Istria, Liguria, Milan and Tuscany secede from Rome; the schism of Aquila even lasting until the year 700.

Besides—if more evidence were necessary—first-hand study of the great disputes concerning dogma in the fourth, fifth and sixth centuries would show that no authoritative control which was universally recognized yet exists at the head of the Church; that although the bishop of Rome as a matter of fact often intervenes effectively, whatever authority he exercises still remains wholly of a *practical* nature.

II

Not a single Patristic writing of the first six centuries asserts the existence of pontifical authority *as a mandatory right,* while many, like the conciliary pronouncements already cited, invalidate it, either in so many words, like the passage in which St. Basil in the fourth century accuses the bishop of Rome of pride, presumption and almost of heresy,[6] or else by implication, sometimes all the more forcibly because the passages occur side by side with formulas which might at first sight create the contrary impression.

Two instances may be quoted. While St. Cyprian in several places displays great respect for "the throne of Peter and the principal Church whence priestly unity had its rise,"[7] yet his point of view does not cease to be that of Iræneus. In confirmation a look is enough at his treatise upon the "Unity of the Catholic Church," which states that all the Apostles had received equal authority and shared similar honor, and that Peter simply happened to be the one of the twelve to whom Christ in the first instance turned in bestowing this authority and honor, his main idea being to fix and safeguard the principle of the unity of the Church on which the integrity of the faith depends.[8]

Again, St. Jerome in 375 writes to Pope Damasius to ask his help in clarifying a formula which is causing disagreement in the Eastern church, and he says: "I know that the Church is built upon this rock; whosoever eats of the lamb outside this dwelling suffers defilement. If a man remains outside the ark of Noah, shall he not perish in the waters of the Deluge?" But to be able to estimate what is back of this bit of politeness at its true value, the following passage must be read from Epistle 146, written by this same St. Jerome: "The Church of Rome does not indeed belong to one species, and every other Church in the world to another. Gaul, Britain, Africa, Persia, the East, India, and all barbarian lands adore the same Christ, following the same rule of truth. If search be made as to where authority lies, the world is much larger than the City (*orbis major est Urbe*). Wherever there is a bishop, Rome, Engubium,

---

[6] Epistles 239 and 214.

[7] Epistle 55, 9; *cf.* Epistles 48, 23; 59, 13.

[8] *De cathol. eccles. unitate*, 4. Such was the passage into which a sentence was smuggled in Rome, in the time of Pelagius II (6th cent.); it runs: "He who forsakes the throne of Peter upon which the Church was founded, and defies it, can he regard himself as still a Churchman?" *Cf.* Turmel, *op. cit.* p. 109.

Constantinople . . . the dignity is the same, its sacerdotal character is the same. It is not the power of wealth nor the humility of poverty which ranks a bishop higher or lower. Moreover, they are all the successors of the Apostles.''

This is indeed the view taken throughout antiquity and in the first centuries of the Middle Ages with regard to the question of the primacy of the bishop of Rome. Back in those days it was not the Pope who regulated the affairs of Christendom and handed down decrees in disputes concerning dogma. This was the province of Councils or Synods, bodies which he does not convene— except, of course, those of peninsular Italy, of which he is the metropolitan. Nor does he preside over them save as the Emperor's proxy, and it is not his place to inspect and ratify their decisions.

Modern Roman theologians have taken pains to make out that the first seven Œcumenical Councils [9]—their canons are still considered by the Greek Church the basis of her faith and discipline—were in one way or another their call to meet, or their proceedings or the confirmation of their action, under the control of the Pope. Although they have made copious use of sophistry in order to convince us, none the less have they failed in their purpose.

These Œcumenical Councils were not convened by the Pope but by the Emperor,[10] without a single exception, nor does he feel obliged to consult with Rome in advance. The Pope was not even represented at all of them; he did not send any legates to either the first or the second Council of Constantinople. He does not preside over them in his own legal right, and his legates experience no difficulty in obtaining precedence; it was solely because

[9] These are the first Council of Nicaea (325), the first of Constantinople (381), of Ephesus (431), of Chalcedon (451), second of Constantinople (553), third of Constantinople (680) and the second of Nicaea (787).
[10] At that time it was really the emperor who figured as head of the Church, even when he had the good taste not to mix up in theology. Theodosius considers the faith he chooses to approve as the principle of the Church's dogmatic unity.

no one present cared to dispute the *honorary* primacy attached to the chair of Peter. He did not settle the order of the day for them, nor direct their discussions; he had no means at his disposal to prevent the adoption of resolutions which displeased him. If, from the second Council, a custom did become established of asking him to approve what had been done, it was as a sign that the discussion was over and peace and unity prevailed, and not in the least because this approval was considered a factor necessary to the validity of the canons. The proof of this reading of the situation is that while Pope Damasius and his successors pretend to ignore Canon 3 of the Council of 381, by which the archbishop of Constantinople obtains the second rank in the honorary hierarchy, nevertheless this canon remains in full force. And when Leo I protests against Canon 28 of the Council of Chalcedon, which gives this very archbishopric of Constantinople the same order of preëminence in the Eastern Church possessed by the Pope in the Western, his protest has no modifying effect upon that decision.

Note that these are canons which have a direct bearing upon his privileges, and affect the hierarchy of the Church materially, because the archbishops of Alexandria and Antioch previously to this period received the second and third "honorary" places. There is yet more to be said. The Eastern bishops in 381 and 451 make an effort to show that the privilege which assures him the first place for himself was his from the beginning; and they find just one circumstance to invoke, namely, that he is the bishop of *ancient Rome,* so that his honorary preëminence seems definitely in their estimation to be derived from the political dignity of his cathedral city!

These things must not be forgotten when it comes time to consider what these same Eastern bishops mean in demanding from the Pope "the word of Peter" in their difficulties, appealing to his judgment in case of need, or examining, like the Fathers of Chalcedon or those of the third Council of Constantinople, that the Apostle himself speaks by the mouth of his successor, in the one case

Leo I, and the other Agathon. All who reckoned on the Pope's approval and hoped to benefit by it, found it to their interest to magnify his authority beforehand, and they did not fail to do so. Their self-seeking protestations assuredly favored the Roman claims, but they were so many illusions to deceive the Pope at first glance and usually were not long in proving themselves false. It remains a truth that his opinions, always of importance *de facto*, and indeed given weight by the other bishops, were not more valid, *de jure*, than their own; the adherence accorded them by the bishops depended upon the advantage which they might derive from them.

It may happen that they create quite a scandal in the Church. This did occur when Pope Liberius aroused a great commotion in the orthodox episcopate by countenancing, for the purpose of obtaining from the emperor his own recall from exile, a doubtful article of faith, and even more by subscribing to the condemnation of Athanasius, the resolute foe of the Arians, in 357. Again, too, Honorius I, elected in 625, was accused after his death of the *monothelist* heresy (the doctrine which maintains that Christ has but one will, and not two, the one human and the other divine), and the third Council of Constantinople (the sixth of the Œcumenical Councils) in 680 censures his memory and has his writings burnt.

How can we fail to note also that St. Augustine, in his treatise on the Unity of the Church, does not even allude to the paramount guidance of Rome in matters of dogma, and that St. Vincent of Lérins, in the fifth century, in his *Commonitorium,* when he is seeking to determine the authentic signs or indications of orthodoxy, breathes not a word of the one which today takes the place of all the others—agreement with the Pope? On the other hand, if any such sovereignty, doctrinal and disciplinary, of Rome had existed, it would have constituted an obstacle in the path of heretics which they would endeavor to overthrow. Instead, the long lists of heresies which have come down to us, from St. Iræneus in the second century to Philastrius and St. Augustine in the fourth and fifth, betray no traces of any systematic opposition to pontifical mastership on the part of any heretical sect whatsoever. The inference then is that no such mastership existed; and this is indeed the truth.

There is more evidence. Somewhat tardily, between the end of the fifth and that of the eighth century, at a time when in practical matters the papal hegemony began to take something like definite shape, for instance, Leo I had already obtained from the Emperor Valentinian III (in 455) an edict sanctioning his domination over the Western episcopate which was based upon the merits of St. Peter and the prestige of the city of Rome. But even then, I repeat, Papacy did not yet constitute a special rank in the ecclesiastical hierarchy. One of the books of the pseudo-Dionysius the Areopagite is devoted to this *hierarchy* as its subject; in it the Pope is not differentiated from other bishops. Isidorus of Seville (631) mentions patriarchs, archbishops, metropolitans, bishops, but not the Pope, because to him the Pope is only the Western patriarch, just as the archbishop of Alexandria is the Egyptian patriarch. He indeed heads the list of patriarchs, but he is not the only one, nor does he differ in grade from the rest. Such is still the point of view of the Spanish monk Beatus, in 789. No one at this time, it is true, is calling in question the prerogatives of the Roman Pontiff, but no one yet interprets them as conferring upon him a position not to be compared with any other and, I might say, *canonically* unique.

Moreover, many of the bishops of Rome at the time we are considering, and not the least important among them, still shield themselves with great care from any claim to govern the Church, while occupying St. Peter's throne with dignity and maintaining what they regard as its legitimate privileges, never sparing either their material aid or their frequently very urgent advice to their episcopal brethren. Of such were Leo I, Pelagius I, and Gregory the Great.

True enough, Pope Leo had a very exalted conception

of his function and possibly he was the first Pontiff to affirm distinctly that Peter lives on ever in the person of his successor, the same Peter whom the Lord constituted the foundation and the head of his Church.[11] Nevertheless, when, in 449, he made known his position in the dispute over dogma raised by the heresy of Eutyches and wrote his "Epistle to Flavian," he does not put forth any claim to impose the doctrine it contains on his own authority without examination. He even explicitly declares that his opinion, in order to acquire the character of a rule of faith, must receive the approval of the other bishops. And if both East and West do receive it well, it is also true that they do so only after it has been examined and judged freely as far as its *orthodoxy* is concerned. To the emperor does Leo himself attribute the rôle of God's agent to maintain the faith and unity of the Church.

As for Pelagius I (555-560) St. Augustine is praised by him for calling attention to the divinely given doctrine which rests the Church upon the apostolic sees as its foundation. He himself teaches that in all doubtful cases the orthodox rule is to be found, in fact, in the apostolic churches. Now the character of apostolic does not belong to the church at Rome alone; it is shared equally by the churches at Jerusalem, Antioch, Alexandria, and yet other cities.

Gregory the Great, at the end of the sixth century, refused to accept the title of *œcumenical patriarch,* or *universal bishop,* which he described as "folly thoughtlessly put forward." He contented himself with the primacy over the churches of Italy, with which custom had already endowed him.

III

Various causes, however, which converged in their working were to lead the bishop of Rome almost of necessity to believe that he possessed *de jure* the primacy of jurisdiction over the universal Church, and to claim it.

[11] Epistle 25, 2.

To begin with, the honorary primacy which he knew to be his due, and which none refused him, readily lent itself to that misconstruction, as well as the custom followed by many churches of seeking an arbiter of their disputes in Rome. The Eastern churches, in particular, in asking of the more steady-going Roman cast of mind a word of counsel which should guide them in their uncertainties and put an end to their interminable disputes, ran to polite exaggerations, as I have already said, and frequently, too, went beyond their true thought in their tokens of deference and submission. So much is this the case, indeed, that their declarations taken literally would seem to signify that at the close of the fruitless disputes which had caused them to stray from the true way of orthodoxy and the real faith, they were consciously returning to full allegiance by soliciting the correction of their error at the hands of the supreme master of doctrine and morals. We know that this is not what they desired to say. But if many theologians of the present day persist in making the same mistake and still think so in the interest of their arguments, how much more would the Pope, in the interests of his direct personal power, and (from his point of view) in the undoubted interest of the Church, be tempted to make the same mistake!

It was moreover in logical accord with the governmental course of development of the Church that its desire for unity, which grew always stronger and had created the episcopate and then in the fourth century placed archbishops over the bishops and "primates" or patriarchs above the archbishops, should not stop short of an absolute monarchy. And, in this event, the monarch could be none other than the bishop of Rome. Not only did he occupy the most famous of the episcopal thrones, but actually he was the *only* patriarch in the West, whereas there were *four* patriarchs who divided between them the care of the Eastern Church,[12] and thus seriously

[12] These were Constantinople, Alexandria, Antioch and Jersualem, the latter recognized in the middle of the fifth century.

weakened their own respective authority. The historical evidence is convincing that if the logical development of the Church was thwarted, and instead of closer union an irremediable breach occurred, it was due entirely to the political circumstances that confronted the Pope of Rome with the Pope of "the new Rome" in the person of the patriarch of Constantinople, the Emperor's bishop, whose secular importance counterbalanced his somewhat lowly ecclesiastical origin. It certainly was doing violence to authentic tradition for the bishop of a see whose very recent and obscure origin at Byzantium seemed to destine it to subordinate rank forever to take first place over apostolic Eastern sees, and become a rival to him who occupied the throne of Peter. When the Greek schism occurred, the Pope was already firmly established in what he believed to be his lawful position. He could therefore only consider the action of Cerularius, which occasioned the rupture in the eleventh century, as a proud and preposterous revolt against legitimate authority. Thus the matter is still regarded by the Romanist theologians of our day.

The situation which circumstances were preparing to the advantage of the Pope found in passages of Scripture an ally with all the means required for making it an ecclesiastically legal one. Many "sayings" attributed to the Lord, rightly or wrongly, themselves yield an interpretation which would justify the forced application made of them. Nevertheless that interpretation is improper and inappropriate. Well known are "Thou art Peter" and the "Feed my sheep," and the "Stablish thy brethren," which today still flash out in letters of gold above the Apostle's *Confessio* around the cupola of St. Peter's at Rome.

Not one of the many Fathers of the Church who, during the first few centuries, had occasion to quote one of these texts and comment upon it, had uttered a single word in recognition of it as the basis of a claim to primacy in favor of the bishop of Rome, and it took *him* a long time to realize that each of them alone and all three together contained something of special advantage to him. From the middle of the fifth century, however, and the reign of Celestinus I, the Pope began to set store side by side with the apostolic dignity of Peter's seat, by *the power of the keys* and *the right to bind and unbind* which the Apostle had transmitted to him. Even so at that time it was but an occasional way of speaking, still far from conscious of its future significance. Nevertheless from time to time the statement reappears more or less distinctly, and more or less widely exploited. Toward the end of the seventh century, in 680, Pope Agathon, to defend the very seriously compromised memory of Honorius I, whom the third Council of Constantinople (the sixth Œcumenical Council) had just anathematized, cites, as a guarantee of the doctrinal infallibility of Peter's successor, the text (Lk. xxii. 32), "I made supplication for thee, that thy faith fail not . . . stablish thy brethren." But this interpretation still seems at that late date to be due to the circumstances of the case, and to be wholly personal. It was totally disregarded, as it happened.

The Pope will cling with increasing confidence just the same to this profitable interpretation and in the end obtain consent to it at least by the Western Church, inclined by disposition to submit to this impulse toward monarchy, which the churches of the East resist only because it would make them subordinate to Rome. History tells us that they accept it in practice with respect to Constantinople. At the seventh Œcumenical Council (the second at Nicaea), in 787, Pope Adrian I has a letter read, one phrase of which, at least, is very significant: "May the word of the Lord be fulfilled. . . . 'Thou art Peter,' whose throne shines in primacy throughout the earth, and makes it the head of all the Churches of God." [13] The Council does not put itself on record in contradiction, because it did not indeed really go as far as to think the direct contrary, but from that time the Pope and the Council no longer interpret his

[13] Denzinger, *Enchiridion symb.* p. 135.

words in the same way. Where the Fathers still only perceived an assertion of the right to "honorary" first place for the occupant of Peter's throne, the pontiff means his words to express privileges belonging to a head of the Church possessing real jurisdiction. On account of this fundamental difference of opinion indeed the conflicts between the Eastern and the Western Churches at last proved irreconcilable.

IV

In the eighth century the actually decisive influences which are going to establish in the practice of the time the power of the Pope, come into play. These influences, anterior to the medieval theory of the Papacy, will raise him to the rôle of authorized head of the Church; they are political in their nature.

For an indefinitely long time the people who dwelt within the confines of the Romania were accustomed to accept the idea that the Eternal City carried within herself the very principle of sovereign authority, an authority vested in the Emperor, since by the will of God he *personified*, as it were, the Roman people. Now at the end of the fifth century the time came when there was no longer an Emperor in the West. For the Western peoples whom the idea of Roman sovereignty still dominated (an idea kept up also by the Church), the bishop elected by the Roman people might to some extent appear to be the heir to his œcumenical prestige. As a matter of fact, this new sovereign was thoroughly ill at ease, between the Byzantine Emperor who continued to consider himself the master of Rome, and the King of Lombardy who desired to seize the city. To free himself both from the tyranny of the one and the impending yoke of the other he appealed to the King of the Franks who, in fact, did rid him of his enemies and granted him his hazardous goodwill.

He made the Pope a prince, by taking seriously a pretended *deed of gift of Constantine's*, forged in Rome probably in the second half of the eighth century,[14] which assigns to the first Christian Emperor the act of granting the constitution of *St. Peter's patrimony.* He confirmed and amplified its rulings. Moreover Charlemagne was willing to admit that the Church should have a spiritual head in Rome, since his Empire, the Empire of the West, reëstablished probably at the suggestion of the Pope, had a temporal head in his own person. He did not forget, however, that Rome formed a part of that Empire, nor to retain his authority there, so that the sovereign jurisdiction of the Pope still remained for some time yet merely nominal.

But Charlemagne's power of domination did not survive him and, thanks to the feebleness of his successors, the Popes were soon free of the Frankish tutelage. At first they gained nothing, but on the contrary lost, for they fell under the domination of the petty Roman barons, and this form of servitude carried St. Peter's successors into strange quarters. During the first half of the tenth century the Papacy seems to have fallen to the lowest depths. Then it was that two courtesans disposed of the episcopal miter in favor of their lovers or of their bastards. It may well be asked point blank how the prestige of the Western patriarch could have survived such a scourge, all the more so because the papal authority neither *de jure* nor *de facto,* neither by bishops nor kings, was yet recognized as that of the lawful sovereign of the Church. The Papacy was saved from disaster, first of all, by the intervention of Otho I, king of Germany. Although this brought it afresh under a foreign hegemony, yet it restored its sense of dignity and supplied the means of guaranteeing it. This very restoration would later on permit it to exploit, boldly and vigorously, the position acquired by the bishop of Rome in the Church of the expiring Roman Empire, of which tradition had kept the memory green. Then too a number of circumstances opportunely combined to further its

---

[14] The first mention of it occurs in a letter of Pope Adrian to Charlemagne in 777.

rehabilitation. One of these was the foundation of the Holy Germanic Roman Empire in 962, which seemed to reëstablish the ancient Roman *unanimitas,* no longer an arrangement between several secular princes, as at the time of Diocletian's tetrarchy, or of the partitionings of the fourth century, but this time between a temporal prince and a spiritual prince, the one, a ruler of bodies; the other, a master of souls. Another of these favoring circumstances was the disorder of the Church, caused by anarchy and feudal barbarism that called for a reform, which to be successful must undoubtedly be the product of coördinated direction. And what other party capable of this direction could be called upon than the Western patriarch? And last of these favoring circumstances to be mentioned here was the enormous extension of the *monastic orders,*[15] for in seeking their own independence in the Catholic Unity which goes deeper than the diversity of dioceses, they naturally tended to confer upon the Church a reality as visible and as tangible as that of the various constituent churches, and exalted it in the person of its head. Certain men appeared who knew how to turn all these circumstances to account, and do so quite simply because they believed with their whole soul that it was their right, and even their duty, before God, and toward men. They established in a comparatively short time the powerful monarchy which has ruled Catholicism from the end of the eleventh century.

V

Nevertheless, as late as the year 1000, the Pope had never once yet, *of his own special authority,* pronounced upon any doctrinal point addressed to the Catholic world, nor interposed his personality between a bishop and his flock in the ordinary management of the affairs of a diocese, nor yet exacted any toll or tax outside the coun-

[15] It must be clearly understood that it is a question of the orders which multiply their houses throughout all Christendom, operating everywhere as real monastic governments superimposed upon states as well as upon bishoprics.

tries immediately obedient to him. But already various documents were current—anonymous forgeries, and more or less brazen—which credited to a distant past with which people were unacquainted and so could not dispute, the ambitions, interests and, at need, the habits of the present, and these were made to serve as a basis of the theory of the rights possessed by the Pope in the Church and in the world. And the profitable example thus set will not be lost: an extraordinary array of forgeries of the same nature will keep the progress of the Papacy company from the dawn of the feudal age to that of the Reformation. Scarcely anybody defends them today. The Romanist theologians and apologists, who abandon none of the results which they formerly were used to obtain, are reduced to apologizing for them. To tell the truth, they do not usually succeed very well either.[16]

How came it that the Roman Chancellery should be so unconscious of, or credulous on, the subject of forgery? We do not know, but this evil seems to have overtaken it early, for it goes back to 451 at the Council of Chalcedon when the legates of Leo I, in the course of their protests against the privileges granted by the Council to the archbishop of Constantinople, produced a copy of Canon 6 of the Nicene Council containing a very interesting addition which proclaimed that Roman supremacy had always been recognized as a part of settled tradition (*quod ecclesia romana semper habuit primatum*). Comparison of this passage with the original Greek at once proved its lack of authenticity. There is no doubt that the legates acted in good faith, and so had the Pope Zosimus shortly before when he stamped the canons of Sardica with the authority of the Council of Nicaea and, in addition, donated them a sense which did not belong to them. In this impervious assurance, which at last will impose its constructions upon centuries of ignorance, lies, if I may say so, the explanation of the spawning power

[16] Cf. Goyau, *Vue générale de l'histoire de la papauté*, p. 40 *et seq*, and for the contrary standpoint, Döllinger, p. 25 *et seq*.

of a practice which it would be necessary to characterize severely if it proceeded from an outright dishonest motive. I do not mean that the conscious authors of these serviceable forgeries were not dishonest from our point of view, but it must be realized also that they were not so from their own. In their day texts were not treated with the respect with which they are surrounded nowadays, and in forging a document for what seemed to them the purpose of authenticating the truth, they believed themselves to be merely repairing a historical omission or a vexatious error in the transmission of records. Thus the redactors of the *Liber Pontificalis* (a collection of biographical notices about the Popes, the oldest parts of which go back to the first thirty years of the sixth century) attributed to the Roman bishops of the earliest ages the temper and the interests of the Pontiffs of their own times.[17] Again, and still in the sixth century, a small armory of apocryphal documents appeared which were designed to oppose the menacing encroachments of the patriarch of Constantinople.

There is no reason to believe that the Popes, however truly they may have been lacking in knowledge and critical faculty, deliberately turned falsehood to account, but it is a fact that they did derive advantage thus and so persistently that the Greeks have some little foundation for saying, as they do, that the fabrication of documents is the characteristic industry of Rome. At these inventions Gregory VII, as well as Nicholas I, will himself be caught, and all the other Popes throughout the Middle Ages. Nearly every pontificate will add its supplement of false documents to this formidable *corpus* whence the theologians, St. Thomas Aquinas among them, will for a long period confidently derive the justification for whatever the Roman Pontiffs may desire to do or to say. Much more guilty than the forgers themselves are men such as Baronius, Bellarmin and different Jesuits who, in the sixteenth and seventeenth centuries, employed

---

[17] The *Liber Pontificalis*, many times touched up again, added to, and embellished, stops short at the end of the ninth century. *Cf.* Mgr. Duchesne's edition.

their erudition and their zeal in the face of considerations of fact and good sense which admit of no reasonable rejoinder, to bolster up a body of arguments for the sake of conclusions drawn from them which they could not consent to abandon. Today, truth has obtained, and keeps, as ever, the last word in its custody.[18]

Toward the middle of the sixth century a Scythian monk, known as Dionysius the Less, who undertook to arrange a collection of canons of the Councils, added to them a certain number of *decretals* [19] of the Popes from Siritius onwards (384-399). His example was followed and the Dionysian supplement gradually grew in length. In itself this assembling together of the special decisions taken by the Popes and the conciliary canons in one and the same collection already possessed the serious disadvantage, from the standpoint of tradition, of appearing to attribute the same authority to both. Besides it served as a cloak for a very handy method of action in case any one wished to justify any pontifical claim whatever to authenticate a privilege already acquired in practice: he had only to invent a decretal and add it to the collection. Who could indeed in those days verify or contest the authenticity of the fresh document? Now toward the middle of the ninth century, at the very time when the Papacy was getting rid of the hegemony of the Frankish sovereigns, a copious collection of decretals began to be circulated, absolutely false, which are known as the *Decretals of the pseudo-Isidorus*. They circulated under cover of the name of Isidorus of Seviglia, whose reputation for learning stood very high in those ignorant days.

There were about a hundred of these documents, attributed to former bishops of Rome, but probably fabricated

[18] It would be wrong to believe, moreover, that opposition with respect to the standing of these forgeries has altogether ceased; even today theologians are to be found who refuse to recognize that the famous *De catholicae ecclesiae unitate, 4,* of St. *Cyprian,* has suffered an interpolation, and who put their confidence in the most desperate arguments.

[19] A *decretal* is the term in use for a reply given by the Pope to a question as to a point of doctrine or discipline which has been referred to him, which is susceptible of a general application.

in the Frankish countries on the left bank of the Rhine. The Roman claims not only found justification in them but at the same time the means of clarifying themselves, although the fact is that the forger had not done his work in order to favor them. He was interested in opposing to the secular power, which the bishops believed to be encroaching upon their own, an authority remote, ecclesiastical in kind, like their own, from which they never expected to have anything to fear. This is why these forged decretals laid down the twofold principle (a) that no conciliary or synodal decision is valid without the approval of the Pope, and (b) that the supreme power in the Church, even in matters of faith, belongs to the Pope. These two principles preserved for bishops tyrannized over by royal personages the right of appeal to Rome.

Nicholas I, elected in 858, at once accepted the forged decretals, and the two principles which were evolved from them henceforward served as the fundamental basis for the thesis of the supremacy of the Pope over the Council, and for the doctrine of infallibility upon which, mainly, the theory of pontifical power is founded.

About the time of Gregory VII, in particular (1073-1085), the work of forging false documents and their systematic utilization, *i.e.* fitting them together into a body of doctrine, reached a magnitude and a degree of openness absolutely stupefying. The events of the past have no means of resisting distortion; after being twisted, reversed, upset, a theory is made from them which becomes a veritable dogma, whilst in the meantime Gregory himself, in 1078, is tranquilly affirming (and, I must repeat, quite in good faith) at a certain synod that he is only following the statutes of his predecessors.[20]

Toward the year 1140 the monk Gratianus, the first professor of canon law in the University of Bologna, blends together the earlier forgeries, adds others, and constitutes a *corpus* which becomes the legal framework

[20] It is naturally impossible to go into detail here; *cf.* Döllinger, *op. cit.* pp. 37, 41, 43, 46, etc.

of the whole "papal system," and of the "authority" beyond dispute. It goes without saying, however, that the procedure which has succeeded so well in the past is not abandoned all at once: the thirteenth century employs it to confer upon the most favorable conclusions of the pontifical jurists the rank of affirmations of principle and of theology. The Dominican Martin of Troppau, archbishop of Gnesen in 1278, does not hesitate to carry back to the early days of the Church the authentic origin of the papal system! This obtains for him great success among the clerics and others imitate him who are no less successful, although it is difficult to maintain that they believe themselves also to be telling the truth. They render the Pope a service, but not Christendom.

It must not be overlooked that we now find ourselves face to face with the work of Jurists and not with the interpretations of theologians. The most active of the Popes, such as Innocent III and Innocent IV, Clement IV, Boniface VIII, are themselves jurists. In their entourage the study of theology, of the Scriptures and of the Fathers is very much neglected. Nevertheless the theologians, in their time and place, did the cause of the Pope service; they brought into the case their arguments. In this way they have helped to establish the doctrine which makes the Pope the vicar of Christ on earth, and no longer of Peter, and all other episcopal authority an appendage of his authority, and reduces the rank of the bishops, formerly his equals, to nothing more than that of his lieutenants and deputies. St. Thomas Aquinas likens their powers and his to those of a proconsul compared with those of an emperor. His personal infallibility is not yet currently admitted, but that problem has been stated and St. Thomas solves it in the affirmative, saying that Christ cannot have prayed in vain that Peter's faith should not fail (Luke xxii. 32).

VI

This theory of the Church has, so to speak, a political aspect: by it the Pope is claiming an authority superior to that of kings and princes. In the Gospel it is affirmed that two swords suffice; [21] Christ certainly meant to say that the government of the world is committed to the charge of the spiritual power and the temporal power, and that the two swords which serve as their symbols have been delivered to Peter. His successor disposes of them and, if he has voluntarily relinquished the temporal sword, he who holds it is responsible to him for the use he makes of it. Before these amazing ideas received decisive, or at least, complete and thoroughly coördinated expression by the pen of a St. Thomas Aquinas, they had been sown broadcast in the world of Christendom by the innumerable army of monks, in the form of still incomplete, but already encroaching theses. These monks spread themselves throughout every diocese of Christendom in which the "houses" of their orders arose, superposed themselves upon and inundated them all. In order to maintain their independence at close quarters with the local ecclesiastical authorities, they willingly proclaim their obedience to the *universal bishop,* who in exchange for the services they render him does not bargain with them over privileges, even to the detriment of the parochial clergy. It is the propaganda of the order of Cluny which thus prepares for the monarchy of Gregory VII, himself a former resident of Cluny, where he became impregnated with the theory which was being elaborated there, of a Church truly sovereign, free of the trammels of the passing age, purified of its errors and led by the Pope in the ways of the Lord. And when the older orders fall into decay, the Mendicant Friars, especially the Preaching Friars, of whom St. Thomas is the supreme pride, will flourish opportunely to continue their work. Their Third Orders will extend their influence in the same direction, and the Inquisition will confirm it.

Next the Pope begins to reserve to himself the right of confirmation over all the bishops, and also the right to

[21] This refers to the passage in Luke xxii. 38, in which the disciples, in reaching the Mount of Olives after the paschal supper, show Jesus two swords, which are their only weapons: *And he said unto them, It is enough.* It is of course understood that this text was interpreted symbolically to support the medieval theory of the two swords.

settle any contested election; his court organizes itself for administrative work, and in it the entire life of the Church comes to a head. He is the supreme arbiter in all the lawsuits of the Church; his legates go in all directions bearing his orders, with authority to represent his person, and to set limits, on the spot, to the powers of the bishops and archbishops, at which the monks from their side are also nibbling away. The pontifical taxes, beginning with "St. Peter's pence," are in operation, and the "Servant of the Servants of God," as he is called (so that the Master's word: *"Whosoever would be first among you shall be your servant"* [Matt. xx. 27] may be fulfilled), begins to live like a sovereign of the age, even if in private life he is an ascetic.

It would be just cause for astonishment to believe that any similar metamorphosis of the authentic tradition of the ancient Church could be accomplished with the unanimous consent of kings and bishops, unless the influence of external causes of great potency were not only favorable, but had to some extent determined and forced this dénouement.

Two facts of capital importance thus exerted from outside a decisive influence in forming the constitution of the Papacy. One of these was the struggle carried on by the Pope against the king of Germany from the end of the eleventh till the middle of the thirteenth centuries. He was obliged by it to formulate and justify his claims; it gave him the opportunity to reckon up his supporters, and add to their number; finally, when he emerged triumphant, he had also gained the prestige of a victory which might appear a manifestation of the judgment of God. It is true enough that when he had destroyed the Hohenstaufen "nest of vipers" the aftermath was only a relapse into Italian anarchy and the creation of a desperate need for money, but his triumph none the less appeared to consecrate his right to rule Christendom.

The second of these favoring outside influences was the Crusades inspired by him, which clearly set him from the beginning of the eleventh century at the head of all the Christians fighting the infidel. The Crusades did not succeed, but their early ephemeral triumph, and the years they lasted, and then too the hope, always springing up again after each setback, of a forthcoming new crusade, enabled the Pope to keep up indefinitely his attitude of supreme head of all believers, and the active champion of the faith. Indeed it is hard to conceive the possibility in this period of any enterprise destined to fortify the faith and extend its domain which did not either initiate with the Pontiff or place itself under his protection.

Last of these favoring outside influences and chief of them all, the Crusades enabled Western peoples to rediscover the East. At least one consequence of this renewal of acquaintance is as important for the Papacy as for the faith. I mean the revival of intellectual activity which will blossom out into Scholasticism and produce the great doctors which exalted the fact and the principle of pontifical sovereignty to the dignity of a dogma.